The Corpse Walker

The Corpse Walker

Real-Life Stories,
China from the Bottom Up

—⟋⟍—

LIAO YIWU

Translated from the Chinese and
with an introduction by Wen Huang

I.C.C. LIBRARY

PANTHEON BOOKS
New York

Introduction and translation copyright © 2008 by Wen Huang

All rights reserved. Published in the United States by Pantheon Books,
a division of Random House, Inc., New York, and in Canada
by Random House of Canada Limited, Toronto.

Pantheon Books and colophon are registered trademarks of Random House, Inc.

This translation is composed of ten new pieces and sixteen pieces that were
originally published in Chinese in Taiwan as part of *Interviews with People from the
Bottom Rung of Society,* published by Rye Field Publishing Co., Taipei, in 2002.
Copyright © 2002 by Liao Yiwu.

The following pieces were previously published: "The Mortician" in *Harper's;*
and "The Corpse Walker," "The Human Trafficker," "The Leper," "The Peasant
Emperor," "The Professional Mourner," "The Public Toilet Manager," and
"The Retired Official" in *The Paris Review.*

Library of Congress Cataloging-in-Publication Data

Liao, Yiwu, [date]
The corpse walker : real-life stories, China from the bottom up / Liao Yiwu ;
translated from the Chinese by Wen Huang.
p.   cm.
ISBN 978-0-375-42542-4
1. Working class—China.   2. Social structure—China.
3. China—Social conditions.   4. China—Economic conditions.   I. Title.
HD8736.5L.56 2008
362.850951—dc22   2007034160

www.pantheonbooks.com

Printed in the United States of America

First Edition

Contents

Foreword

To hear a new voice is one of the great excitements that a book can offer—and through Liao Yiwu we hear more than two dozen original voices that have a great deal to say. Liao is at once an unflinching observer and recorder, a shoe-leather reporter and an artful storyteller, an oral historian and deft mimic, a folklorist and satirist. Above all, he is a medium for whole muzzled swathes of Chinese society that the Party would like to pretend do not exist: hustlers and drifters, outlaws and street performers, the officially renegade and the physically handicapped, those who deal with human waste and with the wasting of humans, artists and shamans, crooks, even cannibals—and every one of them speaks more honestly than the official chronicles of Chinese life that are put out by the state in the name of "the people."

Liao was shaped as a writer by the harshest of experiences: he nearly starved to death as a child and his father was branded an enemy of the people; he was thrown in jail for writing poems that spoke truthfully about China's Communist Party and he was beaten in jail for refusing to shut up; and he discovered in jail the enormous value of listening to others like him whom the authorities wanted to keep forever unheard. So Liao writes with the courage of a man who knows loss and doesn't fear it. There is nothing to make him take notice like an official injunction against noticing, nothing to make him listen like official deafness, nothing that drives him to make us see than the blindness that Communist officialdom seeks to impose. But it is not merely defiance, and it is hardly political polemic, that drives the vitality of the stories in this collection. What makes Liao's encounters with his characters so powerful is the fact that he clearly delights in their humanity, however twisted its expression, and he shows his respect for his subjects in the most fundamental way: he lets them speak for themselves.

There is no question that Liao Yiwu is one of the most original and remarkable Chinese writers of our time. It is, however, truer to say that he is one of the most original and remarkable writers of our time, and that he is from China. Yes, his language is Chinese, his country and its people are his subject, and his stories originate from intensely local encounters. But even to someone who has never been to China, and who can know Liao's work only through Wen Huang's translations, these stories have an immediacy and an intimacy that crosses all boundaries and classifications. They belong to the great common inheritance of world literature.

Liao Yiwu is an original, but it seems a very good bet that writers as diverse as Mark Twain and Jack London, Nikolai Gogol and George Orwell, François Rabelais and Primo Levi would have recognized him at once as a brother in spirit and in letters. He is a ringmaster of the human circus, and his work serves as a powerful reminder—as vital and necessary in open societies lulled by their freedoms as it is in closed societies where telling truthful stories can be a crime—that it is not only in the visible and noisy wielders of power but equally in the marginalized, overlooked, and unheard that the history of our kind is most tellingly inscribed.

Philip Gourevitch
November 2007

Introduction: The Voice of China's Social Outcasts

When the Chinese government tanks rolled into Beijing on the night of June 3, 1989, and brutally suppressed the students' pro-democracy movement, Liao Yiwu was home in the southwestern province of Sichuan. The news shocked him to the very core. Overnight, Liao composed a long poem, "Massacre," that portrayed with stark imagery the killing of innocent students and residents as vividly as Picasso painted the Nazi bombing massacre in the town of Guernica.

Without any chance of having his poem published in China, Liao made an audiotape of himself reciting "Massacre," using Chinese ritualistic chanting and howling to invoke the spirit of the dead. The tape recording was widely circulated via underground channels in China. In another poem written at that time, he described his sense of frustration at being unable to fight back.

> You were born with the soul of an assassin,
> But at a time of action,
> You are at a loss, doing nothing.
> You have no sword to draw,
> Your body a sheath rusted,
> Your hands shaking,
> Your bones rotten,
> Your near-sighted eyes cannot do the shooting.

That tape of "Massacre" as well as a movie he made with friends of its sequel, "Requiem," caught the attention of the Chinese security police. In February 1990, as he was boarding a train to Beijing, police swooped down on him. Six of his poet and writer friends, as well as his pregnant wife, were also arrested simultaneously for their involvement in his movie project. As the ringleader, Liao received a four-year sentence.

Since then Liao has permanently been placed on the government blacklist. Most of his works are still banned in China, where he lives, as a street musician in a small town in southwestern Yunnan Province, under the watchful eyes of the public security bureau. He has been detained numerous times in the past for conducting "illegal interviews" and for exposing the dark side of Communist society in his documentary-style book *Interviews with People from the Bottom Rung of Society*. The twenty-seven stories that appear in this book are translated and adapted from that collection as well as from his recent writings posted on overseas Chinese-language Web sites.

Liao was born in 1958, in the year of the dog. It was also the year that Mao Zedong launched the Great Leap Forward, a campaign aimed at industrializing China's backward peasant economy. The forced collectivization of agriculture and the blind mobilization of the whole country to adopt primitive ways of producing iron and steel led to a famine in 1960 that claimed the lives of some thirty million people.

During the famine, he suffered from edema and was dying. Out of desperation, Liao's mother carried him to the countryside, where an herbal doctor "held me over a wok that contained boiling herbal water." The herbal steam miraculously restored him.

In 1966, Liao's family was deeply affected when his father, a schoolteacher, was branded a counterrevolutionary during the Cultural Revolution. His parents filed for divorce to protect their children from the father's pariah status. Life was hard without his father. Among his childhood memories, there is one he still recalls vividly: "A relative gave my mother a government-issued coupon that was good for two-meters of cloth. But, when mother sold it on the black market to buy food for us, she got caught by the police and was paraded, along with other criminals, on the stage of the Sichuan Opera House in front of thousands of people. After several of my classmates who had seen my mother told me about it, I was devastated."

After high school, Liao traveled around the country, working as a cook, and then as a truck driver on the Sichuan-Tibet Highway. In his spare time he read previously banned Western poets, from Keats to Baudelaire. He also began to compose his own poems and to publish in literary magazines.

Throughout the 1980s, Liao became one of the most popular new poets in China and contributed regularly to influential literary magazines as well as to underground publications that published contemporary Western-style poems considered by the government to be "spiritual pollution." In the spring of 1989, two prominent magazines took advantage of the temporary political thaw and carried Liao's long poems "The Yellow City" and "Idol." In the poems he used allegorical allusions to criticize what he called a system paralyzed and eaten away by a collective leukemia. He claimed that the emergence of Mao was the symptom of this incurable cancer. Alarmed by the poems' bold anti-Communist messages, police searched Liao's home and subjected him to thorough interrogations, depositions, and short-term detention. The magazine publishers were also disciplined; one magazine was ordered to shut down.

Liao's imprisonment in 1990 for his condemnation of the government crackdown on the student pro-democracy movement the previous year was a defining chapter in his life. Ostracized and depressed during his four-year incarceration, he rebelled against prison rules, only to be subjected to abusive punishment: prodded by electric batons, tied up, handcuffed, and forced to stand in the hot summer sun for hours. At one point, his hands were tied behind his back for twenty-three days in solitary confinement until abscesses covered his armpits. He suffered several mental collapses and attempted suicide twice. He was known among the inmates as "the big lunatic."

In 1994, following international pressure, Liao was released fifty days before completing his prison term. (The Chinese government claimed he was being rewarded for good behavior.) He returned home to find that his wife had left him, taking their child. His city residential registration was cancelled, rendering him unemployable and subject to expulsion to the countryside. His former literary friends avoided him in fear. His only possession was a flute, which he had learned to play in jail. Liao walked through the noisy streets in his native city of Chengdu and began his life anew as a street musician.

Liao did not give up his literary pursuits. In 1998, he compiled the volume *The Fall of the Holy Temple*, an anthology of underground poems of the 1970s, which includes works by, or made references to, numerous Chinese dissidents. One of China's vice premiers personally ordered an investigation into the book, calling it a "premeditated attempt to over-throw the government, and is supported by powerful anti-China groups." He was detained again and the publisher was prohibited from releasing any new books for one year.

As the Chinese government tightened its noose on his publishing career, Liao sank further to the bottom, picking up odd jobs in restaurants, nightclubs, teahouses, and bookstores. But his life at the bottom broadened the scope of his intended book about the socially marginalized people that he had befriended. The conversations with his prison inmates and people on the street gave rise to *Interviews with People from the Bottom Rung of Society*. Among the sixty interviews selected for his book were those of a professional mourner, a human trafficker, a murderer, a beggar, a fortune-teller, a burglar, a dissident, a homosexual, a whoremaster, a former land-lord, a schoolteacher, and a Falun Gong practitioner. Like the author himself, all of the individuals were either thrown to the bottom of society during the various political purges in the Maoist era or landed there as a result of the tumultuous changes of today's evolving Chinese society.

The interviews are literary as well as journalistic—reconstructions rather than transcriptions of his encounters with his subjects. Because the interviews required extra sensitivity and patience, he sometimes eschewed the usual tools of a tape recorder and a notebook. Whether he was in prison or on the street, Liao always spent a considerable amount of time with his subjects, trying to gain their trust before conducting any interviews. For one story, it might require three to four conversations on different occasions. For example, he interviewed a mortician seven times and then incorporated all his conversations into one piece.

In 2001, the Yangtse Publishing House published a sanitized and shortened version of the book and it immediately became a best seller. Yu Jie, a well-known independent literary critic in Beijing, called the book "a sociologist's investigative report, which can serve as a historical record of contemporary China." Another independent critic, Ren Bumei, observed in an interview with Radio Free Asia: "All the individuals depicted in the book have one thing in common—they have all been deprived of their right to speak out. This book is a loud condemnation of the deprivation of their rights to speak and an excellent portrayal of this group of unique individuals."

For the first time after the Communist takeover in 1949, Liao introduced the word *diceng*, or "bottom rung of society" to the country. The notion is anathema to supporters of Mao's Communist movement, which is supposed to create an egalitarian society free of prostitutes, beggars, triad gangsters, and drug abusers. As expected, the Propaganda Department and the China News and Publishing Administration ordered all of Liao's books off the shelves, punished his editor at the publishing house, and fired all key staff at a popular Chinese weekly, *The Southern Weekend*, which had carried an interview with Liao and featured his book.

In 2002, Kang Zhengguo, a writer and lecturer at Yale University, met Liao in China and smuggled the complete manuscript out of the country. With Kang's help, the Taiwan-based Rye Field Publishing Company released an unabridged version of *Interviews with People from the Bottom Rung of Society* in three volumes. In the same year, Liao received a literary award from the Independent Chinese PEN Center, and in 2003 he received a Hellman-Hammett Grant, an annual award given by Human Rights Watch in recognition of writers who show courage in the face of political persecution.

I first heard of Liao back in June 2001 when I was contracted by Radio Free Asia to translate an interview he taped with the station, not long after the book was banned in China. The interview piqued my interest in the author. *Interviews with People from the Bottom Rung of Society* reminds me of Studs Terkel's book *Working*, in which Terkel collected interviews with Americans from all walks of life, ranging from a waitress and a telephone operator to a baseball player and a musician, who talked about their jobs and lives in America. *Working* was translated into Chinese in the 1980s, with the title *Americans Talk About Lives in America*. As a college student in China, I read both the English and Chinese versions (my teacher chose the English version of *Working* as a textbook for colloquial American English). *Working* introduced me, and many other Chinese, to the real America and the lives of ordinary Americans, about which I didn't know much before. Similarly, I believe the true-life stories in Liao's book will serve the same purpose for Western readers, helping them understand China from the perspective of ordinary Chinese.

Starting in 2002, I made numerous attempts to contact Liao through his friends in China. The search turned out to be an arduous task because as a dissident writer, he had to move constantly to dodge police harassment. One time he had to jump from a third-story window and run away from Chengdu to escape arrest after he had interviewed a member of an outlawed religious group.

One day in early 2004, I received an e-mail from a friend who was a former visiting scholar at Harvard University. She happened to know Liao pretty well and managed to track him down after she returned to Beijing from the United States. In her e-mail, I learned that Liao had agreed to my proposal of translating his works into English and he had also provided his cell-phone number. I checked the area code and it was from a small town somewhere near the Chinese border with Myanmar.

The two-hour conversation marked the beginning of our partnership. Over the next two years, Liao and I collaborated on the translations through e-mails and telephone calls. Sometimes we talked in our mutually understood codes or through our mutual friends if we believed our conversation was being tapped.

In the summer of 2005, three interviews from Liao's book—the professional mourner, the human trafficker, and the public restroom manager—appeared for the first time in English in *The Paris Review*, in the inaugural issue under its new editor, Philip Gourevitch.

Following the successful *Paris Review* debut, Liao and I selected twenty-seven stories that we feel are both representative of his work and might be of interest to Western readers. We also restructured and shortened the narratives, adding background information to help readers who are not familiar with the political and historical references mentioned in the interviews. As suggested in the title, we hope the book will offer Western readers a glimpse of contemporary China from the bottom up.

Meanwhile, Liao continues to break Chinese government censorship laws by publishing his works on overseas Chinese-language Web sites despite repeated police harassment. In December 2007, Liao was detained and interrogated for more than four hours when he traveled to Beijing to receive the Freedom to Write Award given by the Independent Chinese PEN Center. He is not intimidated. With the help of a Chinese lawyer, he is now suing the government for violating his human rights. "I am trying to overcome, little by little, the fear that's been inflicted on me," he says. "By doing so, I try to preserve my sanity and inner freedom."

Wen Huang
January 2008

The Corpse Walker

THE PROFESSIONAL MOURNER

I met Li Changgeng in Jiangyou County, in the southwestern province of Sichuan, on the way to the picturesque Baoyuan Mountain. Li, a professional mourner, is nearly seventy years old. He was born in the central province of Henan, and despite years of absence from his hometown, he still carried traces of the twanging Henan accent. He looked healthy and tough, half a head taller than a typical Sichuanese. He attributed his healthy constitution to years of playing the traditional horn, the suona—the long, trumpet-belled, Chinese oboe—which he told me requires considerable physical strength. Suona music and wailing are both used to create the mood of lamentation at traditional funerals.

—ɯɯ—

LIAO YIWU: How do you manage to wail and howl over a stranger?

LI CHANGGENG: I entered the mourning profession at the age of twelve. My teacher forced me to practice the basic suona tunes, as well as to learn how to wail and chant. Having a solid foundation in the basics enables a performer to improvise with ease, and to produce an earth-shattering effect. Our wailing sounds more authentic than that of the children or relatives of the deceased.

Most people who have lost their family members burst into tears and begin wailing upon seeing the body of the deceased. But their wailing doesn't last. Soon they are overcome with grief. When grief reaches into their hearts, they either suffer from shock or pass out. But for us, once we get into the mood, we control our emotions and improvise with great ease. We can wail as long as is requested. If it's a grand funeral and the money is good, we do lots of improvisations to please the host.

I left home and came southwest to Sichuan Province at the age of sixteen. Sichuan was a wealthier place than Henan, and people were willing to blow big money on weddings and funerals. I became pretty famous not long after I arrived here. This is a profession, like acting in a play or a movie. Once you have started, you gradually grow into the role. In a movie, the actor follows a script. For mourners and wailers, we follow the tunes of the music.

These tunes—"Sending Off the Spirit," "Pursuing the Spirit," "Requiem," "Calling the Spirit," "Farewell from Family Members," "The Ultimate Sorrow," "Sealing the Coffin," "Transcending to Heaven," "Burial," "One Last Look," "The Searing Pain," and "Oh I Am So Sad"—have been performed for hundreds of years, passed down from generation to generation. There are specific instructions on where to hit the high notes, or drop to the low notes; where to use a cracked voice, or to be high-pitched; where to wail with the effect of a dry throat, or to cry with tears; and where to tremble your body with great sadness or where to sound like you're losing your voice. It has to be very precise.

LIAO: How long can you wail? What was your record?

LI: Two days and two nights. Normally, once the suona starts the opening tune, all us band members will drop whatever we're doing and put on our white linen outfits. Then, in unison, we bow to the portraits of the deceased three times, and kowtow nine times. Then we start two rounds of crying, sobbing, and wailing. It sounds pretty chaotic on the surface, but if you take time to observe us from the side for about an hour or so, you will notice that it is a well-orchestrated chaos. For example, when I sob, you wail. It's like while you're taking a break, I work the shift. Voices are our capital and we know how to protect them. Not even a loud, searing, heartbreaking wail will damage our voices.

People's feelings of happiness or anger can be as contagious as a disease, and spread fast. Of course, we recognize that the family members of the deceased are the lead actors. But often, when they're overcome with sadness, their bodies begin to weaken. Before long all the lead actors have to exit the stage. At this time, we, the supporting actors, enter refreshed and warmed up for the role. Frankly speaking, the hired mourners are the ones who can stick to the very end.

As a hired mourner, you are both a participant and an observer. Sometimes, I will steal a glance or two at the relatives: some of them are truly grief-stricken, thrusting forward to the coffin, hoping to cling to the deceased. Others are just feigning. At that point, we are entrusted with dual roles: we will cry and wail our hearts out, and at the same time act as bodyguards, making sure to stop the relatives from dashing forward to bang against the coffin. After all the relatives have walked past the coffin and made their farewells, we come in to keep the momentum going. Traditions dictate that before the coffin is sealed, about five or six of us will try to thrust forward three times, trying to reach over to the deceased, and the others will seize our shirts to restrain us from touching the coffin. Only when the lid is on and the last nail is finally hammered can we secretly utter a sigh of relief.

We used to treat every funeral like a contest. There were lead wailers and backup wailers, and after the gig was over, members would get together and critique one another's performances. Having loud voices is not enough. You need to know how to perform properly. For example, the chanting of poems involves a well-coordinated combination of appealing introductions, smooth transitions, high crescendos, and strong endings. While performing, you have to control and, sometimes, let go of yourself. Your face, your hands, and your shoulders—every part of your body movement is important. When wailing, we chant stanzas like "You have worked so diligently all your life" or "How could you leave us just when our good days have started?," et cetera. Those are our librettos. We would critique the performance of each stanza so the wailer could improve in the future.

Wailing is more difficult than playing the suona or singing an opera aria. It's acting, but with such subtlety that people don't realize that you're acting. And, in the old days, it was key to our survival. From laying the body in the coffin to the wake, from sealing the coffin to the burial, each time the relatives were brought face-to-face with the deceased, there was a climax of emotional outbursts, and the amount of income we could earn from a gig depended on how well we did with the wailing.

LIAO: I would assume that people in your profession would always have jobs.

LI: I used to think so, too. In the 1940s, the Communists and the Nationalists were fighting a civil war. Refugees flooded my hometown like tidal waves. Unlike those refugees who ran away from danger, we rushed to places where there were deaths. Like musicians in the nineties, performers at that time also formed troupes or bands. My dad was a troupe leader. He used to be a Henan folk-song and opera singer; my teacher belonged to a different band. In those years, when China's central region was embroiled in wars, people lived in total misery, and roadside robbers and army deserters abounded. Nobody was in the mood for operas. In a desperate attempt to survive, my teacher suggested merging his band with my dad's. Their logic was that folks who were alive could live without going to concerts or operas, but they had to hold funerals for the dead. My dad didn't know how to play the suona, but he had a loud tenor voice. When he yelled, he could be heard miles away. As a former opera singer, memorizing over ten wailing tunes was a piece of cake for him.

But it wasn't an easy start for us in Sichuan. People used to hire local bands to perform at funerals. Rich households would hire both a local opera troupe and a group of chanting monks to send off the spirit of the dead. In the city of Chengdu, it was impossible for us to break in. We retreated and traveled down to the Mianyang region. We couldn't get any gigs there either. It was the same situation when we got to Jiangyou County. We decided to settle down temporarily in a poor village about six miles away from the township. To survive, we searched for all sorts of odd jobs just hoping to get three meals a day.

In 1948, an epidemic hit this region. Dead bodies were lying everywhere on the roadside. The epidemic saved our troupe. As you know, disease is an equal opportunity hitter, striking both the rich and the poor. Many of the local funeral bands were quite small, more like a family business, a couple of individuals who would bring their suona to a funeral and do a simple performance. There was no way they could compete with a large troupe like ours. Besides, northerners like us were bigger, taller, and stronger. After a while, our troupe pretty much monopolized the businesses of weddings and funerals. When we played the suona, we showed better stamina than those tubercular locals.

But each region was controlled by triad gangs or bandits. If you crossed paths with them and snatched their business, you could end up with a number of stab holes in your belly. Who dared to take business from them? We couldn't even afford to pay protection money. So, after losing their iron rice bowls to us, local suona players and professional mourners rallied together and enlisted help from a local triad leader, called Red Flag Five. This guy ran a teahouse in Qinglian Township. Red Flag Five sent us a message: either we moved our ass out of his territory, or he'd have someone break our legs and throw us out.

Luckily, we were pretty well-known in the area. There was a local landowner whose family were Buddhists. His nickname was Mediator Zhang. He went, begging for mercy on behalf of us, and offered twenty pieces of silver. With a little bribe, Red Flag Five backed down a bit. He proposed the idea of staging a one-on-one contest. My dad asked: How can we stage a competition when there are no dead bodies and funerals? The triad leader said: That's easy.

The next morning, when we got up and opened the door, we stumbled on the corpse of a beggar, right in front of our house. So we treated the beggar as if he were a big shot and prepared a big ceremony. We purchased a coffin, embalmed the corpse, and dressed him up in fancy clothes. We then carried the open coffin to the township square. Then, both sides began to build their separate stages with the mutually agreed terms. Local suona players, professional mourners, and their relatives raised a large sum of money, and paid big bucks to hire some prestigious players, ready to fight us to the bitter end.

Within half a day, both stages were set up. The two stages, standing opposite each other, were almost fifteen meters above the ground. The open coffin was sitting between them. The grand contest attracted people from villages over a hundred kilometers away. This was the first time ever, since the legendary Pangu created the world, that suona players and professional funeral wailers were dueling for territory.

The contest started with the suona. Both sides played the same tune, "The Ultimate Grief." About several meters away from the stage sat the judges and audience. In the front row were the head of the triad and his lackeys, the county security chief, local celebrities, and rich gentry. I was young and competitive, and decided to mount the stage to start the first round, but my teacher pulled me down. He was in his fifties, but still strong and energetic. He wore a black mourning outfit with a white headband, which was quite dazzling under the sun. He held the suona between his teeth, grabbed the hanging ladder, and with a few big steps he climbed up to the stage. I could see that his opponent was also getting ready on the other side.

A guy in the audience waved a white flag and yelled, "Start!" Music flew out of both players. For a while, the tunes were sharp as a knife stabbing people's hearts. Both players were veterans, very experienced. Half an hour into the contest, it was still hard to declare a winner. At the height of the competition, those with observant eyes could probably see traces of saliva mixed with blood flying out of my teacher's suona. My dad looked very calm. He knew very well that my teacher had good stamina and was quite stubborn. He would never acknowledge defeat. His parents used to call him Mule Head. About an hour later, his opponent began to show signs of fatigue and was gasping for breath. Victory was on the horizon. Suddenly, I saw my teacher's suona snap into two and the guy at the podium flash his white flag. Oh, we were finished. I looked back at the stage and noticed that my teacher's mouth was covered with blood. It turned out that someone had used a slingshot to sabotage him.

I reacted fast, without much thinking, I grabbed the ladder, and the next thing I knew, I was on the stage. My dad was also trying to get on, but the stage couldn't support that many people, and began to sway from side to side. I screamed at my teacher: Teacher, please get off fast. At that moment, the other troupe's members rallied around the stage and blocked Dad's way. He had to give up and stomped his feet, yelling: That little bastard, get off the stage. You are asking for death. Before he even finished, I saw another contestant from the opponent's camp stepping onto the stage opposite me.

It was time for the wailing contest.

My opponent kicked his feet, pounded his chest with his fist, and uttered a thunderous wailing, like a cornered ox. The audience responded with waves of "Bravo." I thought, We're done! I thought about my teacher who was wounded and had lost the contest. I thought about my dad who couldn't possibly survive this defeat. We had been forced to leave our homes and travel thousands of kilometers, trying to bring laughter to those who were alive and wail for those who were dead. Now we ended up in such a terrible situation, getting bullied by the locals. When would we see the end of our misery? This ritual for this deceased beggar could kill our band. What were we going to do? How were we going to survive? If I was not allowed to play the suona, begging seemed to be the only alternative left. Someday, I could end up with the same fate as the beggar in the coffin.

The more I thought about it, the more despondent I became. The more I thought about it, the more suicidal I became. I burst into tears.

I opened my eyes wide, staring at the sky, at the blaring sun, without blinking. I lost all my senses. I couldn't see anything or hear anything. I wailed my heart out. I kept punching myself on the chest and then reached my fists into the sky, as if I were wrestling for life with the Heavenly God. Then the person with the slingshot aimed at me. All I could hear was *bang,* and my head was hurting and spinning. I tried to keep my face upward. As long as my face was not bleeding, I would continue to wail. When the white flag flashed several times to signal my victory, I didn't even notice it. Later on, I was told that my opponent lost his voice way before I did. I still kept on for more than ten more minutes, bringing down tears in the crowds, who began to join and wail in a loud chorus. Even those triad guys had misty eyes. They were heard sighing: We have treated those out-of-towners unfairly. It's so sad. It's so sad to see that kid on the stage.

LIAO: During Mao Zedong's Smashing the Four Old Elements campaign, in the time of the Cultural Revolution, after the Great Leap Forward, were you still allowed to perform?

LI: I've never changed professions, but I have changed the tunes I play. While celebrating China's liberation, everyone loved folk tunes and folk dances. Our funeral troupe turned around and began to play in unison, "The Sky in the Communist Regions Is Brighter." We performed similar revolutionary tunes during the ensuing political campaigns. Singing and performing helped to mobilize the masses. Whatever tunes the leaders wanted us to play, we followed orders. Performers like us were happy if we were fed three meals a day and given a comfortable bed at night. We seldom harbored any discontent or anger. Let me tell you, during the three-year famine, as waves and waves of people died of starvation, I continued to play rosy tunes, praising peace and prosperity. I guess after you act at funerals for too long, you become heartless. In this world, one shouldn't be too hot-blooded. Today, the Party allows you to speak your mind and has relaxed its political control, so you feel encouraged and excited. But if you get too carried away, the Party will send you to labor camps. Then you end up living with your tail tucked between your legs in the camps for ten or twenty years.

LIAO: Your troupe disbanded, didn't it?

LI: We broke up in 1951. Since then, I followed the example of many local suona players: doing farmwork during the daytime, and moonlighting when opportunity arose. Whenever someone got married, had babies, or died, people in the region would come get me because I was pretty well-known. Someone suggested that I form a new troupe and look for gigs. I gave it some careful thought and then said, "Uh-uh, no." If I had a troupe, it would be considered a nongovernmental organization. Which government agency would it fall under? I wasn't aware of any, and in that case my troupe could be considered an illegal organization. If you were labeled illegal, you could be charged with counterrevolutionary activities. I wanted to avoid that.

I did have some auspicious years, but they seem to be so far away now. Immediately after China started its economic reforms in the late 1970s, my fortune changed. The old traditions were revived, and I became popular for a little while. But it didn't last long. Nowadays, people no longer follow the traditional practice of having suona music during weddings and funerals. Fewer and fewer invitations come my way. Country folks follow urban fads very quickly. Young people in the cities watch too many Hong Kong and Western movies. They begin to imitate everything in the movies. People no longer go through the kowtow ceremonies. Of course, country folks can't afford a Western-style wedding, but with a single phone call, they can easily rent a big limousine. That is much more grandiose than the traditional red bridal sedan chair followed by a band of suona players.

I have to stay away from the urban areas and try to find opportunities in the remote mountainous regions. It's really hard because you can never plan anything. Plus, I'm getting old. Traveling is no longer an easy task. I used to have several apprentices, but they have all given up and changed jobs. Young fellow, playing the suona in the old days was never considered a degrading profession. Rich kids might have looked down on us, but they were notoriously phony. Actually, the pioneer and founder of this profession was his holiness, Confucius. In his early years, he played the suona to support his mother. He performed at funerals, dressed in mourner's outfits made from white linens. He was also a professional wailer and coffin bearer. That's why you see the portraits of Confucius or his memorial tablets in many suona players' homes.

We are in a different era. Not so many people want to learn how to play the suona. Nowadays, once a tent for the wake is set up, relatives immediately pull out several mah-jongg tables and play gambling games all night long. The mourners are more preoccupied with winning games than with the deceased. People are not what they used to be. They don't even bother to pretend to be sorrowful.

LIAO: What about funerals? The suona tunes still make the ceremonies more touching.

LI: You seem to be out of touch with the current market economy. My village has easy access to modern transportation. When a person passes away, a family just has to make a phone call. A company specializing in funeral preparations will show up right away, offering a wide range of services from wreath rentals to the organizations of wakes and funeral processions. They call it one-stop service. In the old days, families invited monks to chant mantras to pave the way for the dead to cross to another world. Suona music accompanied the wailing of the devoted children. Nowadays, deaths are considered festival occasions here. People host pop concerts during the wake. Friends and relatives will fight for the opportunity to order songs on behalf of the deceased. These can be any kind of pop songs. Sometimes mourners use a popular song and change a couple of lyrics to make it fit the occasion. People go crazy over that. As for the funeral procession, the children and relatives of the deceased are no longer required to carry the coffin. People use cars or limos. Western instruments lead the procession. With loudspeakers, the funeral music can be heard miles away and everyone knows that a person has just died.

LIAO: You know so much about funerals. I used to hear my grandpa tell stories about "walking the corpse." Is it true that this was a profession, and people used to pay those professionals large sums of money to transport home the body of someone who died hundreds or thousands of miles away?

LI: Correct. In the old days, there were people who specialized in walking the corpse. They normally traveled in the evenings, two guys at a time. One walked in the front and the other at the back. Like carrying a sedan chair, they pulled the body to walk along, as fast as wind. They would utter in unison, "Yo ho, yo ho."

　　If you looked from a distance, you would see that the dead and the living march to the same steps. They used gravity to keep the corpse walking to the same rhythm. It was hard for the trio to change gait and make a turn, never a sharp turn. If you happened to see a walking corpse coming, you got out of the way. Otherwise, it could walk right into you.

I saw this in 1949. A local merchant was accidentally shot by a group of army deserters in Jiangxi Province. This merchant's name was Lu. I helped arrange his funeral. At that time, there was no easy means of water or land transportation to bring his body back home. His friends couldn't bear to bury him in another land. They paid money to those professionals to get his body home. It took them over a week, and when they got there his body looked as if he were alive.

Since most of these corpse walkers slept during the daytime, young people like me were quite curious. I licked a small hole in the window paper, and checked what was in their room. It was pitch-dark. All I could hear was the thunderous snoring. A guy called Xiao Wu wanted to sneak in and steal the wand used by the corpse walkers. We all wanted to see if there was any magic to it. But the moment he stealthily opened the door, a dark shadow jumped right onto him. It was a black cat.

Corpse walkers always brought a cat with them wherever they went. Before they set off, they would move the corpse, which was standing against the wall, the same way they would open a door. They would then carefully move the corpse outside, and support it from the front and the back. After that, a cat would climb all over the corpse three or four times. They called it "electric shock." The three of them would march in unison on the same spot for a while, just like an army exercise. Then they began to move with "Yo ho, yo ho."

LIAO: I still don't know what to believe.

LI: It's a true story.

THE HUMAN TRAFFICKER

Abducting or trafficking in women is a criminal trade that has a long history in China. In the old days, this profitable business was controlled by crime syndicates—the triads—which lured rural girls and women with offers of nice jobs in big cities, then sold them into brothels at a high price. After the Communist revolution in 1949, the government eliminated the triads in many parts of China. The business of domestic human trafficking has now been largely taken over by country bumpkins like Qian Guibao, whom I visited at a detention center in the city of Chongqing. I interviewed him for over two hours; since I was not allowed to bring any recording equipment into the prison, I had to write up the interview from memory.

—————

LIAO YIWU: You look like an honest hick. How did you end up in this trade?

QIAN GUIBAO: My experience was nothing unique. I was a peasant in River Valley Village in Pinggu County, Sichuan Province. Have you heard of Pinggu, home of the famous pandas? In the old days, the mountain next to our village was covered with lush forests and provided us with everything we needed for a living. We would pick up the timber left by the lumber mills and sell it. It was pretty good money. In addition, the mountain was rich in many natural food resources. But as the demand for lumber increased, the trees disappeared fast. Soon the forest was gone. The lumber factory closed, we had no more leftover timber to sell, and it was impossible to plant crops on the bare, deforested mountains. You probably haven't visited my hometown, but you can't make a living there as a peasant. Before I turned twenty-eight, I had violated the one-child family planning policy because my wife had given birth to three girls. I couldn't even afford to buy pants for them.

Everyone else in the village was pretty much in the same situation.

Men would wear pants made from dry grass when working in the field. They left their real pants at home, saving them for holidays and special occasions. In the wintertime, women and girls would be stark naked, huddling next to the stove to do housework. We led miserable lives until 1992, when a couple of young guys in the village decided to take the leather goods that many families had saved for years and sell them at the local market. With the money we got, we bought ourselves bus tickets and left the village. At first we found construction jobs in the county, and then we followed a contractor all the way to the northwestern province of Gansu. We soon gave up the hard labor jobs and I began to go from village to village, doing some small retail business. It was quite an eye-opening experience.

Northwestern China is enormous. In many places, there's nothing but barren desert. It was even hard to get drinking water. Locals would keep the snow in a big pond and the melting snow provided them with drinking water for half a year. In these villages, the men were honest and kind. They loved their women and followed them around. Since most families prefer boys to girls, there weren't too many women in the region. Young men would spend years pinching pennies so they could use all their savings to find a woman to marry. I felt so sorry for them. Each time they saw a woman, their eyes would brighten up with lust, ready to mount her and fuck her immediately.

My hometown in Sichuan was pretty poor, but I hadn't seen any men as desperate as these. As you know, the Sichuan women have a reputation for being industrious, good-looking, and nice to their men. Guys in the northern provinces love women from Sichuan. With that in mind, I saw a moneymaking opportunity.

LIAO: What was your first experience like?

QIAN: I couldn't sell anybody, so I married two of my daughters to two guys in a village in Gansu Province. My in-laws were considered relatively rich in the area. I received six hundred yuan and eight sheep. I sold the sheep to a peasant at the train station for fifty yuan each. So I ended up getting a thousand yuan [about $120]. I had never felt so rich. I was exhilarated beyond control. But a couple of days later, my daughters told me that they had met a few other Sichuan wives in the village. Those women were brought to the village by human traffickers, and guess the price those bastards asked for each woman: over two thousand yuan each. Basically, I lost money in the deal. Damn.

LIAO: You sent your daughters to a faraway place and married them off to strangers for money?

QIAN: What do they know about happiness? My daughters are the children of a poor peasant. As long as their husbands have dicks, that's all I care. The more often women get laid, the prettier they look. Of course with some women, after they give birth to a couple of kids, their looks are gone forever.

LIAO: How did you manage to expand your business?

QIAN: I realized that I could be pretty charming. When I started out, I was a little nervous and lacked confidence. I tried to do some honest business as a matchmaker for the women in my village. But it was really tough. I ran my tongue nonstop and talked up a storm, but my success rate was very low. Women growing up in the mountains had never left their native villages before. It was difficult to show up out of the blue and convince them to leave home and travel thousands of miles to marry a stranger. They wouldn't do it even when I threatened to kill their parents.

I had no other alternative but to entice them with beautiful lies. First I told them that I was running a restaurant in the north and recruiting waitresses to help out. I promised to pay them decent wages and cover their food and accommodations. Those lies didn't fly. So I came up with some new ideas. I had some fake identification cards made and claimed that I was recruiting workers for a textile factory in the north. I told the women that wool was cheap in Gansu since cows and sheep were abundant; it was an ideal location for the manufacture of sweaters and rugs. I told all sorts of lies, and finally some of them worked. Soon I became bolder and bolder. I set up contacts in several major cities in the northwest. My job was to transport the "goods" to a certain location, and my contacts would "distribute" them to the villages.

Practice made perfect. My tongue became as slick as if it were soaked in oil, and I could easily lure a real goddess from heaven into marrying a human on earth. There were many women who would swallow my crap like it was the most nutritious food they ever ate. If they believed in my crap and ended up getting sold, it served them right.

LIAO: You were trading human flesh.

QIAN: Comrade, that is certainly not a nice way to describe it. I didn't run a brothel.

LIAO: Have you ever forced innocent women into prostitution?

QIAN: A virtuous woman will never prostitute herself, no matter how hard you force her. But most women are just like men. They crave adventures and love easy money. It's true that I sold over twenty women in the past five years, but those women came to me on their own. I didn't threaten them with a gun. I wasn't a bandit or kidnapper. You didn't even have to use dirty tricks to lure them. There are so many poor bachelors in the north. I provided a service that linked those love-birds thousands of miles apart. The beginning of their relationships might not sound too auspicious or tender. Sometimes the brides want to commit suicide. But after their initial reluctance or rebellious pro-tests, most of them ended up accepting their fate. As time went by, their lives became better and more harmonious.

   As for being tied up and beaten, it is quite normal in the country-side. A man cannot be considered a good man if he doesn't beat his wife or if he is too old to pick up a cane. Once, my wife and I were car-rying some corn back from the field. I became so horny and wanted to have sex with her. She said she was having her period and that I'd at least have to wait until dark. I wouldn't give up and insisted that I fuck her in the daylight. She then said she was too tired, and didn't want to take off her pants. I got mad. Before I had the chance to grab a wooden pole and force her to strip, she bolted out the door. I chased after her. She jumped in the village pond, attempting to drown herself. Ha! Guess what? The water was only waist deep. She began to cry and scream when her body didn't sink.

   Oh well, those girls that I transported to the northwest had much better luck than my wife. As the saying goes: Beatings and quarrels make good couples. I'm just trying to supply what the market needs.

LIAO: You deceived those women and tricked them into the business. You ruined their lives.

QIAN: I was also trying to provide a solution to a problem that the Chinese government faced. In some northern regions, there are too many bachelors. The regional climate is too dry and people are poor. Sooner or later, there will be disturbances. By taking women over there, I balanced the yin and yang. This helps dissolve young guys' sexual tension. As you know, the matchmaking service in the city collects fees. I was in the same business. Actually, if you deducted the cost of train fare, food, and other miscellaneous stuff, there wasn't much left as profit. Sometimes, after I negotiated with my contacts in the north and sent the girl over, the village bachelor would change his mind because he couldn't afford the fee. We'd have to sell her at a cheaper price.

LIAO: Didn't you worry about bad karma?

QIAN: Bad karma? That's such bullshit. If you read newspapers nowadays, you will constantly come across stories about how someone became enlightened and has finally come to realize the true value of life, blah blah blah. The so-called "value of life" is nothing more than not having to worry about money. When someone earns money without working hard, he begins to bullshit about the value of life. Just like a pop singer, who only needs to open his or her mouth, sing a couple of songs, and the money pours in like crazy. That's why everyone adores pop stars and models. I'm a peasant. Nobody envies the life of a peasant.

    I admit that I lied to them and used deception. But in this world today, could you tell me a person who has not lied to get what they want? The only honest beings are animals, such as stupid pigs.

LIAO: For victims of human smuggling, there is no such thing as a traditional wedding. In many cases, I'm told, the guy's parents hire some fellow villagers to tie up the girl immediately after the human trader hands her over and then the groom rapes her.

QIAN: Rape? These guys are having sex with their wives. You can't call that rape. Of course, you're a city guy. You can meet girls at nightclubs or dance parties, or even at train stations. There are so many ways for boys and girls to meet in the city. If you're a shy guy, you can always join a government-run matchmaking service, or place a personal ad in the paper. If it doesn't work out with one date, you can meet someone else. Poor folks in the countryside are not so lucky. As for weddings, according to the local tradition, as long as you have a ceremony, with drums and horns, and invite everyone to a banquet, you are considered husband and wife. Country folks have been following these traditions for generations. They never follow the so-called "legal procedures." Law just doesn't apply in those regions.

LIAO: Well, the law applies to you. Are you going to get the death penalty?

QIAN: I actively cooperated with the prosecution and they reduced my sentence to life imprisonment. I accepted the verdict and pleaded guilty. But I still can't accept the charges—that I've harmed the general public or caused lots of trouble for the government.

LIAO: Is your human trafficking group still in business?

QIAN: We used to have over ten people. Now, seven are here in this jail. Those guys working in the northwest were thrown into local jails. The two group leaders have been executed. I wasn't listed as a top criminal because I merely organized the goods and didn't abuse any of the women. I persuaded my colleagues not to touch the goods because northerners are pretty conservative people. They want the goods in their original packages. They want to see blood on their wedding night. Once you deflower the girl, you can't get a decent price.

LIAO: Did you only target women from the poorest villages?

QIAN: Mostly, but one time I managed to talk some university graduates into the deal. One of them was working on her doctoral degree at a university.

LIAO: With that ugly face of yours?

QIAN: Damn right. I acted very sophisticated. With those intellectuals, you could never use the lies you'd use to recruit for small companies or textile factories. They would see through your tricks right away. I dropped all my masks. I told them I was a peasant from a fairly well-off region, which was covered with fruit trees and thick forests, an uncultivated Shangri-la. When it comes to bragging about the abundant natural resources of the countryside, I'm an expert. It didn't take long for the female college students to change their minds. Then, I pretended to seek their advice on how to do business. I told them that my village desperately needed some educated folks to go help cultivate the natural resources. I invited one of the Ph.D. students to visit my village so she could refer more students to help my village do business. I told her we would hire college students and pay them high salaries. She fell for it so easily. I've got a remarkably slick tongue. Unfortunately, once you snatch those educated women, they can be a handful. One girl was locked up in a cell for over a week, but still wouldn't cave in to our demands.

LIAO: If I were the judge, I would first cut off your tongue as punishment. It deserves to be cut off.

THE PUBLIC RESTROOM MANAGER

Zhou Minggui has handled human waste for almost all of his life, first as an employee of the state in charge of cleaning public toilets, and now as an independent restroom manager under contract with the city government of Chengdu to manage a large public restroom in the northwestern part of the city. "It's serious business," says Zhou. He's about seventy years old, but he looks pretty energetic.

I had known of Zhou for quite some time. His restroom stands almost next door to my mother's teahouse. But we were simply nodding acquaintances. One night last year, I summoned up enough courage to get over my concerns about losing my social status as an intellectual, and started a conversation with him.

—◦—

ZHOU MINGGUI: Are you coming in to use the toilet or not? It's already past midnight. Based on our rules, I need to charge you extra. How else can I pay my taxes to the city's Environment and Hygiene Department? But since you're a regular client, I'll waive the extra charge.

LIAO YIWU: Grandpa Zhou, I'm not here to use the restroom. I want to take you out for tea.

ZHOU: You don't have to bother. I'm only a public restroom guard.

LIAO: Let's go over to the teahouse.

ZHOU: You are too nice. Is your mom's teahouse still open? Actually, the more her customers drink, the better for my business. When their bladders are full, they come to my place. It's called "mutually beneficial."

LIAO: In this world, there are rich people and poor people, aristocrats and common folks. But when it comes to the call of nature, everyone's equal. Even the emperor has to take a shit.

ZHOU: I have never seen a royal family member taking a shit. If they did, they wouldn't come to do it in this public restroom. Hey, you're a writer, you like to collect material for your articles. Did you know there was an attempted murder here not long ago? About two days ago, a guy was chasing a young woman and she ran into this restroom. I tried to stop the guy at the door but couldn't. All the female customers were startled and began to scream. I sent my son to break it up, but the man took a knife out of his pocket. Nobody dared move. The guy seized the young woman, and was about to slash her face. She went to her knees, begging for mercy.

You know, in many public restrooms, the fertilizer companies put plastic containers near the urinals to collect urine. I grabbed one of these containers and splashed its contents all over the guy. That stopped him. He was soaked. Later on, someone called the police and they took both the man and the woman away. Guess what happened the next day? I saw the man and woman walking on the street, hugging and kissing like lovers. I tried to dodge them, but they came up to me. The guy pointed his fingers at my nose: You motherfucker, how dare you pour all that pee on me?

I didn't reply. He continued swearing at me: You fucker, why didn't you mind your own damn business? Look what you did. My whole body smells like piss.

When I heard that, I lost it. I said: If I hadn't poured the urine, you'd have killed someone!

Then—I couldn't believe it—his girlfriend started to defend him: So what if he killed me? It had nothing to do with you. You're the stinking public restroom manager. We've been dating for almost three years. He's tried to kill me over ten times, but I've survived. Why call the police? We got detained yesterday and our families had to bail us out. When they saw us, they all covered their noses. Our neighbors laughed at us. We've come back to seek compensation for our emotional trauma. Nowadays, everyone in China talks about the rule of law. We're going to sue you.

My son was incensed and got into a terrible argument with them.

He grabbed a copper ladle and was ready to fight. I tried to hold him back, but that bitch jumped out in the street and screamed murder. All hell broke loose. We got quite a crowd. What pissed me off was that the guy pointed at my son in front of the crowd and said: Did you just use that ladle to stir up the shit in the latrine? You're a born toilet cleaner. You even use a shit ladle as a murder weapon. So insulting! That was no shit ladle. It was for cooking. My son threw it at them. The people in the crowd thought it was covered with shit and ran away as fast as they could.

Let me tell you, there's never been any shortage of these scoundrels in our city. They don't have any jobs, they just hang out on the street and make trouble. This jerk I was telling you about still shows up at my restroom now and then. He always teases me: Since you're not too well-off and pinching pennies here, I won't seek any economic compensation for what you did to me. In return for our kindness, why don't you allow me and my girlfriend to use the restroom free for one year.

LIAO: He does sound like a jerk.

ZHOU: Yeah, but I'm not mad anymore. What goes around comes around. In the future, even if someone falls into the latrine, I won't pull him out. When I used to work as a latrine cleaner, I liked to go out of my way to help people. Sometimes, people used to make fun of me and call me the Shit Samaritan. Well, it took me half a month to go through the various bureaucratic hoops before I could obtain the contract to run this restroom. All I'm going to do from now on is guard the toilets and collect the entrance fee.

If I had been born ten years later, I would never have thought to make a living in the restroom business. When I was young, you didn't have to pay to answer the call of nature. All public restrooms were under the supervision of the municipal Environment and Hygiene Department. Later the department assigned each public restroom to its nearby street committee. The street committee then asked the local residents to take care of the restrooms themselves. In the end, nobody was taking responsibility for their maintenance and they got dirty. When it rained, the street flooded with human waste, and cars couldn't even drive through. When the sun was out, the human waste dried up, and the moist stink could bring tears to your eyes. There are still a couple of free restrooms like that in the city, in the old residential areas. But nowadays, most public restrooms have been renovated and it's a good business.

As you know, houses built before the 1970s didn't have indoor plumbing systems. People had to rely on public restrooms. Sometimes, they had to walk quite far. At night, families had to use chamber pots. In the old days, chamber pots painted in red were popular items for bridal showers or dowries. A sturdy chamber pot could last over ten years. In the old days, every morning, families used to dump their chamber pots into the public restrooms or wait for the human-waste truck. Those trucks were more punctual than public buses. While waiting for the truck, people chatted and caught up with one another over the day's gossip. It was quite harmonious.

LIAO: You sound nostalgic.

ZHOU: Yes. I used to drive a human-waste truck. Nobody looked down on me because I was handling shit. My clients called me Master Zhou. In those days, peasants didn't have access to fertilizers, so human waste was quite precious. There were even people who stole shit from the latrines. Sometimes, they would get caught and the street committee would detain their carts. People in that era had no sense of money. There was no such thing as a fine. All they wanted from those shit thieves was a soul-searching self-criticism. During the Cultural Revolution in the 1960s, they would blame the capitalists for poisoning their minds and making them steal. The punishment for stealing human waste was to recite Chairman Mao's Little Red Book.

LIAO: Wasn't that a bit much? Stealing shit wasn't a serious crime, was it?

ZHOU: China's a socialist country. In theory, everything belongs to the government. In the old days, the waste we collected every morning was sent to a collective farm called the Red and Bright Commune, which is famous in our region because Chairman Mao visited it in 1957. They were really proud of that and they still display the plaque Mao gave them. Since the Red and Bright Commune was associated with Mao, and was used as a model for peasants in the rest of the country to emulate, we sent them only the top-quality human waste, to ensure bumper harvests each year. Each time we brought a shipment to the commune, we'd beat drums and gongs and decorate the trucks with red flowers. When they saw our trucks approaching, the peasants would hold large welcoming ceremonies. Many young students volunteered their time to help with the mission.

LIAO: I did similar stuff when I was a kid. On weekends, we would pick horse manure off the street and donate it to the communes. Everybody was following Mao's instructions to support agriculture.

ZHOU: In our profession, our role model was Shi Chuanxiang, who was elected as a representative to the National People's Congress. He met Chairman Mao in person and had a picture taken with him. Everyone was excited that Mao would grant a public restroom cleaner like him such a high honor. We all tried to emulate him. Of course, we didn't have toilet bowls then like we do today. The structure of the public bathroom was quite simple: a wooden platform with many holes in it was laid on top of a pit. The people squatted and relieved themselves through the holes. Every morning, a tube drained the waste from the pit into the truck. One day, the tube was blocked. When I went to investigate, I saw that a fetus had got stuck there.

LIAO: That's awful. Why didn't the woman go to the abortion clinic?

ZHOU: Young man, we're talking about the 1970s. In the last decade people have become more relaxed about premarital sex. In those days, without a marriage certificate, a woman would never have the guts to go to the hospital for an abortion. Premarital sex was considered extremely shameful. If her company found out, the woman's career would be ruined. The stigma would stay with her the rest of her life. As a result, many girls would secretly procure medicine and the public toilet was like an abortion clinic, a dumping ground for dead fetuses. Some girls took the wrong medicine and died. In China, life is cheap.

LIAO: I understand that during the Cultural Revolution, professors were forced to clean the public bathrooms.

ZHOU: Many professors and scholars were labeled counterrevolutionaries, and yes, they were assigned to clean toilets. For people like me
who did this for a living, we suddenly found ourselves with nothing to
do. I wanted to work, but the students belonging to the Red Guard
groups wouldn't allow it. I still got paid, but I ended up staying at home
all day long, sleeping and goofing around. Since I was used to doing
hard labor every day, I got really bored. Sometimes, in the mornings
and evenings, I would sneak out to the toilet to coach the professors on
their technique.

Considering how Chinese emperors slaughtered dissenting intellectuals in ancient times, I think Chairman Mao and the Communist
Party were pretty merciful. Mao emphasized the importance of initiat-
ing mind reform and reeducating scholars. He ordered intellectuals to
engage in hard labor, and at the same time, encouraged working-class
people to read books. Reading books was easy for us working-class
folks. We enrolled in literacy classes, and took courses in history and
politics. That was fun. But when you forced professors to clean toilets,
they considered it a huge loss of status. On the surface they acted as
obedient as dogs. But many of them couldn't take it and hanged themselves with their belts inside the toilet stalls.

People thought it was tragic whenever a professor died while cleaning the restroom. But I was born a restroom cleaner. If I have a sad life,
nobody gives a damn. I think Confucius was right when he said, "All
occupations are base. Only book learning is exalted."

LIAO: Your story triggers a lot of childhood memories. I still remember
those big, spacious public restrooms. We would play hide-and-seek in
them. Sometimes, when we forgot to bring toilet paper, we would wipe
our little asses along the edge of the wall. I constantly got scolded for
that. But I have to say that the public restroom was my second classroom.

ZHOU: What? You call the public restroom a classroom?

LIAO: It was through a hole in the restroom that I saw female private
parts for the first time. It was shocking and exciting. From another
drawing on the wall, I learned about sexual intercourse. I couldn't see
the body clearly. There was only a sectional profile of a male and a

female sexual organ stuck together. I was only eight years old. The only thing we studied in school was the chairman's red books on the Communist revolutions. I had never imagined that in Red China there were people who would draw such dirty pictures. I became indignant, took out my pencil, and wrote beside the picture: This is two counterrevolutionaries doing bad stuff.

ZHOU: Were you one of those kids that does graffiti? That's a bad habit. I just don't understand it.

LIAO: When I was in high school, I used to hate this girl whose name was Wang Xiaohong, because she was such a gossip. So I wrote on the bathroom wall: Wang Xiaohong is a whore. She sleeps with evil capitalists.

ZHOU: You know, it takes me a long time to remove graffiti. It's more difficult than sweeping the floors or even cleaning out the pit. And when I finally erase it, the minute I turn around, new graffiti appears. Restroom graffiti has been in existence since ancient times. The only exception was during the Cultural Revolution. The Red Guards painted Communist slogans all over the place and didn't leave enough room for graffiti artists. On the restroom walls, they printed slogans like "Capitalists Are as Worthless as Shit" or "Counterrevolutionaries Deserve to Eat Shit."

I'm semiliterate so I can't understand much of what people write there. Most of the time, the mere sight of graffiti makes me so mad that I don't even bother to read it. There are limericks, dirty drawings, vulgar phrases, political slogans, and even paragraphs copied from published articles.

LIAO: Those graffiti limericks were much more interesting than the ones we learned in school. I vividly remember one of them, "Love Songs from the Restroom." It goes like this: You are a bird flying in the sky, I'm a cockroach, in shit I thrive. You are flying in circles in the clouds, I'm doing somersaults in the shitty pond.

ZHOU: You're a well-educated person. Why do you memorize vulgar limericks like that?

LIAO: Sorry to embarrass you. But think about it: there are well over a billion people in China. Only a few can get their writings published in newspapers and magazines, and you need to go through rigorous reviews and various levels of censorship. By the time your article gets to the paper, it no longer resembles what you originally wrote. Many people will never have an opportunity to express themselves in public. That's why the public bathrooms have become the venue for free speech.

ZHOU: OK, I admit I saw a very funny one yesterday. It was a limerick to commemorate Chairman Mao. It was pretty easy to remember. It went: Chairman Mao, Chairman Mao, if you rise from your grave you will see embezzlers in raves. Chairman Mao, if you look to your right, hookers and druggies at your side. Chairman Mao, if you look to your left, fake goods are what you get. Chairman Mao, if you look behind your back, laid-off workers are deep in debt. Chairman Mao, if you look down, extramarital affairs are common. Chairman Mao, Chairman Mao, close your eyes, out of sight, out of mind. People want their iron rice bowls back.

LIAO: That sure captures the mood these days. But anyway, is your business good, Grandpa?

ZHOU: Barely. Then again, so many people are unemployed here. I'm lucky to have a business. My monthly profits are about two hundred to three hundred yuan. I'm pretty content with that. And for an old guy like me, managing toilets is easy work. Life is tough and tiring. All my nerves are strained. One of these days, one of the nerves will snap, and then I'll be gone.

THE CORPSE WALKERS

Stories of walking the corpse are popular in both northern and southern China. Most of the time, the tales are so dramatically exaggerated that one has to discard them as fiction. After Li Changgeng, a professional mourner, mentioned corpse walking in a previous interview, many readers wrote asking whether they were expected to believe Li's description of corpse walking. I myself thought it was half truth, half fiction, but recently I heard the following story, which seemed to me quite convincing. On the anniversary of my father's passing I traveled to Lijiaping in Sichuan, where my father was born and where his ashes are buried. After going through the rituals—burning incense, lighting firecrackers, and kowtowing in front of his grave—I paid a visit to Luo Tianwang, a feng shui master, who had selected my father's grave site. Luo is an old family friend, now in his seventies. He looked healthy and energetic; his vision was still keen and his mind sharp, and we spoke for some time.

—⟨⟨⟨—

LIAO YIWU: When I was growing up here, I constantly heard stories about corpse walking from our neighbor, Third Grandma Wang. She told me that people in Sichuan call the practice "yo shi." While "shi" means "dead body," the word "yo" is taken from "yo ho, yo ho," the sounds that corpse walkers chant while they haul the dead body along. Do you think there is any truth to these stories?

LUO TIANWANG: Sure. Corpse walking has never been an officially recognized profession, but the practice had been around since ancient times. When I was young, I had several friends in the business of trading salt. They used to travel by foot on dirt paths to the central provinces of Shaanxi and Henan. By the roadside they would sometimes come upon shops that were closed and empty, with signs up saying "walking corpse across border." These signs were spooky—blowing in the cold wind on a deserted mountain road. When my friends told me about this, I said: When a person dies, he becomes stiff. How can he manage to cross the border? They didn't know, and it wasn't until a couple of years later that I found out how it was done.

LIAO: Corpses crossing borders? Did that mean the border that separates the worlds of the living and the dead?

LUO: No, it meant literally crossing the province or county borders. As I told you, transportation was not very well developed then. The so-called national highway was a rutted dirt road. When a traveling businessman died of a sudden illness or accident, it was hard to transport the body back to his village to be buried in his native soil. And if a dead person is not returned to his hometown, as custom dictates, he would be called a lonely soul and a homeless ghost. So, since buses or trucks weren't available, if the family could afford it, they hired professional corpse walkers.

LIAO: But how could a corpse walk? Was there magic to it? I've heard that corpse walkers would have a black cat climb over the dead body, generating static electricity that would make the corpse move like a puppet.

LUO: That's nonsense.

LIAO: Have you ever seen someone walk a corpse?

LUO: Yes. In the early 1950s, the new Communist government sent a work team to launch the Land Reform movement, which took land from the rich and gave it to the poor. The work team categorized people according to their wealth and beliefs. Rich landowners and Nationalists were deemed enemies of the people, and many were tortured or executed if they couldn't first escape into the mountains or pay off the triads to protect them. Since three generations of my family had been in the feng shui business, we were considered practitioners of superstition, and I wasn't allowed to participate in the land redistribution activities. I had nothing to do, and one dark and overcast afternoon I was strolling along the village road when a bulky, black object suddenly passed me, sending a chill down my spine. The thing was covered with a huge inky-colored robe. The bottom hem of the robe was splattered with mud, and from time to time a leather shoe poked out below. The footsteps were heavy and made a repetitive, thudding noise, like someone knocking the ground with a block of wood. Just then, my friend Piggy scurried up to me and whispered in my ear: That's a corpse.

Piggy's words spooked me, and I ran around in front of the robe. A man was there, walking a few paces ahead of the corpse, wearing a beige vest and carrying a basket filled with fake paper money. In his other hand, he held a white paper lantern. Every few minutes, he would reach into the basket, grab some money, and toss it high in the air. You know the ritual, don't you? It's called "buying your way into the other world." People in the countryside still believe that the fake money is used to bribe the corpse's guardian ghosts so they don't block the road to heaven.

LIAO: So people used to think the world of the dead was equally corrupt. But why the lantern in broad daylight?

LUO: To light the way to heaven. And the white lantern, the fake money, and the black robe helped create an atmosphere of mourning. The lantern also served a practical purpose—but let me finish my story. Piggy and I decided to keep following the corpse walker. The corpse looked a head taller than an ordinary person and wore a big straw hat. Beneath the hat was a white paper mask—one of those sad-looking masks like they wear in operas. The guy at the front would chant, "Yo ho, yo ho," and strangely enough the corpse would cooperate just like a well-trained soldier. He followed the guide with great precision. For example, when the guide and the corpse were climbing some stone steps on the street, the guide said, "Yo ho, yo ho, steps ahead." The corpse paused for a second, then moved up the stairway, step by step, with its body tilting back stiffly. Piggy and I followed the pair for about six or seven kilometers, all the way to a small inn on a quiet side street. While the corpse waited at the entrance, the guide walked into the lobby, tapped on the counter, and said in a low voice: The god of happiness is here.

LIAO: What does that mean?

LUO: Apparently it was a code phrase, because the innkeeper nodded and smiled and stepped out from behind the counter. He bowed to the guide and led him and the corpse to the back of the inn. We snuck into the backyard and found the corpse walker's room because the guide had left the white lantern in front of the door. We tried to get closer but heard an angry shout from the innkeeper. He grabbed my coat sleeve and snarled: Get away, you little bastards. Don't you dare tell anyone, got it?

LIAO: Wasn't the innkeeper afraid of getting bad luck from accommodating a corpse?

LUO: Because the corpse was wrapped up in a robe, no other customers would even suspect anything, and the local people actually considered corpse walkers auspicious, because death is the beginning of life in another world. I later found out that's why a walking corpse was referred to as the god of happiness. There was even a saying: If the god of happiness comes to your inn, good fortune will follow. Of course, an innkeeper could charge three times as much for providing accommodation to corpse walkers.

Anyway, despite the scolding from the innkeeper, Piggy and I didn't want to leave. We hung around in the lobby. Soon the innkeeper returned from the back with a shiny silver dollar in his hand. That was a lot of money in those days—he couldn't contain his excitement. When he noticed us, he called us over, handed us some small change, and told us to run to a restaurant down the street to get fried peanuts, cooked pig ears, pig tongues, and some hard liquor. We were also told to buy candles and fake paper money from a funeral-supply store. The innkeeper said the corpse walker needed to replenish his supplies for the next day's trip. Strangely enough, the innkeeper specifically asked us to get two sets of bowls and chopsticks from the restaurant. He said one set was for the god of happiness.

We ran our errands quickly, and the innkeeper thanked us profusely. He tipped us a couple of coins and invited us to sit down with him for tea. He told us that over the past twenty years, he had accommodated over ten corpse walkers who were passing through the region. We peppered him with questions. He lowered his voice to a whisper: It's not the corpse that does the walking—it's the living. Piggy and I didn't understand. The innkeeper said the magic lies inside that black robe. But he wouldn't say anything else. Piggy said: We live in a new Communist era now. Corpse walking is a practice from the old society. It is now considered superstitious and illegal. There's no need to keep it a secret from us. We won't tell anyone. But if you don't tell us, we'll report you to the officials for renting rooms to corpse walkers. After our begging, then our threatening, the innkeeper told us.

LIAO: What's the secret?

LUO: Inside the black robe, there are two bodies: the corpse and a living person who carries the dead one on his back. During the trip, the person who carries the corpse has to use two hands to secure the body so it doesn't slide off. As you probably know, the body of a dead person becomes as stiff and as heavy as a stone. It takes eight people to carry a coffin. Imagine how tough it would be for one person, wrapped up in a large black robe, to walk hundreds of miles with a dead body on his back. Since it is hard for him to bend his knees, each move must be very stiff and awkward. On top of that, the black robe prevents him from being able to see what is ahead of him. Remember the white lantern that we talked about earlier? The light from the lantern is used to guide the corpse carrier.

LIAO: When does a corpse walker eat?

LUO: Under normal circumstances, corpse walkers only eat one meal a day, and they travel ten to twelve hours without any rest. Since they work in pairs, they alternate days carrying the body. Sometimes a corpse walker's journey can take over a month. With such a long travel time, it is impossible to make the trip during the warm months because the corpse would decay in the heat. Even in winter, corpse walkers have to inject mercury and other anti-decaying solutions into the body. Since clients know how tough the business is, they're willing to pay big money for the service. The innkeeper said people in the profession had to go through years of specialized physical training. They often had good kung fu skills and could defend themselves against roadside robbers.

  Piggy and I were amazed when we heard all this. Piggy wanted to go to the backyard to check it out. The innkeeper stopped him, saying the door was locked. I said: We can put our ears to the door and listen. The innkeeper pinched my ear: If they catch you, they will chop off your ear and serve it as cold cuts with their drinks. Corpse walkers are very private people. Once they get in the room, they never come out again till early in the morning when they set off. It was a slow night for the innkeeper, so we ended up chatting for quite a while. It was pitch-black outside when we finally left. He gave us a couple more coins and made us promise not to tell anyone what we'd seen. He said that if officials knew that he was renting them a room, his business would be closed down.

LIAO: That was it?

LUO: Be patient! I'm not finished. After I got home, I couldn't get to sleep. I was still haunted by images of the corpse walkers. The next morning, I was awakened by the sound of the village chief walking up and down the street banging a gong. He was calling an important meeting for the whole village. I jumped out of bed, grabbed my coat, and ran out into the drizzling rain, skipping breakfast. From all directions neighbors were coming out of their houses.

As I got closer to the village square, I spotted Piggy. He pulled me aside and said in a muffled tone of voice: I have to tell you something. After we split up last night, I kept thinking about the stories the innkeeper told us. Something felt wrong to me. Chairman Mao told us to smash all superstitious practices. Well, those corpse walkers are engaging in superstitious activities—they're counterrevolutionaries! I couldn't let Chairman Mao down. I had to do something—otherwise, I'd be an accomplice. So I got up in the middle of the night, walked several miles to the county offices, and reported the corpse walkers to members of the Land Reform work team. They immediately contacted a unit of the People's Liberation Army stationed nearby. I led the soldiers and members of the work team to the inn.

Piggy's words made me really mad. I slapped him: You weren't supposed to do that. Didn't we promise the innkeeper to keep quiet? Piggy gave me a nasty look: What, you think I'd keep my mouth shut for just a couple of measly coins?

LIAO: So much for the noble revolutionary reasons. It was all about money, wasn't it?

LUO: Not quite. In that era everyone wanted to gain favor with the new government. Piggy was just trying to be part of the group. With Piggy's help, soldiers armed with rifles burst into the inn and rounded up the innkeeper and his staff. They moved silently into the backyard, stopped in front of the corpse walkers' room, and knocked on the door. There was no response. The soldiers had to bang on the door violently before they heard some rustling sounds from inside the room. Who is it? someone asked. That infuriated the soldiers and they broke down the door with their rifle butts. The soldiers jumped inside, waving their flashlights around the room. Piggy, who had witnessed the whole thing, told me that the two corpse walkers were standing in their underwear by the bed, shaking. The corpse, still covered in the black robe, was leaning against a wall. One soldier pulled up the robe and saw that it was the body of a woman, a rich lady—she had permed hair and heavy makeup, and she was dressed in an expensive, green silk *cheongsam*. Neither the village folks nor the soldiers had ever been that close to a rich lady before. Out of curiosity, some poked at her face, while others fingered the material of the dress. Her nose, ears, and mouth were filled with mercury and some kind of smelly liquid, but that didn't stop them from probing.

The two corpse walkers raised their hands over their heads. The soldiers ordered them and the innkeeper to stand along the wall, side by side with the dead body. Since there was no electricity in those days, the soldiers lit the corpse walkers' white paper lantern and began to ask them questions right there on the spot. Piggy said that the whole thing was pretty weird with the room lit so dimly.

LIAO: Who were the corpse walkers?

LUO: They were brothers from Shaanxi Province. The older one was thirty-five, stocky and very muscular. The younger was thirty-one, thinner and taller. Their father had been in the profession for many years and was known in the region as *Guijianchou*—warrior that scares the ghost. The two brothers inherited the profession from him at an early age. They said they had tried to be farmers but gave it up because they couldn't make ends meet. When the soldiers pressed them for information regarding the dead woman, the two brothers looked at each other, shook their heads, and said it was a violation of their professional code to disclose information about the dead. The soldiers slapped their faces and pointed their rifles at their heads, shouting: Chairman Mao teaches us, leniency toward those who confess and severe punishment for those who refuse to cooperate. Scared shitless, the brothers both fell to the floor and confessed everything.

LIAO: Who was she?

LUO: The deceased was the wife of an officer in the Nationalist army. When the Nationalists were defeated, the officer and his wife ended up wandering from place to place. It was wintertime, and the wife caught pneumonia. On her deathbed she made her husband promise to return her body to her hometown for burial. He bought a wheelbarrow, put his wife's body and two suitcases in it, and began pushing it along the winding mountain roads of Xishenba, where he met the two brothers. The weary officer promised to pay them a large sum of money if they would deliver his deceased wife to her native village. They accepted the deal and carried the woman for two months over the treacherous terrain. When Piggy and I saw them, they were only sixteen kilometers from their final destination.

LIAO: What happened to them?

LUO: The soldiers made the two brothers carry the corpse to the county government building. They were locked in a dark room, together with the corpse.

LIAO: Those poor guys. Corpse walking was quite labor-intensive, much harder than farming. They were not exploiters, but working-class people—the allies of Communism.

LUO: I agree that corpse walkers were working-class, and if the corpse had been, say, a poor peasant girl, those two would have gotten off easy. But they had committed a double crime: first, they engaged in a business connected with tradition and superstition; second, they were employed by a Nationalist officer. It was considered quite a serious crime to cooperate with an enemy.

Anyway, in the 1950s, it was not uncommon to see people executed after being denounced at a "speak bitterness" session. So after Piggy told me what he'd done to those corpse walkers, fear took hold of me. Soon the village square was packed with gawking spectators. I could see people's heads moving in the slight drizzle. Loud drums and gongs drowned out the chatter of the crowd. Some who couldn't get in climbed up onto the roof of the grain collection station. Country folk seldom got to visit the city and had no access to entertainment all year long. Public denunciation meetings offered free drama for many onlookers. None of them wanted to miss it.

A makeshift stage had been set up next to the grain warehouse. The newly appointed county chief sat behind a long table in the middle wearing a gray suit like Mao's. Next to him were the head of the government Land Reform work team and three soldiers. About a dozen wooden chairs and stools were placed in the front row. They were reserved for the head of the village militia, the chairman of the newly formed Poor Peasant Revolutionary Committee, and several peasant activists. Soon the loud gongs and drums stopped. The county chief grabbed a microphone that occasionally blasted out piercing squeals. He moved his mouth closer: Let's first bring Zhang Kan, the evil landlord, Liu Chan, the notorious bandit leader, and their lackeys out on stage.

I felt somewhat relieved that the corpse walkers were not called. People standing near the stage shuffled around to make way for the criminals: More than ten people were pushed onto the stage. They were wearing tall dunce caps, their hands were tied to their backs, black cartoon boards hung in front of their chests with characters such as evil landlord Zhang Kan, et cetera. Then the county chief raised his right arm and shouted, "Down with the exploiting class and kill the evil landlords and the bandits!" As if on cue, people all raised their right arms and shouted in agreement. After the slogan shouting died down, some poor peasant activists stood up and began to tell dreadful stories about how badly they had been treated and exploited by those landlords before the Communists came. Their testimonies were followed by another round of slogan shouting. Then the soldiers escorted the pair of them and their lackeys out to an open field nearby, and the whole bunch was shot dead on the spot.

LIAO: What about the corpse walkers?

LUO: After the county chief announced the execution, people started getting restless and asked: I heard some corpse walkers were arrested last night. Where are they? The county chief wasn't about to let them down. About half an hour later, the corpse walkers were paraded onto the stage. People immediately pushed toward the front, trying to take a good look at these people who were supposed to possess legendary powers that could make a corpse walk. The gathering became quite chaotic and several kids were trampled in the crush. The soldiers on the stage stood up and jumped down into the crowd to help maintain order. They tried to push the crowd back from the stage. The county chief screamed on the microphone: Order, order, don't push. Chaos will create opportunities for our class enemies to stir up trouble.

But the people wouldn't back down. Who could blame them? The older brother and the *cheongsam*-wearing corpse had been tied together, back-to-back. The younger brother was forced to put on the black robe and carry the white lantern and the basket with fake paper money. The scary mask was tied to the back of his head. The older brother had a black sign hung around his neck that said "The Lackey of the Counterrevolutionary Corpse." When a soldier pushed the elder brother's head down to show regret, the head of the corpse, tied to his back, appeared to look up. We could see her permed hair and makeup. It was quite a frightening but comical scene. People began to ooh and ahh. A woman in the audience screamed: She is an evil fox!

LIAO: Isn't it taboo to insult a corpse? Didn't people worry about retribution for blaspheming the dead?

LUO: People were so caught up in the moment that traditions and taboos went totally out the door. It was like a circus. The crowd kept getting rowdier. The excitement was quite contagious. Some younger guys tried to climb onto the stage to touch the corpse. The soldiers wrestled with them, attempting to push them down. It was a real mob scene. Then suddenly we heard a loud crash: the stage had collapsed. People were screaming and falling over one another. One soldier raised his gun and fired at the sky several times before the crowd became silent and under control.

Luckily for the two brothers, their kung fu skills came in handy. They were able to dodge the attacks from the mob and survived with some minor injuries. The soldiers then untied the corpse from the elder brother's back and sent both of them back to the dark room. That night the two brothers broke a window and escaped. They were soon discovered by soldiers on patrol, who chased after them for several kilometers. The elder brother, though shot in the leg, didn't want to surrender. As he stumbled forward up on the mountain, he accidentally stepped on a loose stone and fell into a ravine. After that the younger one was caught without any resistance.

LIAO: Was he executed?

LUO: The younger one was allowed to wrap the bodies of his brother and the army officer's wife in straw mats, and he dug a grave and buried them together outside the village. Then he was deported back to his local village with the death certificate of his brother. I heard later that the government charged the elder brother posthumously with "refusing to admit crimes and committing a sacrificial suicide to honor a counterrevolutionary."

LIAO: What an ending.

LUO: But that wasn't the end. Several days later, the village officials had some unexpected guests: the relatives of the Nationalist officer's wife. They had received a letter from the officer telling them to welcome home the body, and they had set up an altar and were prepared to hold a wake. They waited and waited, but the corpse walkers never showed up, and eventually they got word of what had happened at the public denunciation meeting.

LIAO: What could they do? She had already been buried.

LUO: The relatives cried and screamed and went all the way to the county chief's office. They begged him to give the body back. Normally, the county chief wouldn't dare meet such a request for a Nationalist officer's wife. But the fiasco at the public denunciation meeting plus the killing of a corpse walker, who was considered a member of the working class, had made him nervous.

He was afraid that the relatives of the dead woman could take the issue to a higher level of government and get him into trouble. So he let them dig up the body. The relatives then hired some professional mourners, who carried the body home. It was quite a procession in the old-fashioned style, which the county officials pretended they didn't see.

It had been a long journey home for that woman. As for the elder brother, it was really sad that someone who had spent his whole life returning the dead to their ancestral homes should end up getting buried in a place far away from his own home.

THE LEPER

A year ago, I met a medical doctor named Sun outside Shimen-
kan, a village in the mountainous region of Yunnan Province.
Dr. Sun used to have a cushy practice at a government-run hos-
pital in Beijing, but in the midnineties he joined China's
underground Christian movement, and his religious beliefs
eventually cost him his job. Since then, he has been traveling
around Yunnan preaching Christianity and offering medical
help.

About two years ago, while visiting a tuberculosis patient
in Shimenkan, he came across a dilapidated hut hidden in the
woods on the slope of the mountain. Intrigued by this lonely
dwelling far from town, he decided to find out who lived there.
His local guide tried to prevent him, saying that this was the
residence of the village leper. Dr. Sun ignored his advice. The
hut's thatched roof was blackened by decay, several parts of
the clay walls had collapsed, and on a bench outside there sat
an elderly couple, astonished at the sight of a visitor. The man's
name was Zhang Zhi-en and the woman was his wife. Dr. Sun
told me their story and I decided to interview them. After hours
of driving on a winding, red-dirt mountain road, I found Zhang
sitting in his yard, dozing off in the sun.

—⁓—

LIAO YIWU: How old are you?

ZHANG ZHI-EN: I was born in the year of the sheep. So I should be
  seventy-five this year. This is my new wife. She is a horse—seventy-six
  years old.

LIAO: How long have you lived here?

ZHANG: Oh, for many years. I used to live down in Shimenkan at the foot
  of the mountain. But the village people didn't allow me to get close to

them. They said I was contagious. So I just moved up here. Before Dr. Sun visited us, we hadn't talked to a living person for years.

LIAO: How did you contract leprosy?

ZHANG: My bad luck started when I accidentally killed a snake. I don't remember what year it was. I think it was before Deng Xiaoping came to power and began to give some land back to peasants from the collective farms.

LIAO: Deng's economic reform started in the late seventies.

ZHANG: OK. Early one morning I went to the mountain to dig some herbs so I could sell them at the local market. I used to make my living that way. As I was climbing, one of my feet caught on a piece of rock and I fell. While I struggled to get up, I spotted a wild azalea near my foot. The azalea root is a type of rare herb and it can sell for big bucks. So I took a berry hoe out of my backpack and carefully dug around the plant. It turned out the root was quite fat, worth a lot of money. While I was lost in happy thoughts, a snake darted out from the bushes and wrapped its body around the azalea root. It had rough brownish skin, and I saw that it was what we called a Ma snake. I was startled and began to shake. Before the snake had a chance to attack, I hacked at it with the hoe. I missed its head the first time but cut its tail off. The snake's tongue darted out and it writhed in pain. I aimed my hoe at its head and whacked it a couple more times. When I was sure the snake was dead, I dug out the azalea root and went home.

Soon after, I began to be haunted by the experience. My skin itched and I felt cold all the time. I wore a cotton-padded coat even in the middle of summer. I tried all sorts of herbs, hoping to find a cure for myself. Nothing worked. One day, I went to buy some salt at the nearby market and bumped into the head of the collective farm. When he saw that I was shivering with cold in the summer sun, he asked what was wrong. I said I was possessed by the spirit of the Ma snake.

He was shocked and his face turned ugly. Those Ma snakes are holy creatures. They're dragons on earth! It's a taboo to kill them. You're doomed.

LIAO: Doomed?

ZHANG: The collective-farm leader began to spread all sorts of rumors about my disease. Since Ma snakes sound similar to leprosy, *mafeng-bing* in Chinese, he told people that I was suffering from leprosy. He contacted the local leprosy clinic, but their damn doctor didn't even want to get close to me. He examined me from five feet away and said I was suffering from leprosy. I tried to argue with him. He said, Look at your face. It's as pale as ashes. If you don't have leprosy, what else can it be?

Several militiamen from the village put on face masks and gloves and dragged me to the local leprosy sanatorium. I went through several tests and everything seemed to be normal, but they wouldn't allow me to leave. Instead they assigned me to work in the kitchen, where I ended up cooking for other patients for four years. Eventually the director of the hospital realized that it was against Party policy to lock a healthy person inside a leprosy hospital. So they let me out.

LIAO: Did you have any contact with leprosy patients while you worked there?

ZHANG: Of course. We hung out together all day long. It was no big deal. Nothing happened to me. When I got home, the world had changed. Chairman Mao had already died, and Deng Xiaoping had taken over. The commune no longer existed. They'd had a public meeting and distributed all the land to individual households. Since I wasn't around, they didn't leave me anything, not even a piece of dirt. Even if I had been around, they would have told me that I wasn't eligible because I was a leper. So I became homeless overnight—no land and no home. But I didn't give up, and I began to petition the local government. I told those officials: I come from generations of poor peasants. Didn't Chairman Mao say that poor people are the pillars of the Communist society? Why should I have to put up with this shit?

The government offices didn't know what to do about me. Finally, a leader from my village made a proposal: since I was a bachelor and was way past marriage age, he promised to fix me up with a girl from another county. In this way, I could move out of the village and get a wife and some land in another county. Why not? That didn't sound too bad. So I accepted. The girl's name was Xu Meiying. Neither of us was picky. Soon after we met, I thanked the matchmaker, held a wedding banquet, and moved out of Shimenkan. As you know, in the rural areas, women normally move in with the guy's family after marriage. I did the opposite. The locals called me a relocated son-in-law.

LIAO: Did your wife know about your past at the leprosy sanatorium?

ZHANG: She had stayed at the same leprosy sanatorium for a while and was also released, like me, because her test results came back negative. Even so, people were afraid to be around her. That was probably why they fixed us up together. Even now, people here are scared of leprosy. If they think you might have it, they'll immediately lock you up in an isolated ward. Over the years, many healthy people have been sent to the hospital because fellow villagers suspected they had leprosy. So Xu Meiying and I turned out to have a similar history. Before me, she had several boyfriends. None of them had a good reputation. None of them made an honest living on the farm. They were either petty thieves or scoundrels. Compared with the other guys, I was a much better catch.

I moved in and we began to sleep in the same bed. She was about three years younger than I was. When we first lived together, they had just started building this road. That shows you how long ago it was. We farmed together and life was OK.

LIAO: Did you have kids?

ZHANG: No. My wife was sick for many years.

LIAO: I was told that they burned her to death. When did that happen?

ZHANG: I don't remember exactly. I think it's been ten years. She had met an evil dragon and was possessed by its spirit, and we couldn't find a cure. It all started in the spring. As I was plowing the field, another Ma snake jumped out at me. I didn't want to kill it, but the snake looked so menacing. I was scared and smashed it to death. Soon after that was the Qingming festival, when everyone in the village goes to visit the cemeteries and pays tribute to the dead. My wife visited her mother's tomb on that day. After she came back, we had a guest—a relative of hers from Fumin County. She stayed with us for over three months. This relative gave her some colorful new cloth. My wife made a quilt out of it.

LIAO: Wait, I'm lost. Let's go back to the evil dragon.

ZHANG: That night, there was a terrible thunderstorm. Pouring rain. Right before dawn, a big clap of thunder struck. Our whole house shook. Suddenly, the evil dragon appeared along with the thunder, coming down like the lid on a big cauldron. I could see the head of the dragon half-hidden inside the cloud, its tail wagging back and forth over the village cemetery. My wife opened the window and tried to peek at what was going on outside. As soon as she opened the window, I heard a loud scream. I ran in and found her collapsed on the floor. Her eyes were closed and she couldn't say anything. Suddenly she jumped up, screaming like a devil, saying that her head was killing her. Then she lost her eyesight. She also became deaf.

I was terrified and took her to see many local doctors. I spent all of our savings. I forced her to drink every kind of herb that the doctor had prescribed, but she kept getting worse. Nobody knew what had caused her illness. I almost went crazy. News about her illness started to spread all over the village. The stories became more and more dramatic and weird. Everyone in the village began to believe that my wife's illness was an act of retribution for my killing of two Ma snakes. They said I had upset the dragon, and that it had used its magic power against my family as revenge.

I invited the local Taoist monk to set up an exorcism. But the spirit of the dragon was too powerful for him. Then someone introduced me to a blind fortune-teller. He asked me to take him around the house. He sniffed here and there and then left without a word. I never heard from him again. I could tell that Xu Meiying wouldn't be able to live long. I went to talk with her older brother, and then he discussed her illness with the village chief. They both insisted that my wife was suffering a relapse of leprosy. Some older folks in the village even told me that her mother had died of leprosy.

LIAO: I didn't think leprosy was hereditary. Is it?

ZHANG: How would I know? I had no idea what to do. I was running around like a chicken with its head cut off. When Xu Meiying's elder brother showed up, he wouldn't come into the house. He called me outside, and I saw he'd gathered quite a group of people there, including the village chief. Her brother told me that they had come up with a solution that would be good for me. Then, like a school of fish, the village people came to shake my hand, one after another. They all said the same thing: This will be good for you in the long term.

LIAO: What were they talking about?

ZHANG: I had no clue. As a relocated son-in-law, I really didn't have much say in village affairs. If I had tried to argue with them, they would have drowned me with their spit.

   Anyway, the next morning the whole village showed up. They called me outside and asked me to stand apart and not to move. They took the door off, placed Xu Meiying on the door, and carried her away. Her brother told her that they were going to take her to a hospital. She was too weak to respond. He yelled at everyone to step aside, and they carried her out of the courtyard and down to the foot of the mountain. According to tradition, every household in the village contributed a bundle of wood until they formed a big pile. They tied Xu Meiying to the door with ropes and then put her and the door on top of the pile. Someone poured kerosene, making sure the wood was fully soaked. Then they lit the fire.

LIAO: Did you do anything to stop them?

ZHANG: Several guys held me back. All I could see was a plume of black smoke shooting up into the sky until it blocked the sun. Then the flames got really strong. I didn't want to look, but curiosity got the best of me. I craned my neck and stood on my toes. All I could see was a wall of fire. Xu Meiying's body was like a piece of skin that began to curl up. Its color kept getting darker and darker.

LIAO: I can't believe they set her on fire while she was still alive. Didn't she react?

ZHANG: She was blind and deaf. She hadn't eaten for days and she was probably already in a coma. Even if she had been awake, it would have been only seconds before she died. The flames were so strong that I could feel the heat from several feet away. The pile collapsed and her body sank into the fire. Then all the young guys threw their wooden sticks into the fire.

LIAO: What wooden sticks?

ZHANG: In case Xu Meiying tried to jump up and run away. If she had, they would have beaten her back into the fire.

LIAO: What a lawless mob.

ZHANG: What are you talking about?

LIAO: I'm talking about the people who killed your wife.

ZHANG: They did it because they were afraid of leprosy. They had no other choice. The fire lasted for over two hours. No matter how emaciated the person is, it takes that long to melt a human body.

LIAO: Were you sad? Did you cry?

ZHANG: No. Some villagers told me that they saw the tail of the evil dragon coiling around the flames.

LIAO: Do you believe what they said?

ZHANG: Yes, I do. After Xu Meiying's death, I continued to use the quilt she had made. One night I had a nightmare in which a snake as thick and round as a big rice bowl wrapped itself around my body. I couldn't breathe. So I raised my berry hoe and kept hacking at it until my arms were sore and there was blood all over. When I woke up, I found myself on the floor. I had fallen out of the bed. It was so spooky. I didn't dare go back to sleep. The next day I dragged the quilt out into the field and set fire to it. Guess what? The flames shot up as if it were soaked in oil. It smelled like burned flesh. The dragon must have been hiding in there. After the quilt was burned, I buried the ashes. Since then, my house has been ghost-free.

LIAO: Did you collect your wife's remains and bury her?

ZHANG: Xu Meiying's elder brother collected her bones and buried them near the White Sand Hill. But that was not the end of the ceremony. I had to host a banquet to thank the villagers who had helped.

LIAO: They burned your wife and you had to feed them as a gesture of gratitude. Didn't you find that ridiculous?

ZHANG: What they had done was for my own good. I had no complaints against them for eating my food. I couldn't shortchange them. I wanted everyone at the banquet to eat until their stomachs could no longer take any food. As long as they were happy, I was happy. I gave them the food and they did the cooking. The village chief led a couple of guys into my house, took a pig from the pen, and slaughtered it. They also grabbed the dried meat that was hanging under the eaves. They put a pot on top of the stove and began to boil the meat, even before the smoke from my wife's body was gone. They made a huge pot of rice. It was quite festive. Soon it was dark. Villagers, with torches lit, carried big rice bowls and gathered near my house, waiting for the banquet to begin. There were about thirty households in the village. Each family sent its breadwinner to the banquet. I ended up spending all my savings, and it was still not enough—I had to borrow some more. I didn't have enough rice to feed that many people. The village chief pitched in. He said I could pay him back after the fall harvest.

LIAO: Burning a live person to death is a violation of the law. Did you report it to the police?

ZHANG: Why? They were helping me out.

LIAO: You still believe that?

ZHANG: Yes. Everyone in the village thinks that too.

LIAO: Things have changed a lot in other parts of China. I don't see any changes here.

ZHANG: Oh, there are quite a lot of changes here. They built a road some years ago and now it's been widened. People are allowed to do business. Everyone is busy making money. I raise pigs, dogs, and chickens. I'm too old to farm so I leased my land to other people. My current wife and I don't need a lot. So we're OK.

LIAO: How long have you been with your new wife?

ZHANG: About five years. She used to live on the other side of the mountain. None of her children wanted to take care of her. Someone brought her over to me for companionship.

LIAO: Does she know about Xu Meiying?

ZHANG: She's never asked and I'm not going to tell her. I don't think she wants to hear it. For years I haven't been able to talk with anyone in the region. Now that she is here, I have someone to talk with.

LIAO: Do you still think about Xu Meiying?

ZHANG: Oh, well . . . I have to blame the evil dragon. Not long after she was gone, her elder brother's wife also fell under the spell of the dragon and got very ill. According to the Taoist monk who was invited to exorcise the evil spirit, Xu's brother needed to feed the dragon with human brain marrow. So Xu's brother snuck into the cemetery at midnight, dug up a recently buried corpse, and extracted some brain marrow. He took it home to feed his wife. He told me that he could hear the dragon screaming angrily under a bridge.

LIAO: The brain marrow from a dead person is filled with germs and viruses. That's probably what made her ill.

ZHANG: Oh well, I don't know.

LIAO: Time seems to have stopped here. Every day, all you can hear is the sound of wind blowing.

ZHANG: Yes, but we also hear the trucks pass by. We are very grateful to Dr. Sun. His church helped me rebuild my house. I'm now a believer in God. Thanks to God, I have a doctor visit me and take me to a church down on the other side of the mountain every month. Nobody in the church shuns me. They are all very nice. I pray to God every day, hoping that the evil dragon will not come back and harm people again.

THE PEASANT EMPEROR

A week after the Chinese New Year in 1998, I interviewed the forty-eight-year-old Zeng Yinglong, a peasant who proclaimed himself emperor in 1985 and declared his hometown in Sichuan Province an independent kingdom. Zeng was charged with multiple counterrevolutionary crimes, including organizing and leading subversive activities against the local government and the government's one-child policy. Considering the fact that he was a truly uneducated and uninformed person, the court reduced his sentence from the death penalty to lifelong imprisonment. Zeng was then locked up inside a maximum security prison in the Daba Mountain in the northeastern part of Sichuan. Yet he was an optimist by nature, and abided by the prison rules. All the guards and fellow inmates liked him. They jokingly called him "Your Majesty."

During the interview, I noticed that "The Heavenly Son," as we Chinese used to refer to our real emperors, was getting bald on top, but his narrow eyes still shone with piercing arrogance. He was wearing a pair of old army shoes and a short blue jacket over his blue prison uniform. He rolled up his sleeves and talked nonstop for two hours, issuing one edict after another.

—⚭—

LIAO YIWU: Are you the well-known emperor that people talk about in this jail?

ZENG YINGLONG: You should address me as "Your Majesty."

LIAO: OK. Your Majesty, when did you assume your role as an emperor?

ZENG: Your Majesty didn't want to be the emperor. It was his ten-thousand-strong subjects who crowned him. Let me tell you how it all got started: About ten years ago, a giant salamander climbed out of the river and hid inside a crack on a huge rock in the middle of the Wu River. The locals called the rock the "Guanyin Bodhisattva stone." That mysterious salamander could talk like humans. Each night, many village folks could hear the lizard singing a ballad from inside the crack. The ballad went like this: "The fake dragon sinks, and the real dragon surfaces. On the south side of the river, peace and happiness reign." Later on, the story of the singing lizard spread to hundreds of villages in the region. Even small children knew how to sing the ballad. A local feng shui master, whose name was Ma Xing, became really curious and wanted to trace its source. One night, he led a group of villagers to the bank of the Wu River and waited for the salamander to sing. The lizard did sing. Ma and other villagers jumped on a boat and followed the sound to the rock and saw the salamander. That lizard wasn't afraid of the crowd at all. Instead of gliding away, the salamander simply wagged its tail, as if waiting for people to come see him. Ma used a wooden stick to prod its mouth open. He pulled out a three-inch-long yellow silk ribbon. The ballad was written on the ribbon. With his face toward heaven, his eyes closed, Ma began chanting like a monk. Then, holding the yellow ribbon above his head, he knelt on the ground and kowtowed three times. After he stood up, he turned to his fellow villagers and said that he had just communicated with the spirit in heaven and had officially accepted some divine instructions from above.

Your Majesty didn't know anything about that legendary singing salamander. At that time, Your Majesty was on the run from the law. The government had implemented a very tough one-child policy. Local officials dished out very severe punishment to those planning to have a second child. They would go around the village with doctors and knock on doors, checking up on every household. If a woman was found to be pregnant with her second or third child, she would be sent to a clinic for an abortion and have to pay a heavy fine. Also, women of childbearing age had to be sterilized or have a loop installed in the womb. Your Majesty had two daughters, but very much wanted to have a son to carry on the family name. To escape punishment, Your Majesty joined other villagers and secretly moved with his pregnant wife to another province. Your Majesty ended up in the northwestern province of Xinjiang, where he worked on some odd jobs at a construction site. With gods' blessing, Your Majesty did have a son, who was named Yan-ze [meaning Continued Benevolence]. After the baby was born, Your Majesty took his wife and the newly born to Henan Province, where they settled in a city called Xinxiang.

You will probably ask me: How did this part of Your Majesty's life fit the story of the legendary singing salamander? Well, if you remember the ballad, it says "Zhen-sheng-long, or real dragon surfaces." This sounds similar to my name "Zeng-ying-long." Moreover, the ballad mentions that "South of the river, happiness and peace reign." I was in Henan, which means "south of the river." The city where I was staying was called Xinxiang, which means "newly established territories."

A couple of days after his encounter with the salamander, Ma gathered together a group of my subjects. They walked hundreds of kilometers to Henan to meet with Your Majesty. The moment he saw Your Majesty, Ma took out a dragon robe and put it on Your Majesty. Then, Ma and his followers knelt down and chanted: "Ten thousand years to the Emperor." Your Majesty couldn't turn his back on the will of his subjects. Neither could he disobey the will of heaven. Therefore, Your Majesty returned to his hometown as the people's emperor, established a new dynasty, and selected 1985 as Year One of his reign.

LIAO: What was the name of your dynasty?

ZENG: It was called Dayou.

LIAO: What does that mean?

ZENG: "Dayou" means "We share everything." After Your Majesty was crowned, he promulgated the first imperial edict: "We farm the land together, share wealth, and can bear as many children as we wish." The edict became wildly popular among my subjects.

LIAO: How large was Your Majesty's kingdom?

ZENG: Actually, Your Majesty only ruled three counties near the borders of Hunan, Guizhou, and Sichuan provinces.

LIAO: Allow me to be frank with you. According to the court document, you had reenacted an ancient story mentioned in the *Records of the Grand Historian,* written by the famous historian Sima Qian. Based on the tale in the *Records of the Grand Historian,* Chen Sheng, a peasant rebel in the Qin dynasty [221 BC–206 BC], attempted to rally public support against the emperor and justify his claim to the throne by inserting a yellow ribbon inside a fish. Then, the cook "accidentally" discovered the fish and the ribbon, which said "King Chen Sheng." Everyone believed it was a message from the Heavenly God and they all joined Chen's uprising, which eventually led to the downfall of the Qin dynasty. Apparently, Ma Xing reenacted every detail. That needed a lot of elaborate planning. It is hard to believe that after two thousand years, the ancient trick still worked. Did the local villagers truly believe it was a manifestation from the Heavenly God?

ZENG: Shut up. That is awfully rude of you to talk to Your Majesty like that. Your Majesty knows that you are a journalist in disguise and have been sent from the hostile Kingdom of China. Your Majesty refutes all your slanderous remarks.

LIAO: I'm not a journalist. I'm merely an ordinary researcher and writer. If Your Majesty doesn't want to talk with me today, I don't think the opportunity will present itself again for you to tell people outside the jail about yourself, your subjects, and your kingdom. Based on my observations, you are a pretty smart guy, well versed in Chinese history, and harbor grand ambitions. You went a little too far with your ambitions, but it's understandable. You don't want to be a laughingstock for future generations, do you?

ZENG: Throughout history, it's common for a general or emperor to face defeat. What's there to laugh about? But can you promise to record faithfully what Your Majesty tells you?

LIAO: Yes, Your Majesty. I solemnly promise.

ZENG: Let's say the singing salamander part was taken from an ancient Chinese story. But the rest is true. Upon his return, Your Majesty immediately appointed Ma Xing as prime minister. According to Prime

Minister Ma, the Dayou Kingdom, located in a remote mountainous region, was sparsely populated. My subjects were old-fashioned people, bound by thousands of years of ancestral tradition. The concept of big families with many male descendants was deeply rooted in the minds of my subjects. The family planning policy, promulgated by the Kingdom of China, triggered regionwide protests. Many married women had to run off to the mountain to hide in caves and live like barbarians. They would rather eat wild vegetables and drink stream water than go through forced abortion and sterilization. Prime Minister Ma recommended that Your Majesty should take advantage of that popular anti-government sentiment. Ma urged all Your Majesty's staff to visit people at home and propagate the belief that giving birth to children is an inalienable right bestowed upon us by our ancestors. The more children we have, the better off we are. Raising children can be hard, but people in this kingdom are used to poverty and hard life. It won't make too much of a difference whether you raise one kid or seven or eight. Having one more kid means adding one more glimpse of hope to our kingdom. If anyone wants us to give up hope, we will fight with him to the very end.

After mobilizing the masses for over six months, Your Majesty had rallied enough support and laid a firm foundation for the Dayou Kingdom. Your Majesty issued a series of secret imperial edicts urging all of his subjects to exercise their right to big families. If any woman could give birth to more than ten children, Your Majesty would crown her with the title "The Royal Mother."

During this time, a prestigious villager passed away. He had lived past one hundred. In my region, if a person can live to an advanced age, he is treated with great respect. When he dies, the funeral is a big deal. Many people will travel from afar to attend the funeral in the hope that some of the deceased's luck would rub off on them. As a large number of villagers were expected to attend this guy's funeral, we decided to use the occasion to officially proclaim the birth of the Dayou Kingdom. Prime Minister Ma, a feng shui master by trade, spent a lot of time and energy preparing for the funeral. For two days, Ma climbed hills and crossed rivers to scout out an auspicious site for the old man's grave. He finally located a spot pretty far away from the village. We had a wake with an open coffin for a whole week. Monks from a nearby temple were invited to chant sutras day and night. The abbot in the temple also helped select an auspicious date for burial.

Based on local traditions, on the day of burial, the coffin had to be lowered inside the grave before sunrise. In this way, the elder's spirit could be eternalized and rise with the sun. Under Ma's direction, the funeral procession, with the participation of several thousand mourners, started around midnight. A local brass band led the way. Since that old man was an ordinary peasant, his burial was not something for an emperor to attend. But Your Majesty had to humble himself and act like an ordinary villager. As the line of mourners proceeded up the narrow path wrapping around the mountain, the glittering lights of the fire torches carried by mourners mixed with the stars in the sky. From a distance, you couldn't tell the torches from the stars. At this juncture, Prime Minster Ma turned to me and knelt down. He said: Your Majesty, look at this grand spectacle. Heavenly God is on our side.

I agreed with him and beckoned him to move fast and catch up with the procession. The lead mourner, who was hired to howl and chant, had a truly resonating voice. He would howl a line, and people would respond with another. The echo of howling and chanting was so loud that the mountain seemed to be vibrating. "Go, go, do not tarry; Heaven's gate awaits the morn. You rest awhile and arise reborn. To beget a male child, and marry."

LIAO: Interesting. The chanting about reincarnation even rhymed.

ZENG: The true reincarnation had not even manifested itself yet. Finally, we arrived at the burial site. When it was time to start the ceremony, Niu Daquan, who was my chief of staff, gathered ten of the royal guards from my kingdom. Together, they began to perform the sun dance ritual. As the beat of the drums quickened, many people couldn't resist and joined in the dancing. While the momentum was building up, Prime Minister Ma suddenly took off his shirt, and pulled the Dayou Kingdom dragon flag from a bag and waved it in his hand. He stomped his feet, and shook his head in ecstasy. He then took a handful of peas from his pocket, and scattered them into the sky, chanting, "Change, we need change." People immediately crawled on the ground to pick up the peas, which were auspicious symbols of longer life. Suddenly, dark clouds rose from behind the hill, accompanied with loud thunder and lightning. Heavy rain poured down on us, as if Heavenly God had dispatched thousands of warlike soldiers to earth.

LIAO: You guys reenacted an episode from another ancient Chinese fable, "Scattering peas to summon troops." In the fable, a general was cornered by enemy troops. He sought help from the Heavenly God, who instructed him to scatter thousands of peas into the air. After he did that, the sky turned dark. Amid a heavy thunderstorm, those peas suddenly turned into soldiers. According to court papers, you guys reenacted this fable to deceive those uneducated folks in your region. Your friend Ma Xing had checked the weather forecast beforehand and timed the burial ceremony to coincide with the arrival of the thunderstorm. Then, Ma began to scatter peas into the sky, as if the thunderstorm was the result of his magic. I have to commend you for the elaborate preparation.

ZENG: Don't interrupt, please. Please allow Your Majesty to continue. The crowd was stunned by the downpour and dashed for cover. Many knelt down in front of my prime minister, asking him to take back his magic power. Ma granted their plea. Half an hour later, the sky cleared up. After the mourners completed the burial and funeral ceremony, they followed Your Majesty down the mountain and joined the "Dayou Royal Army." Soon, the story of Ma's magic power spread fast, and within two weeks, Your Majesty had recruited over ten thousand subjects.

LIAO: You are such a liar. Again, court papers say fewer than two thousand people had joined your troops.

ZENG: Your Majesty doesn't lie or joke with you. Following that amazing ceremony, Your Majesty led his troops and seized the county hospital. They stormed the building and kicked out the hospital administrator. Then, they went directly to the family planning department and dug out all the contraceptives. They piled them up outside the building and set them on fire. Your Majesty's heroic act could be comparable to the burning of opium in the nineteenth century by Lin Zexu, the famous Qing official who attempted to stop opium trafficking by the British colonialists. Thousands of people cheered us on. Your Majesty then converted the hospital building into his palace. With this accomplished, the prime minister, chief of staff, and other officials donned traditional official garb that they had made, gathered inside the royal palace, and bowed collectively to Your Majesty to show respect and offer their gratitude.

LIAO: I heard that Your Majesty possessed over forty concubines, and housed them in your various "royal chambers."

ZENG: That was the doing of my prime minister and chief of staff. Initially, Your Majesty declined the offer, saying that the kingdom was still in its infancy and hard work lay ahead. How could he indulge in sexual pleasure while nothing had been accomplished for the kingdom? But members of the cabinet begged Your Majesty to reconsider. They argued: Throughout history, in every dynasty, the emperor owned concubines housed in various palaces. If traditions were not followed, rules would not be in order. If rules were not in order, Your Majesty would lose credibility. We appreciate your determination to serve your subjects first and not to indulge in sexual pleasures. However, you have to follow the royal tradition.

LIAO: Where did Your Majesty acquire those concubines?

ZENG: Every one of the nurses who used to work at the county hospital was selected and made my concubine. Several of my cabinet members recommended their daughters. However, Your Majesty was very busy handling the day-to-day court business. He seldom had time to shower love over the Queen, who had spent half of her life with Your Majesty, much less those concubines.

LIAO: Your Majesty's court seemed to be very corrupt. I can't believe court officials were willing to sacrifice their daughters so they could curry favor with you. I now understand why you chose the county hospital as your palace.

ZENG: Your Majesty attacked the hospital first because burning the evil contraceptives was an effective way to gain support from the villagers. But Your Majesty was a little too preoccupied with the hospital and neglected the threat posed by the county police. Later on, the Chinese army was summoned and they surrounded the royal palace. Your Majesty led his troops to fight back. But unfortunately Your Majesty was captured in the initial battle. My chief of staff, Niu Daquan, moved all the concubines to the back of the palace and ordered them to jump into a pond there. He told them to commit suicide and die as martyrs. The water in the pond was too shallow. Those women were pushed into the water, but they couldn't drown. So my chief of staff became desperate. He took out his sword and chopped the heads off of two concubines. He had really lost his mind. I guess the pain and sadness of losing the kingdom were too hard to swallow.

LIAO: I thought your chief of staff and your prime minister possessed the magic power to manipulate wind and rain. Why couldn't they scatter peas into the air and summon enough troops to fight the government troops?

ZENG: My prime minister straightened the dragon flag, and was planning to perform his magic when a bullet hit his stomach. He was a heroic guy. With a loud howl, he managed to stand up and move a few steps forward before plopping down to the ground.

LIAO: Your kingdom collapsed a little too fast, didn't you think?

ZENG: It was the will of heaven. Since my chief of staff killed two people, he was given the death penalty. Your Majesty and several cabinet members in the kingdom were charged with the crimes of overthrowing the Chinese government and were thrown into jail. But Your Majesty finds it hard to obey the Chinese law. Just think about it: Generations of Your Majesty's family were buried in his kingdom. If you trace Your Majesty's ancestral line, it goes all the way to the Song dynasty, over a thousand years ago. Don't you think Your Majesty should have the right to establish his kingdom there? His kingdom is poor because crops don't grow very well there. There was not enough manpower. If family planning were to succeed there, Your Majesty would be guilty in the eye of his ancestors for not doing the right thing. Moreover, Your Majesty wouldn't allow foreigners to go in there and carry out those brutal procedures on women in his kingdom.

LIAO: What do you mean by foreigners?

ZENG: Anyone living outside my kingdom is considered a foreigner.

LIAO: So, in your eyes, I'm also a foreigner.

ZENG: Correct. No matter how big or small the country is, they should treat one another as an equal. Each should send an ambassador and establish diplomatic relations. What do you think if officials from my country go to yours to implement a policy of "having as many babies as you want"? Would you accept it?

LIAO: Is this the reason for your repeated requests for appeal?

ZENG: Correct.

LIAO: Imagine if every Chinese were to follow Your Majesty's example, there would be millions of self-crowned emperors. You've been locked up in this jail for over ten years. How are the government and jail authorities treating you?

ZENG: Your Majesty is fairly knowledgeable about Chinese herbal medicine. The prison authority has assigned Your Majesty to take care of the prison clinic. In many ways, it's been a heavenly blessing. Your Majesty gets to read the newspapers every day, and has been informed of what's going on outside. The Dayou Kingdom was very backward and isolated. Your Majesty hopes to work hard while in jail and obtain a reduced sentence so he can go back to serve his subjects soon.

LIAO: Do you still want to be an emperor?

ZENG: Your Majesty has learned that poverty cannot sustain a kingdom. If he wants to eliminate poverty and become rich, he needs to learn about technology. In the past, Your Majesty diligently perused history books while neglecting the changes happening outside his home. Since he was put into jail, Your Majesty has widened the scope of reading. He has just been enrolled at a correspondence college.

LIAO: An emperor wants to go to college? That's quite refreshing. I heard that Your Majesty tried hard to get permission to attend this correspondence college. You wrote an "imperial edict" to prison officials. In your letter, you addressed the two prison officials in charge as "members of my royal cabinet."

ZENG: It costs money to go to college. Your Majesty wrote that "edict" with the intent to commend the two prison officials for their good work. At the same time, he hoped to ask for financial help with tuition. Little did Your Majesty know that his well-intentioned letter was misunderstood. The officials came to his cell and scolded him harshly.

LIAO: Has the queen ever visited here?

ZENG: Your Majesty has already banished her from the royal family.

LIAO: So you two are divorced. Have your children changed their names?

ZENG: It's a long story. Your Majesty is in a sour mood now, and cannot continue.

LIAO: Here is my donation of fifty yuan [US$6.40]. I hope Your Majesty can get other sponsors to pay for your tuition. I wish you the best.

THE FENG SHUI MASTER

I bumped into Huang Tianyuan, the then ninety-year-old feng shui master, on a small mountain path in September of 1998, when I was visiting friends in Gongtanzui region, Sichuan. Huang helped villagers achieve optimum balance and harmony through the location and orientation of tombs and cemeteries.

—⁂—

LIAO YIWU: Are you Mr. Huang, the famous feng shui master?

HUANG TIANYUAN: Don't listen to other people's lies. I'm not a feng shui master. Please don't ask me for any feng shui–related advice.

LIAO: Actually, I'm from out of town. I'm not interested in finding out about the feng shui in this area. About twelve years ago, I worked for the folk art agency here. My director, Peng, and I used to visit villages along the You River to collect folk music and arts. One day, Director Peng came here to seek advice from you because his deceased father had appeared in his dreams many times. When he and I showed up at your house, you asked Director Peng to prepare a bowl of clear water and hold the bowl in front of you. I was puzzled by the ceremony and asked: What can you see in the water? Your answer contained two words: The soul. After examining the water for a couple of minutes, you urged Director Peng to bury his father's ashes to appease the old man's soul. But Director Peng said: I have already buried my father's ashes. Upon hearing that, you tapped a burning incense stick on the side of the bowl three times and asked: How come your father's ghost is still angry? Director Peng was so scared that his face turned ashen white. He immediately knelt in front of you and said: You are right, Master! I lied. It turned out his father's ashes were still stored inside an urn at his house and he hadn't had the opportunity to bury it yet. Do you remember that?

HUANG: I know Director Peng, but I don't remember the ceremony. I don't do that anymore. I have given up my practice.

LIAO: How come?

HUANG: It's a long story. During the past decade, feng shui consulting and fortune-telling have become quite popular in this area. People consult feng shui masters before the construction of houses for both the living and the dead. My specialty is to advise people with choosing burial sites. One year, I was so busy. I offered consultation to at least fifty families.

LIAO: Why, was there a high death rate that year?

HUANG: No, no. The advice was for the living. In this area, people spend money choosing spots with good feng shui for big and lavish tombs while they are still alive. Tombs with the right feng shui can bring good luck for your descendants.

I have worked hard for the folks here all my life and accumulated a little fortune from my business. I've just turned ninety. It's time for me to take care of myself. So, two years ago, I left the business to my nine-year-old apprentice, who is a feng shui prodigy. One day, after my retirement, the former chief of our township asked me for help. So I walked around and picked a piece of land for him. Upon my recommendation, he hired a contingent of stonemasons, bricklayers, plasterers, and tillers, who worked nonstop for three months and converted the spot into a private cemetery. The township chief then moved all of his ancestors' tombs from seven kilometers away to the new spot. He also ordered the craftsmen to build a grave for himself, which was more spacious than his house. After the project was completed, the chief hosted a huge banquet, with twenty tables full of guests. I was invited but didn't go. I got my butt out of there as soon as I could. If a person becomes too greedy, he starts to carry bad energy. I was too afraid he could pass the bad energy on to me.

LIAO: The spot you picked for him was supposed to be auspicious. Why did you try to run away?

HUANG: People of different status are provided with different feng shui specs and with different levels of design. A good feng shui design requires the complete harmony of yin and yang elements. It should be neither inadequate nor excessive. The chief of the township broke all the rules of moderation. He heaped on himself the luxuries normally accorded to a provincial governor. You probably have heard about it. Inside his tomb, there was a long list of modern luxuries: a stone replica of a luxury car, a stone bed carved in the shape of a dragon boat, a room set aside for a nightclub with karaoke equipment. He even built a nice carved stone chair, specifically reserved for his meeting with the president of a multinational corporation in the world of the dead. He also specifically requested the company of "young ladies." But the stonemason lacked the proper skills and none of the statues of young women looked pretty. You could hardly tell from their faces whether they were men or women. Building a tomb should be a private affair, but the township chief made it a huge public event.

It's hard to blame him. Throughout history, there have been many people like him. For example, Emperor Qin Shihuang [259 BC–210 BC] defeated other kingdoms and united China. After he established the Qin dynasty, he racked his brain and tried to figure out how it could last forever. While searching for an immortal pill, he also began to build his own grave. He wanted to take his wealth with him. Guess what? He ended up dying at the age of forty-nine. Soon after his death, his empire crashed. Do you see any difference between Emperor Qin Shihuang and our government officials? They are in constant pursuit of gain for themselves and their descendants. When you overdo it, you achieve the opposite result.

Please excuse the digression. Since the township chief made a big deal of his tomb, he soon caught the attention of the local media. The pictures of his tombs were all over the paper. The county government read the report and sent out an investigative team to check how the tomb was financed. They found out that the chief had embezzled public funds. It became a huge scandal. A whole bunch of people under him—the village chiefs and the village party secretaries—were all implicated. They had all followed his bad example by illegally occupying public and private lands, and embezzling public funds to build their own tombs. Many peasants also followed their lead. Those who couldn't afford to get advice from a feng shui master began to build their own tombs near those of the officials. As you can see from here, there are several rows of empty tombs on the sunny side of the path.

LIAO: Were you implicated in the scandal?

HUANG: And how! The township chief blamed me for all his criminal activities. He told everyone that he had fallen into my superstitious trap. He said I had encouraged him to embezzle public funds to support his tomb-building project. He accused me of ruining his career and fortunes as well as those of his descendants. Then, many other party officials followed suit. They went to the police with the same accusations against me. Overnight, I became a criminal who was responsible for the revival of superstitious activities in the region. I had to run away and hide inside my own tomb for several months. Nobody knew where I was. They caught my nine-year-old apprentice and made him a scapegoat. The TV station shot a documentary about how the nine-year-old feng shui prodigy was a quack and deceived people with his tricks. After the documentary was aired, many people started to harass my family members. The public security bureau detained them for interrogation. Luckily, none of my family members knew the location of my hiding place.

As the investigation expanded, police began to target other feng shui practitioners. They ended up arresting over twenty of them. Those poor guys were publicly denounced at village meetings and paraded through the streets along with other criminals. I heard several of the younger feng shui guys have been sent to a reeducation camp around here.

Two years ago, there used to be an area in the marketplace for blind fortune-tellers and feng shui masters. I used to have a booth there and was in great demand. Many considered me a regional treasure. But police raided the area and made it illegal to practice fortune-telling and feng shui.

LIAO: Are you still on the run?

HUANG: No. Once the campaign was over, people forgot about me. Besides, I'm in my nineties. What can they do about me? I'm too old to do any physical labor if they decide to send me to the reeducation camp. If they do lock me up, I could corrupt more people in jail by giving them feng shui advice. Believe it or not, people love this kind of stuff. During the Cultural Revolution, the Red Guards also clamped down on feng shui and fortune-telling activities. But I never stopped my practice because there was always a need somewhere. People secretly invited me to their homes and asked for my advice.

LIAO: Yesterday, I walked around the area you just mentioned. It was empty. Apart from those who have been sent to the local reeducation camp, where are the rest of the fortune-tellers and feng shui masters?

HUANG: They have all gone to the neighboring provinces of Guizhou and Hunan. Modern transportation has made it much easier to move around. Sometimes, people in Guizhou and Hunan don't like outsiders to come in and invade their territories. Then, the Sichuan practitioners will travel to the coastal regions of Fujian and Zhejiang provinces where people are getting rich and desperately need the advice of fortune-tellers and feng shui masters. It's pretty easy to do business there. All you need to do is to show off a couple of your normal tricks and the locals will be all over you. However, it's a different story here. Since there is an oversupply of fortune-tellers and feng shui masters, you have to have solid skills to make money.

LIAO: I think the central government has launched a nationwide campaign against feudalistic and superstitous practices.

HUANG: You must be talking about witchcraft. I call that superstition. Recently, as feng shui and fortune-telling are out of favor, Witch Chen's business has started to pick up. Her house has been packed with customers. That witch only knows one trick: burn some fake paper money to appease the ghost and mix the ashes with water. She then has people drink the water, saying that it will cure them of illness. Apart from the water trick, she will also put on a Taoist costume and dance in a circle, mumbling to herself and screaming. She claims that the spirit of the Empress in Heaven possesses her, and the empress can help drive any illness or evil spirits from the patient's body.

Who knows what kind of ghost has possessed her. She is illiterate, and can't read a single character. But she charges people fifty yuan [U.S. $6.40] per session. I don't know why people take her seriously. Mixing water with paper ashes is pure crap. Huh, when I was on the run from police, that woman profited from my misfortune. In this world, feng shui changes all the time. One minute, luck appears on the east, and the next minute, it moves to the west. It's like catching a mouse inside a quilt—you pounce on this end, and the mouse escapes from the other.

LIAO: Do you think your good luck will return soon?

HUANG: I bet it will. At the moment, people are very desperate and they all go visit Witch Chen. Once they realize that witchcraft doesn't work, they will begin to miss me. I grew up reading the books of Confucius. I spent years poring over the I Ching, the Book of Changes, and all the Taoist classics. I studied Chinese medicine for many years. In the old days, a person with my knowledge and talents would have been picked by a governor or an emperor to be his adviser.

LIAO: With your advanced age, you are still filled with ambition. It's really admirable.

HUANG: I was very ambitious, but, as you know, I haven't had too much luck in this life because the feng shui surrounding my ancestors' tombs doesn't have any extraordinary features. I've spent several years studying and surveying this region, and finally located a precious spot where "the floating dragon falls between the penholder." Based on my astrological calculations, the Huang family will prosper after I depart from this world.

LIAO: Could you explain a little more? I'm confused by the "floating dragon falls between the penholder" line.

HUANG: You know the mountain range here is called the Mountains of Penholders because there are three penholder-shaped mountains. I walked around the area with a compass many times. The spot for my tomb nestles right between the first penholder-shaped mountain and the second. Also, if you use binoculars, you will see the Wu River wending its way through the same area between the first and second mountain. In many ancient Chinese legends, the Wu River harbors a floating dragon. A poet once described the Wu River as "the floating dragon falls between the penholder." Do you get it? I will reside in the same spot as the dragon, which will bless my future generations. Unfortunately, this treasured spot has not been discovered yet. Otherwise, with such good feng shui, this place should have produced an emperor. Sadly, the only famous thing we got here was a tribal headman.

LIAO: Back in the old days, a headman was quite powerful, like a little emperor who could get away with anything. Legend has it that the local headman had seventy-two tombs built all over the region with the same designs. He had those fake tombs constructed to confuse grave robbers. After he died, his descendants were instructed to murder or bury alive every single person at his funeral, including the coffin bearers. As a result, his tomb still remains a mystery and nobody knows which one of the seventy-two tombs is the authentic site. Countless numbers of grave diggers have combed through the area to locate the headman's body and the treasures buried with him. So, based on your calculations, it's fairly likely that the real tomb could be right here, under our feet.

HUANG: I don't think that headman's final resting place is somewhere around this prime spot. Otherwise, his descendants would have made it big. Well, on the other hand, he might have picked a good feng shui spot, but the natural and physical environment has changed. The good feng shui might have evaporated.

LIAO: Now that you mention it, I have noticed that the feng shui around here is really good. Look at the setting sun, resting glowingly between the two penholders. There is a nice heavenly breeze now. I can even smell a subtle fragrance.

HUANG: The scents actually come from the herbs that I have planted. The soil is so fertile. I planted over twenty different kinds of herbs in the springtime, and by summer leaves are sprouting all over the place. These herbs are more filling than crops. When I'm hungry, I simply harvest some herbs and chew them. The feeling of hunger will be gone right away. If you get some of these herbs, you can mash them into a thick paste and smear them around your mouth, your ears, under your armpits, and around your asshole. It will help prevent illness and drive away all sorts of bugs and evil spirits. Nowadays, I go days without eating. I simply sleep inside my tomb. My tomb is very dark inside. If a bug gets into my mouth, I can catch it with my teeth. Those earthworms taste pretty good. Snakes or scorpions are all scared of me.

LIAO: Those snakes and scorpions are dangerous.

HUANG: Nowadays, people are more poisonous than snakes or scorpions. In the sixties and seventies, people hurt one another as a result of Mao's political campaigns. In the nineties, people hurt one another in order to make more money. People are so degraded and selfish. Confucius used to call China a nation of formalities and kindness.

LIAO: Sounds like you are still smarting from the experience with the township chief. Can I go take a look at your tomb?

HUANG: That's top secret and I wouldn't allow anyone to see where my tomb is. I have spent years building it. For an old guy like me, it's no easy job. Since you are so persistent, let me give you a rough idea where it is. Look at that huge rock near the cliff. Half of it sticks out in midair. The base of that rock is surrounded by many smaller ones. All the rocks are connected seamlessly, as if they are bonded together with cement. Nobody knows that there is actually a secret tunnel under the rocks that can reach my tomb. It used to be a tiger's den. In 1961, a male tiger roamed around on this mountain. One day, the tiger became desperately hungry because most of the trees had been cut down and all the small animals killed. So the tiger went down to the villages for human prey. All the villagers came out with torches, beat their gongs, and chased the tiger all the way up to the mountain. They cornered the tiger near that rock. With no way to escape, he climbed up on top of the rock, jumped into the ravine, and killed himself. The villagers retrieved the tiger's body, skinned him, and barbecued the meat. Over a hundred people showed up and each one got a small piece to munch

on. Later on, I heard that was the last tiger in the border region
between Sichuan and Guizhou. After the tiger was killed, I went back
to the rock and discovered his den, which was about twenty meters
deep. So I dug a tunnel under it and converted the den into my tomb.
Since then, I go stay there for a couple of days every month. I enjoy
staying there because Ruan Hongyu is lying somewhere nearby. With
her company, my nostalgia for this world is being diminished day by day.

LIAO: Ruan Hongyu?

HUANG: Do you remember the courtyard house by the side of this road?
That was Ruan's house.

LIAO: Of course. She was a famous blind singer and had a great voice. I
visited her once. She was in her eighties and her singing was as vibrant
as that of an eighteen-year-old. I used to put a tape recorder in front of
her and tape her singing folk songs. She would sing one song after
another for hours.

HUANG: Yes, that was her. She has been dead for six years.

LIAO: What happened to her house?

HUANG: The courtyard has long been demolished. Ruan was a tough
woman and she has become pretty dominant in the world of the dead.
When a dead person is too strong, she affects the energy flow. The living will suffer. Her descendants had to move to find a new place so
they could breathe.

LIAO: Was there anything going on between you two?

HUANG: I pursued her when we were both young. I'm three years her
junior. We used to sing love songs to each other from across the mountain peaks. She was a pretty mountain flower and had many suitors.
When it came to singing folk songs, nobody was her match. Singing
folk songs from mountain peaks is a traditional courting ritual in the
region. A boy and a girl sing to each other from separate mountain
peaks all night long. It is like a contest. If the boy can defeat the girl,

she will be his. I only competed with Ruan for half of the night and then acknowledged defeat. She lost both of her eyes during the Cultural Revolution. The Red Guards beat her up for singing decadent love songs. She was very stubborn and competitive all her life, but never made it big outside the area. So, after she passed away, I picked a nice resting place for her. The spot is close by and is very auspicious, better than the plot where her husband is buried.

LIAO: She was married to someone else?

HUANG: I think she married the wrong person. I wanted to borrow the feng shui from the world of the dead to correct her mistakes.

LIAO: She is dead. How can you correct her mistakes?

HUANG: I wanted us to be husband and wife in the other world.

LIAO: You are like the legendary Liang Shanbo and Zhu Yingtai, who didn't get to live in the same house when they were alive, but ended up buried inside the same grave.

HUANG: You can think whatever you want. I will join Ruan Hongyu in her grave. After we reunite in our afterlife, our family fortune will definitely take a turn for the better. As the saying goes, "When the floating dragon falls between the penholder, it heralds the thunderous rising of three generations." Within three generations, the Huang family should be able to produce a regional lord, with thousands of acres of land bestowed on him by the government.

LIAO: Okay. But, Master, how could you share such good feng shui with an outsider like Ruan Hongyu? Aren't you married yourself?

HUANG: I was. My wife died in the 1960 famine. Millions of people died from starvation that year. There was no way for me to afford a tomb with good feng shui. I just randomly found a spot, dug a shallow hole in the ground, and buried her. As you can tell, she was born poor and died poor. With her bad karma, she could spoil the good feng shui for my descendants if I'm buried with her after I die. However, if I'm buried alone, the yin and yang won't be in harmony. For this reason, I have to join Ruan Hongyu after death.

LIAO: I'm so confused by your idea of using Ruan Hongyu to benefit your descendants.

HUANG: Lao Tse, the founder of Taoism, once said: If you can explain what the way is, it is no longer the good way. Therefore, I cannot fully explain the mysterious karma that was bestowed on me and Ruan Hongyu.

LIAO: Have you shared your afterlife marriage plan with your family? As you probably know, you have no control once you die. Also, I don't think Ruan's family will allow you two to be buried together.

HUANG: This matter concerns the well-being of many generations to come. I will certainly tell the children of both families. I think they will understand. Actually, I have long prepared for our afterlife together. I'm going to let Ruan occupy this spot first. In this way, if our children do not respect my will after I die . . . I would move in myself when I'm still alive.

LIAO: I think they will freak out if they know about your plan.

HUANG: I have done enough for my children and it's time they understood me. My children have moved to the township. They are now living crammed inside the tall buildings with their kids on a noisy street. I like peace and quiet and refused to go with them. I'm an old man and I don't want to be a burden to them. Also, once Ruan Hongyu was gone, my only reason to live in this world was also gone. Even though I still helped people with their feng shui designs, my soul had already left. At the moment, my life is coming to an end, reaching zero. Zero is nature. The mountain is my home.

LIAO: Master Huang, it's not like we still live in ancient China, where you can find a remote place to live like a hermit. The mountain here, the river there, none of the pristine scenery will last. Soon, a developer will come and convert the area into a tourist site. If tourism business is good, I bet they will build a big entrance at the foot of the mountain, and market it as a newly discovered forest park. People would come from all corners of China on boats or by air. It's hard to believe that your tomb can remain hidden and the good feng shui can remain intact for twenty years after that.

HUANG: Your mind is filled with many inauspicious thoughts. You'd better go visit your friend in the village. It's getting late.

THE ABBOT

In the spring of 2003, while climbing Fengqi Mountain, about sixty kilometers west of Chengdu, my friends and I stumbled upon an ancient Buddhist temple hidden in a thicket of trees. Guangyan Temple, also known as the Gu Temple, harkens back to the Sui dynasty (581–618 AD). Built on the slopes of a mountain, the temple is divided into two parts: an upper and a lower section. In the upper section, I encountered a scene of neglect: overgrown plots of grass, and crumbling pagodas, which housed the bones of deceased Buddhists. Two halls of worship were in ruins. In contrast, the lower section was abuzz with the noise of activity generated by a long stream of worshippers and tourists. The chanting and the strong smell of incense wafting from the newly renovated halls reminded me of its recent prosperity.

The then 103-year-old Master Deng Kuan was the abbot in the Gu Temple. He lived in a spartan room at the back of the lower courtyard. Unlike those abbots in the movies, Master Deng Kuan didn't look distinguished at all: he was short, with small eyes, and always wore a yellowish woolen hat. He had to sit by an electric heater all the time because he was extremely sensitive to cold. The master was a heavy smoker and puffed on his tobacco pipe every few minutes. At the urging of his nephew, he also took a couple of sips of milk through a straw. He was extremely hard of hearing. Each time I asked a question, I had to shout in his ear. Eventually, after much shouting, coupled with occasional interpretations by his nephew, I managed to piece together this interview.

In September of 2005, one year after this interview was completed, I read in a local newspaper that Master Deng Kuan had passed away.

—◁ꕥ▷—

LIAO YIWU: Master, you look really good, very healthy.

MASTER DENG KUAN (DK): I was just hospitalized for two months in Chengdu. I'm falling apart. My body is stiff. Amitabha, Merciful Buddha. Now that I can't move around that much, I have a lot of time for meditating and thinking. I've been thinking a lot about the things that have happened to me in this life. Unfortunately, I'm only lucid half of the time. Some days, I'm so out of it that I have no idea where I am, what day it is, and who is standing beside me.

Have you read anything about our temple? In the Ming dynasty [1368–1644], Emperor Zhu Yuanzhang gifted this temple with an official name, "Guangyan Buddhist Temple." Later on, Master Wu Kong, Emperor Zhu's uncle, became enlightened at this temple. If we count him as our first abbot, I'm now the eighth abbot in the past six hundred years.

I was born in 1900 when China was still under the Qing emperor Guangxu. My secular name was Chen Jingrong. Since my family was poor, my parents sent me to this temple at the age of seven so I could get fed. So that was how I started out as a monk. My teacher, Master Zu Run, was an eminent monk in the region. He was well-known for his knowledge and his righteousness. Apart from teaching me the Buddhist scriptures, he also invited scholars to the temple to teach all the young novices how to read and write. Thanks to him, I grasped the basic literacy skills in a few years.

In 1928, I walked over ninety kilometers to Chengdu to get ordained in a big temple there. Following my ordination, I was enrolled at a Buddhist school run by Master Chan An. After I graduated in 1930, I studied at two more temples, and continued to receive guidance from various eminent monks. In 1944, after a decade and a half of traveling and studying, I returned to the Gu Temple. Initially, I worked as an official greeter, coordinating daily worshipping activities. In 1947, I was promoted to be the abbot. I stayed in that position until the Communist takeover in 1949.

LIAO: Your life has spanned the entire twentieth century. If we use 1949 as a dividing line, your life is pretty much divided into two equal phases. But you seem to play down the first half of your life with only a couple of sentences.

DK: When you turn one hundred, and look back on the early part of your life, a couple of sentences are sufficient. Otherwise, I can go on for three days and three nights. I have personally benefited from the teachings of over thirty grand masters of Buddhism. You could write a whole book about every single one of them.

LIAO: Sorry for the interruption. Please go on with your story.

DK: This temple was first built during the Sui dynasty. Since then, over thirty convents and temples have been built along the Qingcheng mountain range, with Gu Temple as the main center of worship. At one time, this temple housed over a thousand monks. Over the centuries, as old dynasties collapsed and new ones came into being, the temple remained relatively intact. This is because changes of dynasty or government were considered secular affairs. Monks like me didn't get involved. But the Communist revolution in 1949 was a turning point for me and the temple.

After 1949, the new government launched the Land Reform movement. Many former landowners in the region were targeted. Several were executed, their property seized and redistributed. One day, a government work team raided the temple. The team consisted of government officials and peasant activists. They set up a tribunal inside the temple to dispense justice. They called me a "rich temple owner" and declared that I was under arrest. My captors dragged me onto the stage, stripped me of my *kasaya*, and forced me to stand in front of a large crowd of villagers, with my arms pulled up behind my back in the jet-plane position. One by one, peasant activists stood up to share with the crowd about my "crimes." I was accused of accumulating wealth without engaging in physical labor, and spreading feudalistic and religious ideas that poisoned people's minds. Some even suggested investigating my past activities under the Nationalist government because I was collaborating with the rich to exploit the poor. At the end of each speech, the head of the work team would stand up and shout slogans like "Down with the evil landlord!" and "Religion is spiritual opium!" Then the whole crowd followed his lead with slogan shouting. Emotion soon ran very high: people spat at me, punched and shoved me. About thirty to forty monks were hunched over side by side with me on the stage. They were categorized as "bald lackeys of the rich landowner." The landowner was, of course, me.

LIAO: This is the first time I heard about the term "rich monk."

DK: It came as a shock to me as well and it was hard to cope with those unfair charges. All monks abide by the vow of poverty. In the pre-Communist days, many of us came from very poor families. Once we accepted the teachings of Buddha, we vowed to stay away from all human desires. In this vast province of Sichuan, there were over a hundred temples. No matter which temple you go to, you will find the same rule: monks pass on the Buddhist treasures from one generation to the next. Since ancient times, no abbot, monk, or nun has ever claimed the properties of the temple as his or her own. Who would have thought that overnight all of us would be classified as rich landowners! None of us had ever lived the life of a rich landowner, but we certainly suffered the retribution accorded one.

LIAO: What happened after those "struggle sessions"?

DK: Soon the struggle sessions turned into public beatings. Getting spat on, slapped in the face, and kicked in the back were common occurrences. Many times the local militia would show up at the temple at random and drag me to a room for interrogation. During one interrogation in the wintertime, a village militia chief and his men stripped me of my shirts and pants, and then hung me from the ceiling. It was so painful that I passed out in about ten minutes or so. They poured cold water onto my body. When I came to, my right arm was dislocated. Even today I still experience excruciating pain when I try to raise this arm. Sometimes I was beaten up for some ridiculous reasons. One time, an official called me to his office and ordered me to turn in one hundred golden bowls that I had allegedly hidden inside the temple. The official said a junior monk had revealed the secret to the work team. I had no idea what he was talking about. I didn't even own a regular porcelain bowl, not to mention a bowl made of gold. When I told them that I didn't know, they accused me of lying and hung me from a tree. Then, several villagers went to search the monks' living quarters. Believe it or not, they did find one hundred bowls in the corner of the kitchen. To their disappointment, however, they were bowls made of pottery, not gold. Finally, I understood what the whole fuss was about. Since each bowl could hold only one *jin* [500 grams] of rice, we called it the "*jin* bowl"—which sounds the same as "gold bowls" in Chinese. The situation was truly hopeless.

By the way, during the Land Reform movement, the local government seized all the Buddhist treasures and confiscated hundreds of hectares of pristine forest and farmland from the temple. We were not alone. Temples around the whole country suffered a similar fate.

LIAO: I have checked some historical records and found that many prominent monks suffered persecution during that time. For example, Master Kuan Lin from Chengdu's Wenshu Temple was brutally tortured by local peasants. They broke his legs and arms, and pulled his teeth out. He collapsed and passed out on the floor. His torturers thought they had killed him. Out of fear, they sent him to the hospital, and luckily the doctors were able to save his life. Master Qing Ding at Zhaojue Temple was sentenced to lifelong imprisonment in 1955. That was because he had been a cadet in the Huangpu Military Academy under the Nationalist government before he became a monk. He ended up spending twenty years behind bars. Master Wei Xian, the former abbot at the Ciyun Temple near Chongqing, was arrested in 1954 for his efforts to establish a Buddhist school. He was jailed for twenty-seven years. The list goes on.

DK: The Land Reform movement was just the beginning of a series of disasters that befell the temple. In 1958, Chairman Mao launched the Great Leap Forward campaign, calling people in China to find ways to mass-produce iron and steel so China could catch up with industrialized nations like the U.S. It was also the beginning of the collectivization campaign. No household was allowed to keep any private property or to cook at home. People were ordered to eat at communal kitchens and dining halls.

I put myself at the mercy of heaven and decided to go with the flow. I registered with the local village leader, who gave me permission to lead ten monks to look for iron-containing rocks in the mountain, and to participate in the production of steel. Peasants built a makeshift furnace inside the temple. We were a bunch of laymen and had no idea what an iron-containing ore looked like or how to produce steel from those rocks. The government sent a young scientist, who gave us a quick thirty-minute crash course. Then, confident in their newly acquired knowledge, people rolled up their sleeves and worked in groups to scout the mountain for iron-containing rocks. Many villagers ended up by gathering lots of dark-colored rocks and stones, and dumped them into the furnace.

Meanwhile, the local government also called on people to donate every piece of metal they had in their homes: farm tools, cooking utensils, basins, locks, metal hoops, even women's hair clips, and to melt them down to produce steel and iron. There was a popular slogan: To turn in one piece of metal is to wipe out a foreign imperialist. We monks didn't even have a home, but we didn't want to lag behind the others. We sniffed around the temple like dogs. We found incense holders, metal collection boxes, bells, and locks. We pried and hammered off the metal edges of the wooden incense tables, and even smashed and knocked down the small bronze statues on the four corners of the temple roof.

Near the entrance of the temple, there used to be a pair of royal cast-iron cauldrons given by Emperor Yongle in the Ming dynasty. None of it survived the Great Leap Forward. Since the royal cauldrons were huge, made with thick cast iron, it took over twenty strong and tough men to smash them with large sledgehammers. The loud echoes of the hammering sound could be heard miles away. Besides, melting those thick, ancient cast-iron pots was no easy job. People chopped down hundreds of big trees to fuel the furnace.

It wasn't long before the mountain was stripped bare. When I first entered the monastery here, there were hundreds of hectares of trees, many of which were rare species, such as ginkgo, nanmu, and ancient cypress. But during those crazy years, they were all cut down. Have you seen that big thousand-year-old tree outside the temple? The tree was left untouched because it grew on a cliff and people couldn't reach it. Nowadays, visitors have been telling me how precious and beautiful that tree is. Little do they know that there used to be seven big trees around here, each was thick enough for three people to circle around. That one left was the ugliest and quite useless. The other six were cut to feed the furnace.

It's really hard to imagine what happened then. People were exhilarated by Chairman Mao's lofty vision of building a strong socialist country. I was assigned the task of working the bellows to keep the fire in the furnace going. I used to practice kung fu at the crack of dawn every day to stay fit and healthy. That rigorous training helped build up my stamina. While most people were on the verge of exhaustion and some had even collapsed, I was still full of energy, working the bellows nonstop for hours in a half-squatting position beside the furnace.

LIAO: You were almost sixty years old around that time, weren't you?

DK: Yes, I was. But even the twenty-year-olds were no match for me. Villagers secretly gave me a nickname, "The Steely Mountain Soldier." Anyway, after days and nights of hard work, we finally saw some results—a bunch of hard irregular-shaped pig iron. Some looked like beehives, with small pieces of rocks sticking over their surfaces. We waited until those lumps became cold and solid. Then we tested their quality by hitting them with a hammer. Guess what, they immediately crumbled into small dark pieces. So did our hope.

LIAO: Since you worked so hard during the Great Leap Forward, did the villagers think that you had redeemed your past wrongdoings?

DK: Not exactly. After the steel production campaign turned into a total failure, people resumed their daily routine. At night, after eating at public kitchens, they had nothing else to do. Once again, public rallies against the bad elements were resumed as a form of entertainment. We were at the whim of the village leaders. Whenever or wherever they wanted to hold a struggle session, all of the class enemies would be at their disposal. From 1952 to 1961, I attended over three hundred struggle sessions.

In those difficult years, I constantly thought about a legendary tale relating to the Gu Temple. In 1398, when Zhu Yuanzhang, the founder of the Ming dynasty, died, his grandson Jianwen was crowned emperor. Jianwen's uncle, the prince of Yan, possessed a strong military base in the north and formed a serious threat to Emperor Jianwen's power. They engaged in a four-year armed conflict that eventually ended the reign of Jianwen. The prince of Yan usurped the throne. He called his era "Yongle" or "Perpetually Jubilant." Emperor Yongle spent several years purging China of Jianwen's supporters in a brutal manner. His nephew, the deposed ruler, escaped and then disappeared. Several years later, there was a rumor circulating that Jianwen had turned into a monk and was hiding inside the Gu Temple. One day, a spy dispatched by Emperor Yongle spotted the deposed emperor and relayed the news to the palace. The emperor immediately sent an assassin over. Right before the assassin arrived, Jianwen caught wind of it and disappeared. His would-be assassin found a poem written on the wall of a worship hall: "Traversing the southwest in exile for forty long years, gray has tainted my once dark mane. Heaven and earth I once reigned, but now nothing remains. Not even a hut to rest my soul. Rivers and streams pass by silently; where do they flow? Grass and willows turn green year after year; this old countryman is choked with tears." The assassin jotted down the poem and presented it to Emperor Yongle. He read it aloud; tears streamed down his face. He waved the long sleeve of his robe and sighed: Let my nephew go.

LIAO: What a story. How did that relate to your predicament then?

DK: Emperor Yongle ruled China with brutality. His police and spies were planted all over the kingdom. Even so, Jianwen, his former nemesis, could find shelter inside the Gu Temple. But in Communist China, a harmless monk had nowhere to escape to.

LIAO: Chairman Mao certainly tried to wipe out the spirit of Buddha, and every other form of religion.

DK: No human being possesses the power to destroy Buddha in people's hearts. This is because Buddha is as essential to us as the air we breathe and the water we drink. That's where all kindness, forbearance, compassion, and wisdom originate. I would never have survived that difficult period had it not been for my belief in Buddha.

Let me tell you a story. A poor old lady named Wang lived near the temple. She secretly helped me for many years. Since I was a counterrevolutionary, she couldn't talk with me when there were people around. While I was working in the field, she would walk past me, and stop briefly, pretending to tie her shoelaces. Then, she would bang her sickle on the ground a couple of times to get my attention. After she left, I would dash over to the place where she banged her sickle, and pick up the corn bread she had left there for me. It was in January of 1960, the onset of a nationwide famine. Many folks in the village had already died of starvation. That lady squeezed food from her tiny ration and saved it for me. She was the reincarnation of the Goddess of Mercy. Even now, I can still remember her courage and generosity and pray for her soul.

By 1961, half of the people labeled as members of the bad elements had starved to death. To reduce the number of people on the food ration roll, the local government simply deported me back to my birthplace in Chongqing County. I moved in with a distant nephew and lived the life of a peasant. In 1966, when the Cultural Revolution began, the Red Guards took the place of the village militiamen and became my new tormentors. I worked in the rice paddies during daytime and was forced to attend public denunciation meetings at night.

LIAO: So how did you manage to survive the various political campaigns?

DK: Buddha says: If I don't go to hell, who will? I had to suffer to redeem the sins of my previous life. Otherwise, the suffering could befall someone else. That was how I motivated myself to live. Eventually, I simply resigned myself to adversity.

In those years, the worst part was that all Buddhist teachings were banned. We were not allowed to pray. Sometimes I would close my eyes and silently chant some scriptures. But then some villagers found out and reported it to village officials. I ended up getting more beatings for refusing to mend my feudalistic, superstitious ways.

LIAO: As an eminent monk, it must be very hard to live without praying or reading the scriptures.

DK: It was difficult. Deep in my heart, I never gave up my belief in the benevolence of Buddha.

For a while, I thought that I would be destined to farm and lead the life of a secret monk for the rest of my life. However, after over seventeen years, the tide started to turn. One day in 1978, a friend from out of town stopped by and told me that new leaders in Beijing had relaxed the government's religious policy. People were allowed to openly practice Buddhism.

Initially, I didn't quite believe his words and wanted to find out myself. But I didn't dare to tell anyone because the local government was still clinging to the old Communist doctrine, even though Chairman Mao had died two years before. If I got caught, I was sure to get myself and my nephew into trouble again. So, I waited for a couple more days. One night, after the whole village was asleep, I quietly packed my bags and left. I ran and walked for about sixty kilometers in the darkness. By noon the next day, I arrived in Chengdu, and went directly to Wenshu Temple. There, I reunited with about thirty monks who had just returned. It was quite an emotional reunion for us.

I stayed at Wenshu Temple for over three years, working as a greeter and presiding over Buddhist ceremonies. Since I was pretty good at performing the "releasing the soul from purgatory" ritual, I gradually established quite a reputation in the region. In 1984, I think it was on July 15 on the lunar calendar, I was welcomed back to the Gu Temple to continue my service to Buddha. Over ten thousand residents showed up and filled every corner of the temple. People lit firecrackers nonstop, and the smoke shrouded the temple like a thick fog, which lingered around for quite a while before drifting away. There were gongs booming and bells pealing. It was quite a festive spectacle.

LIAO: You were eighty-four years old that year. When you smelled the smoke of fireworks and saw the crowd, how did you feel?

DK: My feelings were of joy and sadness mixed. From 1949 to 1978, China experienced the longest period of retribution for sins in history. For twenty-nine years, there were no real monks in Chinese temples.

LIAO: But in those crazy years, the government still kept the Buddhism Association.

DK: The Buddhism Association was simply an empty shell. All the monks were defrocked and put under the supervision of the village party chief. In many small temples around here, lay peasants kicked the monks out and converted the temples into residential quarters.

For myself, I felt lucky that I was still alive. I didn't have time to dwell on the past. I was already old and ailing like a candle's flame fluttering in the wind. The temple was in disarray with dilapidated buildings and broken walls. Weeds were growing everywhere. I couldn't find a single room without a leaking roof. Wherever I looked, I saw the tragic results of manmade damage and years of neglect.

About thirty monks and lay Buddhists joined me at the temple. We didn't even have enough beds. Many had to sleep on the floor. Occasionally, snakes and rats would sneak under our quilts. The young monks were very scared. I would often tell them: The rats are cold too. Let them in so they can get some warmth and good sleep. Even now, rats constantly get into my quilt, and a couple of them will snuggle under my chin. They are like my kids. One time, a naughty rat dragged my rosary beads away. So I scared it with the words: You little rascal, what do you need that rosary for? You can't eat it. Bring it back. If you don't, I'm going to kill you with rat poison. It must have heard me. Not long after, the rosary beads showed up beside my bed.

LIAO: You have done a great job restoring the Gu Temple.

DK: You are too young to see what the temple was like before. It's far from being restored. Have you ever visited the upper part of the temple?

LIAO: Yes, I have.

DK: The Receiving Hall is being reconstructed on its ruins. If you pass the crumbling Hall of Burning Candles, you will see the forest of pagodas, where generations of Buddhist monks were buried. The tall pagoda in the middle held the body of our grand master Wu Kong, the first abbot of this temple. Grand Master Wu Kong had seen through the secular world at an early age and had always wanted to be a monk. When the prince of Yan deposed Emperor Jianwen, the grand master was traveling in India and Tibet to study Buddhism. On his way back, he stopped at this temple and experienced enlightenment. He shaved his head and was ordained here. Grand Master Wu Kong read extensively and became a well-known Buddhist scholar and practitioner. He reached nirvana, and passed away while in meditation, with his body in a lotus position. His disciples consecrated the Wu Kong Pagoda to hold his body. After over 550 years, the body miraculously remained intact, with no signs of decay. It became the most precious Buddhist treasure inside the Gu Temple.

LIAO: I stood in front of the Wu Kong Pagoda and noticed that the shrine lies empty now. The characters engraved on both sides of the shrine are hardly recognizable.

DK: The characters were supposed to express the grand master's ecstatic feelings of being enlightened and coming to the realization that "all worldly things are empty and transient, like the floating clouds." During the Land Reform movement, a leader of the local militia led a group of armed peasants into the temple in the name of "eliminating superstition." They started in the upper section. When the militia leader stopped in front of the Wu Kong Pagoda, he seemed to have been taken over by demonic forces. He raised his rifle with its bayonet, screaming, "Kill that Buddha!" He stabbed into the preserved body of the grand master twenty or thirty times. Soon, the rest of the mob joined him. Pieces of the grand master's body were strewn on the ground. Then he ordered his fellow militiamen to round up all of the monks and parade us on the street for several hours. After we returned to the temple, we found out that the flesh on his body had already dissolved in the soil, leaving only his bones. When the bell struck midnight, I held back my tears, went secretly up to the forest of pagodas. It was painful to see his bones scattered on the ground. I quietly gathered every single piece and carefully put them in a bamboo basket. I found a place on the ceiling beam of the Guanyin Hall. With a makeshift pulley, I managed to send the basket up and put it on the beam. I thought it was going to be safe there, but I was wrong.

During the Cultural Revolution, the Red Guards from the nearby schools launched an assault on what they called the Four Old Elements: old customs, old thinking, old habits, and old culture. They ransacked the temples, burning and destroying anything that had survived the previous political campaigns, including the worshipping halls.

Let me give you some background. In the Ming dynasty, Emperor Yongle had commissioned the construction of five halls of worship with glazed tile roofs. Despite their normal wear and tear, those buildings remained preserved and survived the craziness of the 1950s. One day in 1966 I snuck away from my hometown and climbed up the mountain to take a look at the temple. Before I approached the main entrance, I heard the singing of revolutionary songs. There seemed to be a lot of people in there. I walked closer and hid behind a tree. There were red

flags everywhere, with the characters "Revolutionary Fighters" embla-
zoned on them. A large group of young people were on the roof of the
Daxiong Hall—singing while pulling the glazed tiles out and then kicking them off the roof. I just stood there in a daze. After the roof had
been stripped, the Red Guards began to punch holes in it. Inside the
Daxiong Hall, there were eight floor-to-ceiling stone columns decorated
with engravings of poems and paintings by well-known artists and cal-
ligraphers. The Red Guards tied thick ropes around the columns and
pulled the ropes in unison until the columns collapsed. It was too traumatic for me. I just left.

I was told later on that the Red Guards toppled the other four halls
with similar barbarous methods. When those buildings collapsed, people could feel the vibrations from far away, as if an earthquake had hit
the region. Like the ancient saying goes: "No eggs can remain intact
when the nest is destroyed." As I mentioned earlier, I put the bones of
Grand Master Wu Kong in a basket and hid it on the ceiling beam of
the Guanyin Hall. When the hall was demolished, the basket mysteri-
ously disappeared. Nobody knows what happened to the treasure.

Thanks to those young zealots, the whole upper section is now in
total ruins. There is no way to rebuild those halls. In addition to demolishing the worshipping halls, the Red Guards also burned hundreds of
royal edicts issued by emperors from various dynasties. They destroyed
paintings by famous artists, as well as rare editions of books and scriptures, and smashed hundreds of Buddhist statues.

LIAO: In other words, most of the buildings we see now have been reconstructed in recent years?

DK: Since 1984, many pious Buddhist followers have begun to donate
money and manpower. Little by little, we are able to build new worship
halls and sculpt new Buddhist statues. It is starting to look like a temple now. Let me tell you: It will take at least 20 million yuan [US$2.4
million] just to restore half of the temple to its original scale. You know
the saying: The fire burns high when everyone adds wood to it. We
have set up a stone tablet, engraving the names of those who have contributed over 100 yuan [$12]. There are several thousand names on the
tablet. A private entrepreneur has recently donated 30,000 yuan
[US$3,500] to dedicate a jade Buddha statue in the newly built Receiv-

ing Hall. We have other revenues from the sale of incense and candles, as well as from our teahouse.

LIAO: Do monks have to pay taxes?

DK: We wouldn't mind paying regular government taxes. But with the decline of moral values, corrupt officials, both big and small, are trying to milk what they think is a fat cow. Administratively, our temple is under the supervision of the Bureau of Religious Affairs, which is a subsidiary of the Department of United Front. Officials there are always looking out for ways to fatten their pockets. If we don't pay money as a tribute to those "servants of the people," they will threaten either to expel monks from the temple or to sell part of our temple to a private developer. As you know, many small temples in the area that resisted have been sold to private investors.

LIAO: You are a well-known religious figure in the community. How could they dare to do those things to you?

DK: Those Communist officals dare to do anything. Do you want to hear this? The car driven by the director of the United Front Department was paid for by the monks. He ordered each temple to contribute at least 5,000 yuan [US$625] so he could buy a luxury model. One time, the head of the county Religious Affairs Bureau visited me. I invited him to have tea at my private living quarters. He slammed the door shut, banged on the table, and pointed at my face: You turned a deaf ear to my request. I want your temple to contribute 100,000 yuan [US$12,500] to the road construction fund. I knew very well that the central government had already allocated funds for the road project. Local officials had embezzled a large portion of the money. They wanted the monks to fill in the funding gap.

LIAO: You could report him to the central government or sue him, couldn't you?

DK: Monks take forbearance as a virtue. So I told the official: Monks beg alms. We rely on the kind contributions of Buddha's followers. We'll pay when our collection reaches the amount you have requested. He responded impatiently: Give me a deadline. I said calmly: If we can collect the sum tomorrow, we'll give it to you tomorrow. If we have it in the indefinite future, we'll pay you in the indefinite future. Upon hearing that, he became furious and began to swear at me with four-letter words. His loud swearing was heard by many worshippers in the temple. Several of them stormed in and eventually kicked him out. Corruption is a sin, but Buddha has mercy.

A couple of months ago, some officials showed up and set up their mah-jongg tables right inside the temple. They played that gambling game all day. Some ended up losing money. They walked into my room and wanted to get a loan from me. I did "lend" some to them. You know they will never pay back. Besides, they made a mess here, with food and cigarettes butts all over the floor. Before they left, they came to the worshipping hall, put their two hands in front of their chest, palm to palm, and knelt in front of a Buddha statue, chanting, "Amitabha," Those scoundrels, what can you do? Right now, the Religious Affairs Bureau takes charge of all Buddhist, Taoist, and Muslim temples, as well as the Christian churches. The officials are so powerful, and can destroy you at a whim. The chief of the Religious Affairs Bureau shamelessly calls himself the parent of all gods. Many people use the phrase "covering the sky with one palm" to describe the government power over religion.

LIAO: This is ridiculous.

DK: Throughout ancient history, no matter how incompetent the emperors were, or how corrupt and decadent the royal courts became, one never heard about officials blackmailing and harassing monks.

LIAO: This is the first time I have heard about it, too.

DK: With all of this corruption going on, I don't know when I will be able to raise enough money to pay for the restoration. I just have to let nature take its course.

LIAO: But, Master, you have already done a great job in restoring the temple to its former glory. You are now considered a Buddhist treasure in this whole region.

DK: That's an exaggeration. Have you seen the newly restored Scripture Building?

LIAO: I've seen the outside, the white walls with black tiled roof. The building reflects the simplicity of the Tang dynasty [618–907] architectural style. I was told that the name engraved on the front of the building was given by Yu Youren, a well-known politician under the Nationalist government. His handwriting was far superior to those of Ming emperor Zhu Yuanzhang and Qing emperor Kang Xi, both of whom left their marks here.

DK: Mr. Yu Youren was climbing the Qingcheng Mountain in 1944. He overheard some monks talk about a Buddhist encyclopedia. The book, published in 1372, was a compilation of well-known Buddhist writings in seven thousand volumes. The whole project took thirty-one years to finish. Several hundred scholars and craftsmen were involved in the editing, hand-printing, and volume-binding of the book. Emperor Zhu Yuanzhang ordered two sets, each of which weighed over three tons. One set was lost in a major fire. The second set was stored here inside the Gu Temple. This Buddhist encyclopedia and Grand Master Wu Kong's preserved body were the crown jewels of this temple, attracting Buddhists and scholars from all over the nation. The legendary tales surrounding this rare book greatly piqued Mr. Yu's curiosity. He came into the temple and spent several days poring over the book. When the former abbot asked him to write a couple of words, he raised his ink brush and with one long stroke he wrote, "Scripture Building." His calligraphy, like a flying dragon, was later engraved on the building's front wall.

LIAO: With your permission, may I go up to the building and take a look at the book?

DK: The book is no longer here.

LIAO: Has it been destroyed by the Red Guards?

DK: Amitabha. No. In the summer of 1951, Yao Tixin, an intellectual, was appointed the Chongqing County chief. He had read about the book in the county almanac. Shortly after his appointment, he visited the temple and went up to the Scripture Building to examine the treasure. It was in the middle of the Land Reform movement. Many monks had been banished to the countryside, and I was going through those struggle sessions. Yao emerged from the building and issued an order to his subordinates: Since the abbot has been declared an enemy of the people, the temple doesn't have the manpower and resources to maintain custody of this rare, voluminous treasure. The building will be sealed. He then invited some experts from Chengdu to make an appraisal. After they confirmed that the books were authentic, he packed the volumes into boxes and mobilized over a hundred porters to carry those boxes on shoulder poles—three tons total—all the way to the Sichuan Provincial Library in Chengdu. It's been there for over fifty years.

LIAO: Thank Buddha that the book was protected. Otherwise, it would not have escaped the fire of the Red Guards.

DK: County Chief Yao must have been the reincarnation of a Buddhist guardian warrior. Other government officials were not as farsighted as he was.

LIAO: During the past several hundred years, how did the monks manage to keep the book of scriptures from decaying?

DK: Once a year, all the monks in the temple would gather and bring those volumes out under the sun. Our method was quite primitive. We were not allowed to touch the pages with our hands. We used a thin bamboo sliver to carefully turn over every single page to allow the mustiness to escape. Then we would put special tobacco leaves inside the book to prevent book-eating moths. Several hundred pounds of tobacco leaves were brought in every year. Airing the book was an annual tradition that had been passed down from generation to generation.

LIAO: Now that things have gradually returned to normal and there are no more political campaigns, are you planning to move the book back?

DK: In the past, it was the crown jewel of the temple. Now, it's a national treasure. Any request to transfer the book has to be approved by the State Council.

LIAO: Aren't you allowed to take a peek at it?

DK: There are all sorts of rules, and I haven't had the luck to revisit the book yet. But the rigorous system put in place has not been foolproof. A monk in Peng County managed to use 12,000 yuan [US$1,500] to bribe the curator. He then made a pirated copy of one volume and sold it overseas. I heard he made quite a fortune. I have gathered several abbots in the region and made a plea to the provincial government, saying that the temple should own the copyright to the book. Nobody listened to us.

LIAO: I don't think staff members at the Sichuan Provincial Library will do the book-airing ritual and put tobacco leaves inside each volume every year. I wonder what will happen to the book.

DK: Everything has its preordained fate. We just have to let it go. By the way, you sound like someone who truly possesses the mind of an intellectual. Let me give you a picture as a gift. This is the picture of the body of Grand Master Wu Kong. The photographer's Buddhist name was Xu Kong, and he used to live in Gu township at the foot of the mountain. In the 1940s, he was the first in the region to purchase an old magnesium flash camera. He carried the camera to the temple and took a picture of Grand Master Wu Kong's body. He then sold the picture to a newspaper and the picture got lots of attention from the public. He eventually used this picture as a passport to visit Tibet because Tibetans were pious Buddhists and they worshipped Grand Master Wu Kong. When the Tibetan guards saw the picture, they all prostrated themselves on the ground to show respect. Guess what, he used his special status to travel back and forth between Tibet and Sichuan Province smuggling opium. He was never caught. During the Cultural Revolution, he was persecuted for his association with the temple. Other people also reported his opium-trafficking business to the authorities. The Red Guards tortured and locked him up in solitary confinement for several years. But he never admitted that he was the photographer for Grand Master Wu Kong's picture. The day before he died, he sent his relatives to look for me in my hometown. I did go see him. After I arrived, his eyes were wide open and he was gasping for breath. I held his hands, one of which was making a fist like a ball. He murmured to me: "Wu Kong, Wu Kong." Tears streamed down his cheeks. He then opened his fist and handed me a tiny negative, wrapped with layers of soft tissue and cotton. Before I even had the chance to say anything to him, he was gone.

This picture has been around for sixty years. Look at Grand Master Wu Kong and how well his body was preserved—his face looked so kind and calm, his two earlobes hanging low, he looked divine.

LIAO: You have so many amazing stories. By the way, I have seen a portrait of Communist leader Deng Xiaoping in the hall for worship. He is not a Buddhist. Why do you put his picture up there?

DK: Without Deng Xiaoping, the temple would have been gone. He was the one who reversed Mao's fanatical policies in the late 1970s, opened up China to the outside world, and relaxed government control over religion.

LIAO: During the past hundred years, you have experienced many ups and downs. You can't attribute all your sufferings to karma and to the retribution of sins in our previous life, can you?

DK: I have lived for over a hundred years. I'm gradually ambling my way to the ritual of reincarnation. As a Buddhist, one needs to contain displeasure, anger, and complaining. I have tried to abide by these principles during the past decades and try not to dwell on my past. In recent years, many of the villagers who participated in torturing me have come to seek help because they are poverty-stricken and can't send their grandchildren to school. I have given them money and support. The money is not mine. It was raised from Buddha's followers. It's a sin to keep the money. I remember very well what those villagers did to me in the past, but I don't harbor any ill will toward them. When you start to blame and hate people, retribution will befall you.

Remember that local militia leader who committed the atrocities on Grand Master Wu Kong's preserved body many years ago? He was so evil and full of hatred. Several years later, someone told me that the militia leader had found a big lump growing on his groin. He traveled all over in search of a cure but nobody could help. Eventually, his lower body became rotten and foul-smelling. He died a most wretched death. After he was gone, his wife and children starved to death during the famine in 1960. It was very sad. But how do you explain this phenomenon?

THE COMPOSER

I first heard of composer Wang Xilin in 2001 when I was in Beijing for a book release party. While I was chatting with friends, Wang's name came up because the Beijing Municipal Government had just banned his concert series. Liang Heping, a guest I met at the party, had known the composer for many years. This is what Liang told me:

The Cultural Department of the Beijing Municipal Government had signed a contract with Wang Xilin in 1997, promising to raise funds and host a series of concerts featuring the composer's symphonies in 2000. Over the years, preparations went smoothly. A well-known Swedish violinist had been invited to grace the opening in Beijing.

At about 9 a.m., November 24, 2000, the rehearsal was about to start. As a courtesy, Conductor Tan Lihua invited Wang to say a few words to members of the orchestra. Wang, dressed up nicely for the occasion, walked up to the stage and declared in his resounding voice: *The twentieth century is finally behind us. In the past hundred years, we witnessed many unforgettable events, such as the two world wars and the great many innovations in science and technology. However, I believe that the biggest event in the twentieth century is the fact that Communism has been painstakingly pursued and then relentlessly abandoned by mankind.* Wang's remarks met total silence, but he was too preoccupied to even notice the shocked reaction. He bowed politely and exited the stage.

One week later, authorities in Beijing suddenly notified him that his concerts had been canceled. It was then that Wang realized the stinging consequences of his big mouth. He stormed into Liang's home, stamped his feet, and said regretfully: *Damn, I should have added "except in China" to my statement . . .*

During the Chinese New Year in 2004, I had the opportunity to hear Wang Xilin's Symphony no. 4 at Liang's house. The symphony, named Sorrows of the Century, had been banned three years before. Liang also played tapes of the composer

singing Chinese folk songs as well as his improvised speeches.
While listening to the tapes, I felt a strong urge to meet this leg-
end.

*   With the help of Liang, I finally met Wang Xilin at the end*
of January. Wang, 67, was quite capricious. During the six
interviews I had with him, Wang was shedding tears at one
moment and then playing old tunes on his violin the next. He
said those old tunes helped stimulate his fading memories.

—ᴍ—

WANG XILIN: I remember seeing an old Soviet movie. I've forgotten its
    name. It was made during the temporary political thaw following
    Joseph Stalin's death. In the movie, a kid questioned his father who
    had served as a prison guard under Stalin. The kid asked: When you
    worked inside the gulag, did you ever shoot any prisoner in the back?
    The father refused to answer but the kid kept pressing for answers.
    Eventually, the father couldn't stand the guilt and committed suicide
    by jumping out the window of his apartment building. This scene has
    stayed in my memory for many years. It reminds me of what happened
    in China under Chairman Mao. Nowadays, when I look at people
    walking on the street, I keep thinking to myself: Have they ever perse-
    cuted or tortured others? Have they ever betrayed their comrades and
    trampled on the bodies of others to advance their own political career?
    How many parents are being haunted by their blood-tainted hands?

LIAO YIWU: How do you assess your own past? Can we start from the
    beginning?

WANG: I joined the Communist army in 1949, when I was only twelve
    years old. I was a boy soldier and grew up in the big revolutionary fam-
    ily of the army. Those adult soldiers literally raised me. Since I was so
    young, the commander assigned me to a group of army musicians and
    performers, who taught me how to play all sorts of traditional musical
    instruments. Our job was to entertain the troops stationed in the north-
    west. I picked up things fast and soon made quite a reputation for

myself. As I got older, the Party saw the potential in me and sent me to a music school run by the Central Military Commission. In 1957, I was admitted to the Shanghai Music Academy.

LIAO: It was quite a smooth ride, wasn't it?

WANG: I was really lucky. My civilian life started after I entered college. However, I still wore my military uniform and was quite active in the newly launched anti-Rightist campaign. Soon, I was elected chairman of the student union and head of the Communist Youth League. I despised those students whose sole focus was to study music, especially Western music. As a devout revolutionary, I treated the college as a place for political campaigns and physical labor. I frequently cut classes and volunteered myself at local communes nearby, working in rice paddies or digging canals. During the Great Leap Forward in 1958, we built a furnace in the middle of the college playground and tried to produce iron to support the country's industrialization campaign. It was so crazy.

In the first three years, I didn't learn much about music. It wasn't until 1960 that things started to change. The Great Leap Forward turned out to be a big disaster. The Party was forced to adjust its policy, and Mao's radical ideas temporarily took a backseat. Normalcy returned to school.

LIAO: Since you missed so many classes, what did you do?

WANG: It was like waking up from a weird dream. I looked around and saw some of my schoolmates, whom I used to call "the bourgeois musicians," were getting attention from the Party. Musicians, such as pianist Yin Chengzhong, became celebrities and patriots after they had won awards at international competitions. My classmates began to look down on me, treating me like a country bumpkin who seemed to major in physical labor.

It was also at that time that my family got hit with political problems. My physician brother had lost his sanity and starved to death in the famine. My sister, a former government official in the northwestern city of Lanzhou, was labeled a Rightist. She appealed her verdict, but the provincial government downgraded her even further, making her a counterrevolutionary. It was very upsetting. I decided to shun politics and focus on learning some practical skills. I began to take a strong interest in composing. In my final year, I met a professor who had just returned from the Soviet Union. Under his tutelage, I made rapid progress in Western music composition and soon became the top student in my class.

LIAO: I heard that you composed a well-known quartet while you were in school.

WANG: The professor who coached me was a pianist, and composition was not his specialty. So I learned everything from books. I read over thirty different types of books related to quartets, and took careful notes. In the summer of 1961, I literally moved into a music studio, sweated for over forty days, and finally completed a twenty-five-minute string quartet with three movements. I presented my work to Ding Shande, the dean of the academy. His daughter liked it tremendously. She was the head of a female string quartet group. Her group rehearsed and recorded the piece, which became quite popular.

LIAO: Your hard work certainly paid off.

WANG: I was surprised by the achievement I accomplished on my own. For the first time, I realized that I had found my calling. After graduation, I was assigned to the China Central Radio Orchestra, which specialized in folk music. I was quite upset because my passion was to compose symphonies. So I told the school authority that I wasn't qualified for the job because I didn't know much about Chinese folk music. At first, they ignored me. I simply stayed at the college guesthouse and bugged the Party secretary every day. Eventually, they couldn't stand it and reassigned me to the symphony orchestra.

LIAO: How did you get away with bucking authority like that?

WANG: I was young and quite fearless. That was the only time I lucked out. After I began working at the symphony orchestra, I immediately took on the task of composing my first symphonic piece. First, I requested a piano. Leaders at the orchestra thought I was overly ambitious and arrogant. They turned down my request. One day, I found an old piano in the corner of a warehouse. On the spur of the moment, I called some of my friends and asked them to help move the piano to my office. As we were carrying that big sucker over, I got stopped by an administrator who ordered me to return the piano to the warehouse. I did, but he reported me to the director. I got a terrible reprimand. The director accused me of being too individualistic. He sent me over to a village and ordered me to work in the field for one month as punishment.

In the fall of 1962, Chairman Mao initiated another political movement—the Socialist Education Campaign. Mao referred to the campaign as inviting Communist leaders to come downstairs from the bureaucratic tower and "take baths" to cleanse themselves. The campaign was first kicked off as a pilot project in agencies directly under the control of the central government. In the fall of 1963, the symphony orchestra held a meeting, welcoming staff to pour "hot water" and help "bathe" our leaders.

LIAO: Didn't Mao do the same in 1957, when he encouraged intellectuals to criticize the Party? He called his tactics "baiting snakes out of their caves." When people took his bait, he smacked them right on the head.

WANG: I know. Most employees became cautious and numb to the campaign. At the kickoff meeting, many women nonchalantly knitted sweaters while guys simply lowered their heads, saying nothing. I was this hot-blooded idiot who felt compelled to stand up and offer leaders at the symphony orchestra a "hot bath."

First, I questioned the Party's policy in music. The Party called on composers to create more revolutionary music, incorporate more popular Chinese folk and ethnic music into our work, and make symphonies easily adaptable for radio broadcasts. I said the current policy was restrictive, shortsighted, and detrimental to the development of Chinese symphonic music.

Second, I criticized the unfair treatment of musicians who had returned from overseas. I used the example of Lin Kechang, a well-known violinist and conductor. He grew up in Indonesia and had graduated from a music university in Paris. When Mr. Lin joined our orchestra, he was put under a deputy director who knew nothing about music. Mr. Lin felt miserable. I said: It's ridiculous to put a political appointee in charge of the works of musicians.

I went on and on for two hours. Initially, I was quite diplomatic and cautious with my words. Then, half an hour into my speech, I got carried away. My mind totally lost control and my criticism became more blunt. While I was talking, I saw the deputy director and several other officials were busily taking notes.

LIAO: I bet those guys were busy collecting material against you.

WANG: Yes, they were.

LIAO: What was the Party's reaction to your speech?

WANG: Several days passed and nothing happened. Then, a rumor started to circulate, saying that I was the ringleader of a counterrevolutionary clique within the orchestra. I tried to find out more from my coworkers, but people shunned me like a disease. Zhang Haibo, the first flutist at the orchestra, was the only friend who still talked with me. He and I secretly met at a small restaurant one night, and I had the opportunity to vent my frustrations and fear about the rumors. He was very sympathetic and told me to be cautious.

In the next four weeks, I was like an eagle locked up in a cage covered with black cloth, feeling trapped, tortured, and clueless. Finally, in the fifth week, the Party leaders felt they had tortured me long enough with their silence. They sent me a note, saying that the director wanted to see me. When I walked into his office, the director stared at me from behind his desk. That steely look made me nervous. He uttered a sigh, like a father to his wayward son. Well, the director had joined the Communists in the 1940s. He was a seasoned revolutionary. From the look of things, I could tell that he probably wanted to save me.

The director opened his mouth, uttered another sigh, and said softly: Comrade Xilin, do you know that your speech was a serious political mistake? Why didn't you discuss it with me before the meeting? As your supervisor, I could have told you what to say and what not to say. Right now, it's too late. The nature of your mistakes has changed. Your speech has been considered a direct attack against our Party.

His words scared me. I cried. The director continued, You strayed away from the revolutionary path and pursued a bourgeois goal of composing music to pursue fame. You are as arrogant as a rooster, oblivious of the rules and the criticisms of the masses. You removed a piano from the warehouse without permission and created a bad precedent. After receiving reeducation through labor, you still stick to your old ways. You are hopeless.

Several times I felt the need to defend myself, but the director waved his hand to stop me. Then he offered me an olive branch: Despite the fact that you have gone in the opposite direction and seriously hurt the revolutionary feelings of the masses, the Party will open its arms to embrace you, but on one condition—you have to openly admit your mistakes. Comrade Xilin, the Party raised you in the army and sent you to school to study music. Do you know that it takes three thousand peasants working for five years in order to feed and support a student in college? How could you do this to the Party and to the great masses who have fed you?

I was in a state of total shock. The director talked to me for over one hour. In the end, he told me to dig deeper into the root cause of my mistakes and beg forgiveness from the masses and the Party.

I was touched by his willingness to save me. I had witnessed the punishment the Party had dished out to those Rightists back in 1957. I didn't want that. So I promised, with tears flowing and nose running at the same time, that I would do some serious inner examination.

During the next several days, I wrote day and night nonstop. It was ten times more intense than composing my music. I condemned myself multiple times. I piled up a list of the most vicious words to curse myself. I called myself a stinky bad egg. I used all the political jargon available, such as "individualistic, bourgeoisie, and Right-wing opportunist" to label my mistakes. I truly believed that I deserved hundreds of slaps on my face and hundreds of buckets of shit over my head. Like many intellectuals in that era, I sucked up to the Party, hoping that I would be exonerated. When I finished, the report was almost as thick as a small book.

LIAO: My father used to do the same thing. During the Cultural Revolution, he compiled more than a hundred things which he claimed were his crimes. My father grew up in a landlord's family. When he was two years old, one tenant used to carry him on his back and take him to a market. My father even listed that as his "willful exploitation of the working class."

WANG: We were all baring our hearts to the Party. After I submitted it to the director, he asked the Communist Youth League to organize a staff meeting inside a big performance studio. The sound quality there was excellent. In front of over a hundred people, I read aloud my self-criticism. My talk lasted two and a half hours. Several times, I had to stop to wipe my tears. In the end, I felt dizzy and it was like my throat was on fire. Everybody was quiet. I thought they were really touched by the thoroughness and sincerity of my speech. Then—

LIAO: There was a power outage?

WANG: Don't I wish it! Someone stood up. It was Niu Jun, the secretary for the Communist Youth League. He played Chinese bamboo flute in the orchestra. He spoke with his piercing tone: That is so fake. Let's not be deceived by Wang Xilin's confession. Let's fight back against the attacks by Wang and his counterrevolutionary clique.

After Niu Jun sat down, a municipal government representative stood up and set the tone: Comrade Niu is absolutely right. Wang Xilin's father was a county sheriff under the Nationalist government. His sister is a convicted Rightist and counterrevolutionary. He covered it up and snuck into our revolutionary ranks. Now, after years of hibernating, he finally jumped out to attack our Party. Comrades, remember what Chairman Mao teaches us: "Never forget class struggle." This is a class struggle between the proletariat and the bourgeoisie. We need to be tough. Meanwhile, I also urge everyone sitting here today to examine his or her behavior and to see which camp they want to be in.

I felt like dying. Before I joined the army, the Party knew everything about my family. They had cleared me of any connections with my parents. I just couldn't handle the new accusations. I collapsed onto my seat like a sand castle at high tide.

LIAO: I thought the director wanted to save you and give you a second chance.

WANG: That was what I thought too. Later on, I realized that it was orchestrated by the local municipal government because they wanted to "kill the chicken to intimidate the monkeys." They wanted to make sure that no one in the orchestra dared to challenge the Party again. I became the unfortunate sacrificial chicken.

LIAO: Did the director talk with you again?

WANG: Yes. In the period between the fall of 1963 and the spring of 1964, I was ordered to do self-criticism at every public meeting and almost every staff member had the chance to denounce me. Soon, they ran out of material. One day, the director called me again to his office, with the same fatherly look, the same gesture, and the same sigh. After I had experienced months of nightmarish public condemnation and isolation, the director's fatherly look was quite comforting. I began to cry like a child who has been beaten up by bigger kids on the block.

He said: Comrade Xilin, I hope you have learned something from the past month. Don't blame other comrades for their tough attitude toward you. You should be thankful. The Party has confidence in you. Our Party has successfully reformed the last emperor of the Qing dynasty and many former senior Nationalist officials. If those big shots can change, so can you.

My tears just kept flowing. I thanked him profusely. Then he said: We know that you constantly hang out with some members of this orchestra and vent your complaints against the Party. We know everything. We want you to describe in detail every conversation or meeting you have had with other people. Honesty will get you leniency.

Sensing the hesitancy in my eyes, the director patted me on the shoulder and said: The Party needs to help other comrades who have committed similar mistakes. Don't feel guilty. This is a serious class struggle and you are doing them a favor by bringing them back to the Party. After this campaign is over, all of you will be treated as good comrades.

I was a strong believer in the Party's policy—Cooperation leads to leniency. So, I made a list of one hundred incidents where my co-workers and I had made inappropriate remarks about the Party and leaders of the orchestra. In the process, I betrayed my friends, such as the first flutist Zhang Haibo and trumpeter Chen Yingnan.

LIAO: Under the circumstances, I guess you didn't have too much of a choice.

WANG: It was a total betrayal. I had too much faith in the Party. After I submitted my list, which I titled "My Second Confession About the Counterrevolutionary Clique Within Our Symphony Orchestra," the director asked me to read it aloud at an all-staff meeting.

LIAO: You called your friends members of a counterrevolutionary clique?

WANG: Yes. The director implied that associating my mistakes with a more serious criminal label would make me sound more sincere. Anyhow, on the list I included my friends and a lot of other people. I didn't even dare to raise my head. I simply read the list mechanically. The meeting became very tense. Initially, people held their breath, waiting to hear who would be the next to be implicated. It was like I had one hundred grenades hanging around my mouth. Each time I uttered an item, I could hear an explosion in the audience. Soon the volume of their responses got louder and louder. One woman suffered a nervous breakdown right there. Let me give you an example of what I put in the list: On the morning of September 6, I bumped into so-and-so. I heard him cursing the Party secretary for not allocating him a new apartment. Then, on the evening of January 19, so-and-so told me over lunch that he thought the deputy director was a jerk.

I finally finished the reading in three hours. As I was uttering a sigh of relief, the whole studio was filled with anger. Each time I mentioned a new name, that person would jump up and try to interrupt me, calling me a liar. They called me all sorts of names—"a vicious Rightist, a hypocrite who deserved to be cut into pieces." People also started to bite one another with vicious accusations. In the end, my counterrevolutionary clique became bigger and bigger. More than thirty people were implicated. If it hadn't been for the security guards, there would have been fistfights. I would have been trampled to death.

My confessional list moved the whole campaign to a new stage. In order to clear their names, people started to expose the "crimes" of others. For a while, people were spying on one another, trying to collect damaging material to destroy one another.

The emotional ups and downs of the campaign took a heavy toll on my mental health. I started to lose control of myself at several public meetings. The daytime denunciation meetings extended into my dreams. I would scream in my sleep. When I was awake, I would draw the curtain and became afraid of sunlight. I was in constant fear of getting arrested. Each morning, when the loudspeaker in the courtyard started blasting the famous revolutionary song, "Chairman Mao Is Our Savior," I would jump out of bed, shaking with fear. This paranoia has haunted me for twenty-some years. Even today, when I see a big portrait of Chairman Mao, I literally have goose bumps.

LIAO: Did you seek treatment?

WANG: Initially, they said I was afraid of light because I had harbored too much darkness in my heart, and that I was paranoid about getting arrested because I hadn't come clean about all my crimes. Finally, as my illness worsened, they realized it was for real. So they sent me to a mental hospital. The mental illness seemed to run in my family. When my sister was charged with being a Rightist, she had similar symptoms. In my case, I was doing better after getting treatment. At the same time, the number of public meetings was reduced because people were tired of hearing the same crap over and over again. Soon, they seemed to have forgotten about me. I had more time to myself. So I became restless and began to write music again. I finished a symphony, which I named *The Yunnan Musical Poetry.*

LIAO: I've heard it before. It was a great piece.

WANG: After over twenty years, the piece was finally recognized. I recently won the first prize at a national music contest. It has been played in thirty cities around the world.

LIAO: It is amazing you could compose that masterpiece under those difficult circumstances.

WANG: If it hadn't been for my music, you would have seen me in a mental asylum today.

LIAO: Let's continue with your story. What happened afterward?

WANG: In April of 1964, the Communist Youth League officially expelled me from the organization. The next day, the director called me to his office. Once again, he said with that fatherly tone: Comrade Xilin, you did a good job admitting your mistakes and exposing the mistakes of others. Considering your positive and cooperative attitude, we have decided to assign you to work for a music and dance troupe in rural Shanxi Province. This will give you the opportunity to thoroughly reform yourself.

LIAO: How could you still trust that guy?

WANG: Don't forget that I started receiving Communist education at the age of twelve. I was very brainwashed. I bowed and expressed my gratitude to him. You know what? Some of the friends that I had betrayed got worse treatment. Many members of my so-called counterrevolutionary clique were assigned to the desert regions of Gansu Province. So far, I haven't had the guts to contact any of them.

LIAO: Did you take the assignment?

WANG: Of course. Amazingly, I didn't feel depressed at all about my change of fate. I packed my belongings and left for Shanxi the next day. The troupe I worked for was on tour all the time. They traveled from village to village. Each time we arrived at a place, I would cook, prepare hot water for the actors, load and unload trucks, set up the stage and play an extra if needed. I believed that doing menial jobs would change my stinky bourgeois outlook on life.

Several months later, the local leaders realized that I could compose. They ordered me to write lyrics for a choral piece. I did. There were four chapters: "Praising the Stalwart Commune Members," "The Leaders of the Local Party Are Excellent," "The New Look of Our Village," and "Three Communist Flags Wave in the Wind." Then I was in charge of conducting a chorus of twenty people and an orchestra of thirty musicians. At the opening, many local leaders showed up. They loved my work. The head of the local propaganda department praised me in front of the audience by saying: Wang Xilin has gotten rid of the burdens of his past and he will have a bright future.

For a while, I thought I was finally getting a new lease on life. Then the political climate changed fast. In 1966, the Cultural Revolution started. The local Red Guards checked my personal files and uncovered my past problems. Within days, I was brought back to the public denunciation meetings. All the good work I had done was considered new crimes which aimed to deceive people. Remember the propaganda chief who praised me at the concert? He was accused of being a capitalist admirer and was locked up in a cowshed. Since he liked the lyrics I wrote for the chorus, the Red Guards condemned my work as blades of poisonous grass.

I was the lone enemy in the performance troupe. They paraded me around, with a dunce cap on my head and a black cardboard sign around my neck. I had some new criminal labels: "An escaped Rightist, a hidden counterrevolutionary, a class enemy who covered up his family history . . ." All the self-criticisms I had written before amounted to nothing. I started all over again. The political instructor, who was illiterate, monitored me every day. To regain their trust, I used the same trick. It was like writing a symphony: I put myself as the C major, the main theme. I condemned and slandered myself mercilessly. Then, I divided up people around me in different minor themes or variations.

LIAO: Did it work?

WANG: Through self-criticism, I made myself an odious enemy of the people. Big-character posters were pasted all over the walls of the county office building. Most of them were directed at me. I was reassigned to take care of the boilers.

In 1968, at the peak of the Cultural Revolution, local factory workers took over the county government to clean out "a capitalist citadel." They rounded up all of the disgraced county officials, former landlords, and me, and threw us in a warehouse, which used to be a Japanese army concentration camp. We slept on the floor. Our windows were nailed shut. Our captors practiced what they called "using physical torture to touch the souls." Beatings were quite frequent. In my group, a guy named Cao Yuzhu had been a lighting engineer for the performance troupe. One time, he had said jokingly to his intern that Vice Chairman Lin Biao looked too sick to lead the country. The intern reported him to authorities. Cao was arrested on charges of slandering the successor to our Great Leader. When the Red Guards paraded Cao on the street, they hung all sorts of lightbulbs around his neck to make fun of his work.

During the day, we were forced to work in the fields. Whenever there was a public criticism meeting, we immediately dropped our work and showed up on the stage in our usual jet-plane positions.

Oftentimes, all the bad guys were strung together and we walked from county to county. Most of the meetings took place in the village square or inside big warehouses. Sometimes, we had to attend smaller meetings at someone's home. That was the most painful. After my usual confession of how I was afraid of light, people would kick us or slap us since we were in close proximity. Some sadistic folks would order me to kneel on wooden boards filled with nails. Kids would pull my hair or ears.

One night, it was almost 11 p.m. I heard a knock on the door. I got out of bed and opened the door. Before I knew what was happening, someone attacked me, blindfolded me, tied my hands behind my back with ropes, gagged me with a piece of dirty rag, and dragged me away like a hostage. I could sense that I was led outside into the field. Then they pushed me down into a big hole on the ground, with lots of loose dirt under my feet. I thought I was going to be buried alive. So I moaned and groaned in despair. A few minutes later, I could feel warm water pouring down on my head. Someone peed on me from above. Then they pulled me out of the hole and took me to a warehouse. Two young guys pushed me against the wall, took the rag out of my mouth, grabbed my head, and banged my face against the wall. My nose was broken like a ping-pong ball. Then I heard a familiar voice behind me: Did you steal the little box from the archives office?

I could tell the voice belonged to Zhao Baoqin, a member of the performance troupe. Realizing that they were only looking for a stolen box, I became somewhat relaxed. I told them no. They took off my pants and whipped me a dozen times until I was bleeding. It hurt so much. After two hours of beatings, they still couldn't get anything out of me. So they let me go. The next morning, I found out that two other disgraced officials had similar interrogations the night before.

LIAO: Did you ever think of escape?

WANG: Many times. For several years, I followed the performance troupe. All the actors would sit on the horse-drawn cart. A couple of counterrevolutionaries like me would walk behind the cart, carrying luggage and props. We traveled all over the region, regardless of rain or snow. It was very hard. Eventually, there were rumors saying that all the counterrevolutionaries would be sent to jail. So I discussed this with two other "bad guys" and we planned our escape. I secretly bought a pair of rainproof shoes and a water bottle. As we were ready to implement our plan, my mother showed up. She was in her seventies. As a little girl, she followed the ancient tradition and bound her feet.

My mother carried a small sack of flour, a big porcelain bowl, and some clothes. She stayed at my dorm and waited for me to come back. But an official went to my dorm and told her: Your son is a counterrevolutionary. He is under investigation; you are not allowed to stay with him. My mother was so confused: My son joined the Communist army at the age of twelve. How could he rebel against the Communist Party?

I was then released temporarily so I could find a hotel for her. My poor mother didn't want to spend money on a hotel. She repacked her stuff and left the next day.

In the mid-1970s, after I regained freedom, I used to go visit my mother once a year in the city of Lanzhou. She helped raise my sister's two children. I would send her fifteen yuan [US$2] a month.

Upon her release from the labor camp, my sister was transferred to a rural village outside Lanzhou. She continued to suffer humiliation at public meetings. A couple of times, she ran back to my mother's house in the city to visit her children. But the street committee found out and they sent her back.

My mother died on January 13, 1978. Before her death, she suffered from bronchitis and heart problems. We couldn't afford to put her in the hospital. But a friend of mine, who was also a musician, had married a high-ranking army officer. With her help, the hospital admitted my mother. Three days later, my mother, who used to live frugally in slums, became really uncomfortable and kept saying: Take me home. It's too expensive here. Before I had the chance to move her, she died. I hired a horse-drawn cart, sent her body to a crematorium, and brought her ashes home. She was eighty-two years old. Her hands were like dried tree bark, distorted from years of hard work.

LIAO: What happened to your sister?

WANG: She is now in her seventies and looks older than my mother. She is still quite insane, talking to herself all the time. It's horrible.

LIAO: In China, musicians are low-class performers for hire. Few dare to challenge authorities. Many musicians, writers, and artists have become favorites for being the Party's mouthpieces. For example, poet He Jingzhi became the minister of culture for writing revolutionary poems filled with lavish praise for new China. Singer Hu Songhua became famous and enjoyed the "People's Artist" title for thirty-some years for singing one song, "The Song of Praises." Master Wang, you had superior skills and possess all the qualities to be a "Red" artist like He Jingzhi and Hu Songhua. Yet you ended up getting purged not only in the Mao era, but also under Deng Xiaoping and Jiang Zemin. I guess it has a lot to do with your honesty. Maybe you should learn to be a little shrewd?

WANG: I have never stopped trying to suck up to the government. But my voice is too loud and my mouth is too big. As I said earlier, my trouble began after the two-hour speech in 1962. For fourteen years, I was detained, interrogated, beaten, humiliated, trampled, and abandoned. Even so, I have always tried to use my music to please those in power. During the Cultural Revolution, I composed many revolutionary lyrics while working in the boiler room. Those lyrics included "The Red Sun in My Heart," "Revolutionary Rebels Are Not Afraid of Violence," and "Walking on the Wide Path of the Cultural Revolution." No matter how hard I tried, the Party never gave a damn. You know, for many years, we Chinese were forced to accept the notion that our beloved Party was more endearing to us than our parents. From my experience, I think the Party is worse than an ugly ruthless stepmother.

LIAO: I heard your Symphony no. 4 a couple of weeks ago. The symphony combines some local mourning tunes in Anhui Province; I mean the suona music is so haunting. Then there were the angry dissonant sounds of drums and bass . . . Your music is so autobiographical, harsh and dark.

WANG: Damn right. My music is devoid of tenderness or love. It's like a big dark lake, which contains all the mud, tears, blood, sighs, and screams from its surrounding rivers. That's why it's heavy, deep and dark. Some sissy artists used to say that love is everything. That's total bullshit. When your right to live is being threatened, where do you get love? On June 4, 1989, when soldiers opened fire at students and residents, one thousand shouts of love couldn't even stop a single bullet.

LIAO: Aren't you a bit too harsh on humanity?

WANG: In those turbulent times, I craved love and humanity. One time at a public meeting, I stood on the stage in a jet-plane position for four hours. My body hurt and my mouth was dry. After the meeting, an old lady came over and handed me a bowl of water. The bowl was not very clean and the water tasted a little weird. But she was so brave to care for a class enemy like me . . . Many years later, I still think of that bowl of water. Unfortunately, I didn't get too many of those warm and fuzzy things in life.

LIAO: You look like a tough guy, but you are really quite sentimental and vulnerable inside.

WANG: From my appearance, people think I'm very tough. I'm tall and have a loud voice. But inside here, I'm constantly begging for mercy from my captors. Time after time, they ignored my begging. In the past, I have requested the government many times to reverse its verdict against me. My requests have gone unanswered for many years.

But, music has sustained me. For many years, authorities in China despised twentieth-century Western music: Igor Stravinsky's works were considered too decadent, Richard Strauss was reactionary, and Dmitri Shostakovich a monster! We were at least fifty years behind the West in musical development. It wasn't until the 1980s that China opened its door to the West. We Chinese finally realized that there was so much that we had missed.

Since the late 1970s, I've been trying to catch up. I have produced over thirty different types of works. I have written Symphony no. 3 and no. 4. I'm writing no. 5 now.

LIAO: I have read several news stories about the success of your music abroad. Your symphonies have been played in over twenty countries. People here seem to be indifferent to your works. I can't believe you get paid ten yuan [US$1.30] per hour for teaching a class. An orchestra here fired you because playing your symphonies didn't bring them a profit.

WANG: We are going from a dogmatic Communist society to a commercially driven one. Everyone is busy making money. They don't hear the sufferings and pains of my generation. That indifference doesn't change me or my music. I compose for a different reason. I'm composing a series of elegies for the whole nation, for the millions of victims who died uncalled-for deaths or suffered under Maoism. If Shostakovich's music was testimony to the horrors of the Stalin era, my music will be . . . I don't want to finish the sentence here. I guess my music will come in handy on Judgment Day because it is eternal.

THE RIGHTIST

*Feng Zhongci, 75, was my uncle Liao Enze's neighbor and
friend. He lives in an apartment building near Chengdu's West
Gate Train Station. Feng and his wife have two children, both
of whom are married. In the 1950s, Feng was a promising leader
of the Communist Youth League at his university. But during
the anti-Rightist campaign, he was labeled a Rightist and lived
many years in the desert region of Xinjiang Uyghur Autono-
mous Region.*

*I visited him on a recent August afternoon. His room was
tiny and hot. He acted like an old-fashioned scholar, formal and
overly polite. There was no air-conditioning in his apartment.
During our conversation, both of us were sweating profusely, as
if we were locked inside a dim sum steamer. Several times, I
told him to take off his shirt, but he politely refused, saying it
was improper to entertain a guest with a T-shirt on.*

LIAO YIWU: I want to chat with you about the anti-Rightist campaign. I
want to know how you became a Rightist.

FENG ZHONGCI: I don't have much to talk about.

LIAO: Uncle Feng, I've come a long way. You can't let me leave here
empty-handed. You can at least talk about the political climate in that
era, can't you? I didn't realize that over 500,000 innocent people were
persecuted during that period. Most of them were intellectuals. Some
got labeled Rightists simply because they had written a letter to a literary magazine or because they had expressed their doubts about the
Communist Party in their personal diaries. That's pretty hard to believe.

FENG: What happened in the 1950s might seem strange and abnormal
today. But in that era it was very common.

LIAO: Were you one of those who became Rightist because you had spoken out against the Party?

FENG: Not really. I came from a proletariat family. I was politically active and supported the Party wholeheartedly. At the beginning of the anti-Rightist campaign, I was ready to stand up and fend off any attacks against the Party.

LIAO: You aren't kidding me, are you?

FENG: No. I was head of the Communist Youth League at my university. I joined the Party in my sophomore year. Before my graduation in 1957, I was the first one to write an open letter to the Party and pledged to answer Chairman Mao's call and take assignment in the remote poverty-stricken areas. However, the Party secretary had a private conversation with me, saying that they needed politically reliable graduates like me to help with the anti-Rightist Campaign. They wanted me to stay on after graduation and take over the school newspaper. He said, We need to seize this important forum from the hands of the counterrevolutionaries.

LIAO: If you were so pro-Party, how did you end up being a Rightist yourself?

FENG: I became a Rightist because of my personal life.

LIAO: Lifestyle problems?

FENG: Please don't use that word to judge me. The word "lifestyle" has different interpretations at different times. In those years, you could be executed for having lifestyle problems. For example, if a guy had premarital sex with a female classmate, it could be a serious crime.

LIAO: If your Rightist label was not lifestyle-related, what was it?

FENG: I got it because my wife's family fell into the category of "reactionary bureaucrat and landlord." Her uncle had served in the Nationalist government as a chief of the drug enforcement agency. He was executed not long after the Communist liberation in 1949. Her father, a big landlord, had made a young woman his concubine. So because of her family, my wife, Wenxin, shouldered a huge political burden at college. She tried to concentrate on her studies and kept everything to herself. She was quite antisocial. I was just the opposite, very gregarious. I had many friends. When I was with a group, I felt like a fish in water. But somehow I found myself attracted to Wenxin's aloofness. There was something mysterious and beautiful about her. I just couldn't get over her. I began to hang out with her in 1956.

LIAO: I can imagine the challenges of dating someone who was incompatible with you politically. My sister used to date a military officer during the Cultural Revolution. Before a military officer or a government official got married, the Party had to conduct thorough background checks on the future spouse's family before granting approval. My sister's boyfriend had to break up with her because my grandfather used to be a landlord. In your case, how could her questionable family background make you a Rightist?

FENG: This is how it all started. Initially, I tried to get together with Wenxin in the name of helping her with political studies. During our study sessions, I would engage her in conversations about art, music, and our families. Gradually, she began to open up to me. One time she told me that she was very close to her father's concubine. I immediately warned her to strengthen her political standing by separating herself from the decadent concubine of a landlord. She didn't say anything. One day, she suggested that we take a stroll outside the campus. After we were out on the street, she led me to a courtyard house inside a deep alleyway. She didn't tell me who we were visiting.

As we entered the shadowy courtyard, I saw a woman squatting by a well, hand-washing clothes. She had long black hair and long slender fingers. She had quite an elegant figure. When she smiled, her pale face exuded a kind of sadness. That woman was Wenxin's stepmother, the concubine. She poured tea for us. Wenxin then begged her stepmother to play the piano for us. She wiped the dust off a piano in a corner of the living room and played a variation on "The Sky in the Communist Regions Is Brighter"—the revolutionary song that we had sung hundreds of times in large groups. She probably did that to ingra-

tiate herself with me. She either knew I was a diehard Communist supporter, or she simply wanted to show that she was in tune with the
times. Strangely enough, that uplifting revolutionary song totally
changed character under her long elegant fingers. The tune became
rottenly bourgeois, with so much tenderness, elegance, and sadness, as
if it had been a woman's whisper and sigh on a quiet starlit night. For a
brief moment, I was mesmerized.

After I walked out of that courtyard house, I began to question
myself. As a Party member and the head of the Communist Youth
League, how could I have succumbed to her decadent music so easily?
Where did my political upbringing go?

LIAO: Were you really that radical?

FENG: Yes. I was. But, on the other hand, I was a college student. Before
1957, the stuff they taught at colleges was not as radical and dogmatic.
We had some access to Western books and were allowed to listen to
Western music, which had some positive influence on me. Anyhow, as
I was wrestling with my political beliefs, Wenxin grabbed my hand and
said: She likes you. Otherwise, she wouldn't play the piano for you. I
said angrily: This was the first time that I had come into contact with a
member of the decadent ruling class. Are you trying to corrupt me? So
I turned around and walked away. Wenxin was still standing inside the
alleyway, which seemed darker and frightful. To me, she was like someone standing in the shadows of the past. She caught up with me and
said: Let me tell you the story of my stepmother. Before she married
my father, she had a lover. He was her music teacher. Her family
strongly opposed the relationship because the teacher didn't have any
money. Eventually, she bowed to her family's pressure and became my
father's concubine. After their marriage, my father realized that he
couldn't really change her mind about her music teacher. So he gave up
on her. After the revolution in 1949, she and my father filed for divorce.
Then she went to look for her lover, who had relocated to the central
city of Xian. When she got there, she found out that her lover had
already died of tuberculosis. All she saw was his tomb. The experience
devastated her. Two months later, she returned to Chengdu and has
lived alone since. Before my father passed away, he had forgiven her
and gave her that courtyard house. She had never gotten over the death

of her lover and started to lose her sanity. She would cry and laugh for no reason. Since she and I were of similar age, I felt a lot of sympathy for her. I come occasionally to take care of her.

After listening to Wenxin's story, I was kind of touched. It was like a bourgeois movie produced during the pre-Communist days. So, I asked her: Why are you telling me this? She shrugged her shoulder: I try to bare my heart to the Party. You can report me if you want. I don't care.

I felt so hurt by her mean remarks. I turned my head away to hide my tears. At that moment, I also experienced something that I had never felt before. I was in love with Wenxin.

LIAO: Did the Party interfere in your love affair?

FENG: Not at the beginning. Luckily, very few people knew about our relationship, and my meetings with Wenxin were not that frequent. Then, in 1957, Chairman Mao introduced the campaign called "Let one hundred flowers bloom and a hundred schools of thought contend." Many intellectuals responded with enthusiasm. Through lectures, published articles, and big-character posters people around the country began to voice their views and question the leading role of the Party. Initially, Chairman Mao welcomed the criticism. With his endorsement, local officials were quite tolerant. Meanwhile, the dissenting voices from intellectuals got louder and the criticisms became more severe and radical. Some even suggested the end to the one-party rule and called for the establishment of a Western-style democratic system. I still remember the remarks of Ge Peiqi, a well-known scholar from the Beijing People's University. In one of his articles, he said that China belonged to the six hundred million Chinese, including the counterrevolutionaries. China didn't belong to the Communist Party alone. It was wrong for the Party leadership to assume that "the Empire is mine and I am the Empire." The Communist Party shouldn't be too arrogant, naively thinking that if the Party collapsed, the whole country would collapse. That was not the case. Those who opposed the Communist Party were not traitors . . . Ge just went on and on. Criticisms like Ge's had far exceeded the government's limit of tolerance.

At my university, many students actively joined in the national chorus of criticism. Like I mentioned before, Wenxin was a quiet girl and had never been active in politics. But I encouraged her to speak her mind. Eventually, with my repeated encouragement, she summoned her courage and stood up at a departmental meeting. She said: The Communist Party has long advocated the idea of democracy and equality. That meant students with a nonproletariat family background should be able to enjoy equal rights. During my four years at the university, I have endured all types of discrimination. I was denied the opportunity to join the Communist Youth League. I work really hard and have gotten top grades. But I have been accused of being a bourgeois scholar. Chairman Mao has said on many occasions that the Party should offer a way out for children of nonprogressive families, as long as they draw a clear line between themselves and their landlord or capitalist parents . . .

After Wenxin finished, I clapped my hands loudly, but only a few people joined in the applause. I could see displeasure on the face of many student leaders. I had always followed the Party line closely. At that meeting, I miscalculated. I naively thought that by speaking her mind, Wenxin could get other people to understand her better. She could get more sympathy from her classmates. Little did I know that I had gotten Wenxin into trouble.

One month after Wenxin's first public speech, the political climate turned dramatically. Chairman Mao came out and declared that the movement had brought out the most dangerous class enemies who had previously been in hiding. With those remarks, the anti-Rightist campaign followed. One after another, many intellectuals fell from grace. The purge soon spread to my university. Students were mobilized to expose and report on their classmates and teachers. The school authorities compiled a list of those they considered to be potential Rightists and distributed it to all the departments. The Party secretary asked students and faculty to select the Rightists through voting. Wenxin became a top candidate for Rightist.

LIAO: Wasn't it ironic that people were actually asked to decide who should be persecuted by casting their votes?

FENG: Yes. In this way, the decision would reflect the will of the people. On the day when the vote was cast, the Party secretary of my university showed up and presided over our department meeting. Of course, there were lots of grievances against me. Some questioned my relationship with Wenxin. Since I was on his priority list for promotion, the Party secretary defended me furiously with blatant lies. He said: Comrade Feng contacted Wenxin frequently upon secret instructions from the Party. Many of you here might have thought that Wenxin is a quiet student. But she harbors deep hatred for our new China. That snake, in the form of a beautiful woman, has finally been exposed in broad daylight. We wouldn't have been able to accomplish this without the hard work of Comrade Feng. The Party is considering granting Comrade Feng the honor of "Outstanding Leader of the Communist Youth League." I couldn't believe what I was hearing. Wenxin stood up, looked in my direction with extreme anger. Her face turned ashen and then she collapsed to the floor. Ignoring the stares from people in the room, I carried her in my arms and dashed to the school clinic. Even as I was doing that, the Party secretary continued with his lies: Comrade Feng is doing the right thing. Even though Wenxin is a member of the enemy, we need to help her out of our revolutionary humanity.

LIAO: That was quite dramatic.

FENG: Well, before Wenxin regained consciousness, I left the clinic in a trance. Then leaders of the Communist Youth League came to talk with me. They wanted me to review the list of Rightists in my department and then sign off on it. With my signature, they were going to submit the list to the city government. I refused to sign the paper, which included Wenxin's name. When the Party secretary and the president of my university heard about it, they came to my dorm and tried to talk me into signing it. I knew that my refusal could jeopardize my future. But I was quite stubborn and didn't budge.

The university president warned me: The Party has spent many years training and nurturing you. You should understand your boundary and don't trash your future. I retorted: The Party should be honest and transparent. Why would the Party secretary lie about my relationship with Wenxin? The president patted me on the back and said, Don't you know that the Party secretary tried to protect you from the criticism? I didn't agree: Wenxin should be treated as our ally. She has betrayed her family and is willing to join the revolution. But the president laughed at me: Don't be fooled by her act. If she is as progressive as you have suggested, why did she take you to visit her father's concubine? She attempted to entice you into her world and corrupt your revolutionary spirit. We know everything you and she did. I was flabbergasted. The Party secretary continued: You are the one who is insane at the moment. You would throw away your political future for the sake of that woman.

I became incensed and started to argue with the president: I don't agree with the charges against Wenxin. I swear to the Party that she is nowhere close to being a Rightist. The president banged on the desk and yelled at me: You'd better think before you open your mouth. Your judgment has been clouded by your emotions. For a young hot-blooded guy like you, it's understandable. But human emotion has to succumb to reason and political thinking. Chairman Mao teaches us, there is no such thing in the world as pure love. You can't love an enemy. I was so irrational and blurted out something that I had never said before: I love her. The Party secretary looked at me and softened his tone: OK. You have to make a choice between that woman and the Party. I said again, very firmly: I love her.

Two weeks later, I was expelled from the Party and was labeled a Rightist as well as a bad element.

LIAO: Were you officially dating Wenxin at that time?

FENG: No, we were just friends. She liked me but certainly not as a boyfriend. She was just grateful that I was willing to talk with her since none of her classmates wanted to have anything to do with her. Wenxin changed my political views. Before the Communists came, my family was so poor that I had to beg on the street. One time, I knocked on the door of a landlord, asking for food. The guy let his dog out to chase me away. As the dog was barking at me, I barked back. I ended up biting half of the dog's ear off. That incident made me hate that landlord. After 1949, the Communists told me that it wasn't that specific landlord who was merciless. The whole ruling class was evil. Since then, I started to despise all people who belonged to the landlord or capitalist class. But talking with Wenxin helped me see things differently. I no longer believed in Mao's "class struggle" theory.

LIAO: So what happened to you?

FENG: Have you read the American writer Edgar Snow's book, *Red China Today*? In the book, the author interviewed an American-educated Chinese intellectual who had returned to China to join the revolution. That intellectual became a Rightist. This is how he described his experience: "Everybody in my bureau, from the office boy or scrubwoman up, can tell me how bourgeois I am, criticize my personal habits, my family life, my intellectual arrogance, the way I spend my leisure, even my silences. I have to sit and take it . . . Some people prefer suicide rather than submit to it. It took me years to get used to it but now I believe it has been good to me." This is exactly what happened to me and Wenxin. After graduation, I was denied a job. I stayed at home and had to attend public denunciation meetings. In the old days, I was the one who was in charge at those meetings and always criticized others. Then, as a Rightist, I was the target all the time. Like the guy in Snow's book, I got used to it, especially after I had kids.

LIAO: Did you ever regret your decision?

FENG: No. Many people felt sorry for me, for what they called "my sudden irrational act." But I think it was a good thing. Between the Party and a woman, I picked the latter. People need to put their personal life first, don't you think, young man? We joined the Communist revolution so we could live a better life, have enough to eat, marry a beautiful woman, and raise a family. This basic concept was totally distorted in the Mao era. All we talked about were the abstract ideas such as the Party and the People. Private lives were considered something disgraceful. You can't marry the Party or the People, can you? We used to hear phony stuff like "So-and-so has been nurtured by the Party and the People." What do the Party's breasts look like?

    I would really regret the rest of my life if I had signed the paper and supported the Party's decision to punish Wenxin and other Rightists. Things have changed today. We really should thank Deng Xiaoping for ending the era when humans lived like ghosts, devoid of any feelings or emotions.

LIAO: How did you make Wenxin love you?

FENG: After I became a Rightist, I was somehow at peace with myself. I wrote her a love letter. One night, I snuck out and stopped by her stepmother's house. I pushed the letter in through a slit in the door and rushed back home. I sent five or six letters that way and never got anything back from her. I made lots of inquiries and found out that Wenxin had been exiled to a state farm in Aksu, in Xinjiang. So I went to look for her. I took a train, and then a long-distance bus. By the time I got there, I had literally no money in my pocket. I begged my way around. Then I was detained by the local police for migrating without a permit. They were going to send me to a detention center in the middle of the Taklimakan Desert. I told them that I was looking for Wenxin. It so happened that the detention center was not too far away, on the northwestern side of her farm. Authorities contacted the farm, found Wenxin, and confirmed my story. The day they dropped me off at her farm, I saw her picking cotton in the field. Her face was so tanned and she looked healthy—reform through hard labor had done some good to her health. Anyhow, when I called her name, she hardly recognized me. It took her quite a while to realize that the guy with the disheveled look in front of her was her beloved Feng Zhongci.

The rest is just history, nothing extraordinary. We were both Rightists. In that sense, we were quite a match. Since I went all the way to court her, she couldn't reject me, even though I wasn't her ideal companion. After we asked permission to marry from the authorities at her farm, they were quite accommodating. They issued her a travel certificate and granted her two weeks of vacation. So we came back to Chengdu and obtained our marriage certificate from the city. Then, after the wedding, we both applied for the cancellation of our city residential permit and moved to Xinjiang. A counterrevolutionary couple was willing to relocate to China's frontier to support the socialist revolution. Nobody had objections to that. Since Aksu was so far away from the political center, our lives were really unaffected by the ensuing political campaigns. In the late 1970s, when Deng Xiaoping reversed the Party's earlier verdict against Rightists, we brought our two Xinjiang-born kids back to Chengdu and reunited with the rest of our families. This is pretty much my life. I have to say that right now, I'm pretty contented.

THE RETIRED OFFICIAL

When famine first struck Sichuan in 1960, I was two years old. Since my mother couldn't get enough milk or food to feed me, I was dying from severe edema and my body puffed up like a loaf of bread. Thanks to an herbal doctor, I miraculously survived, but millions of other children and adults didn't. Experts believe that an estimated thirty million people starved to death in the 1958–1961 famine. Zheng Dajun, a retired government official, headed a government work team at a rural region in Sichuan around that time. He witnessed the devastating impact of the famine, which he said was a shameful chapter in the history of the Chinese Communist Party.

I met Zheng in June of 2002 at a resort in Huilonggou, Chongqing County. Zheng was seventy-two years old. He was short with broad shoulders and looked very distinguished. Before his retirement, Zheng had held senior positions in the Sichuan provincial government.

—⚉—

LIAO YIWU: When I was growing up, we normally referred to the 1958–1961 famine as "three years of natural disasters." The government attempted to cover up its mistakes by blaming the famine on drought and flood, even though many areas hit by the famine had mild weather conditions during that time.

ZHENG DAJUN: Most people knew exactly what had happened, but nobody dared to challenge the official version. That part of the history has been treated as a "state secret." In 1959, Marshal Peng Dehuai wrote to Chairman Mao and criticized his extreme policies which had led to the disasters. Marshal Peng was purged and persecuted to death during the Cultural Revolution. Things have changed now. From the information that has been made public we have learned that the famine was mostly manmade. I think the Communist Party owes an honest explanation and apology to the Chinese people, especially the peasants.

LIAO: I don't think that's going to happen soon. Could you tell me about your experience during those three years of hardship?

ZHENG: I joined the Communist army to fight against the Nationalists in 1948, at the age of eighteen. Two years later, after the new China was founded, I was demobilized and assigned to work in the rural areas. My job was to mobilize peasants to participate in the Land Reform movement. Since my family couldn't afford to send me to school when I was a kid, I was illiterate. So I worked during the day and took literacy classes in the evenings. I made good progress in my education and as a result, I was promoted very fast. By the time I turned twenty-six in 1958, I had become the deputy director of the County Agricultural Task Force.

In the 1950s, people were passionate about the new Communist government and would do anything the Party called on them to do. For example, Chairman Mao said sparrows ate the crops and needed to be eliminated. Soon, a nationwide campaign was launched and everyone turned out to chase and catch sparrows. After two years, sparrows nearly disappeared in China. Little did we know that killing sparrows would disrupt the delicate balance of nature. Sparrows ate crops, but they also ate bugs, which flourished and brought disasters to many areas after the sparrows had gone. But passion was running so high that nobody dared to question the practice in a scientific way. Similar things happened in the Great Leap Forward campaign.

In the spring of 1958, the county chief dispatched me to inspect progress on the Great Leap Forward at the Second Production Division of Dongyang Commune. Let me give you some background because many young people don't know much about that period. The late fifties were a critical period for the Party. The split between the Soviet Union and our country began to widen. The world's two largest socialist countries started turning hostile to each other. Increasingly, the Soviets threatened to withdraw financial aid. Chairman Mao and the Central Party Committee realized that China had to become *zili gengsheng,* or self-reliant and independent. We had to transform our country into an advanced industralized country within a short time. That was why

Chairman Mao launched the Great Leap Forward campaign. The slogan at that time was "We are running toward an advanced Communist society."

The region where I stayed was hilly country, with very fertile land and mild weather conditions. It was famous for rice, wheat, corn, beans, and sweet potatoes. However, after the Great Leap Forward started, people were in such haste to produce results that they began to discard traditional ways of farming. The commune leaders followed instructions from the Party and ordered peasants to use a new method called "reasonable density," which had been invented by a Soviet scientist. Based on that new method, furrows were plowed very deep. Rice or wheat seedlings were planted very densely. The Party claimed that the method could increase the grain output ten times. Newspapers carried big photos of densely planted rice, with headlines like "Peasants in Such-and-Such County Have Produced Miracles." Many peasants knew that it was an impossible task, but nobody wanted to be labeled "backward and conservative." They began to follow suit and experiment. Members of the Dongyang Commune planted and packed the seedlings as tightly as possible in one *mu* [0.164 acre] of farmland. Initially, those green seedlings looked terrific. Not long after our work team left, a friend from the region told us that many had died and the surviving ones didn't pollinate or set. The commune leaders got really worried because another inspection team sent by the provincial government was coming. So they ordered peasants to pull twenty *mu* of healthy rice planted in the traditional way and move them over to a small plot right before the inspection team arrived. As expected, the inspectors left, fully impressed. Reporters wrote a long feature with a big picture of the commune Party secretary. He was seen smiling and waving. The article attracted many admirers and visitors to the region. It became quite a circus. Nationwide, officials tried to outbid one another in producing agricultural miracles. Deception became quite common at that time.

In the fall of 1958, our country switched its focus from agriculture to steel production. Our slogan was *chao-ying-gan-mei*—"surpassing the U.K. and catching up with the U.S." For the second time, the county sent me to Dongyang Commune with a work team. All the peasants, old and young, men and women, climbed up the nearby mountain. They cut down trees to fuel backyard furnaces and searched for iron ore. Meanwhile, officials went from door to door, ordering peasants to hand over their pots and pans, metal doorknobs, and farm tools for smelting. They kept the furnace going day and night. There was nobody harvesting crops, which were left to rot in the field. The mountain was stripped of forest. To cap it off, the "iron" they produced was totally useless.

LIAO: After the peasants handed in their pots and pans, how did they cook?

ZHENG: All private property had been confiscated to pave the way for a full-blown Communist society. They told the peasants to dismantle their stoves for a communal kitchen set up for each village. It became illegal to cook your own meal at home. In one village, all families moved into a big warehouse so they could live together as a big social-ist family. Prior to collectivization, many families had raised pigs, sheep, and chickens. Then the commune seized all the animals and penned them in the commune lot.

The second day after our arrival, the Party secretary took us to a communal kitchen at lunchtime. When we walked in, everyone stopped eating, stood up, and welcomed us with applause. Then they began to sing "Socialism is good." On behalf of the work team, I asked the peasants if they had enough food to eat. They all raised their voices and shouted in unison, Yes. Then a singer from the village performed to the accompaniment of bamboo clappers. He was singing something like this: Peasants no longer depend on heaven or earth for their liveli-hood. They depend on Chairman Mao and the Communist Party, which has brought happiness and bumper harvests.

I walked up to each table and shook hands with everyone. I noticed corn bread piled up on their tables. Two big pots filled with sweet potato porridge sat in the corner of the kitchen. Each peasant, regard-less of age, was allowed four big pieces of corn bread with all the por-ridge they wanted.

One peasant came up to me and complained that the bread and porridge didn't last long: We need to have some meat or oil. The Party secretary pushed him away by saying: If you work hard, China will become a true Communist society. When that takes place, we will have an abundant supply of meat. You can eat a whole pig if you want.

The guy walked away, with a confused expression on his face. The Party secretary told me to ignore him.

Then he escorted six of us into a private dining room, where a table full of "twice-cooked pork," "stewed pig intestines," and roast chicken was waiting. I asked why we were treated differently. The Party secretary answered: The commune leadership had a meeting yesterday and decided to slaughter a pig and some chickens to show our respect for the county work team members. In those years, it was very common for local officials to bribe work team members so they could report good news back to the government. In response, the Central Party Committee had promulgated strict rules to crack down on corruption. So we were very prudent. I told the commune Party secretary to bring us some corn bread and porridge and dish out the meat to peasants during dinner.

In the late fall of 1960, I led another work team to Dongyang Commune. That was my third trip. Things had changed dramatically. The Great Leap Forward distracted peasants from their farmwork. Crop yields were reduced, but peasants had to fulfill the government grain quotas. In many places, commune leaders had turned over the grain that peasants saved over the years to meet the quotas. Peasants were left with little food for the winter.

The once prosperous communal kitchen was in disrepair. The wall separating the kitchen and the dining hall had been demolished because peasants accused cooks of embezzling food. They wanted to see exactly what the cooks were doing. At lunchtime, hundreds of people lined up, each carrying a bowl in their hand. They looked feeble. Lao Wang, a fellow work team member, told the Party secretary not to disturb the lunch crowd. We simply stood outside and watched. The dining hall looked very empty. All the tables and chairs had gone. The food served at lunch was porridge mixed with vegetables, rice, and husks. After people got their share, they squatted around in various circles. Most poured the porridge into their mouths quickly, then they all licked their bowls very attentively, as if they were going to swallow the porcelain container. One local official who was our aide told me in private that having the rice and husk porridge was considered a special treat. Under normal circumstances, they could only have sweet-potato soup. We were really shocked. At the county level, food was scarce but each official was guaranteed a fixed amount per month. Nobody was starving there. Seeing the crowd here, I felt really guilty.

After peasants finished their meals, the Party secretary led us into the dining hall and yelled loudly: Please welcome the comrades from the county work team to our commune. Everyone stood up and began to applaud rhythmically while shouting the slogan three times: The communal kitchen is good. We have excellent food. Thanks to Chairman Mao! Thanks to the Party for leading us onto the socialist road! Before their slogan shouting ended, several people collapsed to the floor, too weak to stand up for so long.

That evening, the work team called a public meeting, where I relayed the latest news to the peasants: Considering the extremely difficult situation in the rural areas, the Party had decided to reverse some of its earlier collectivization policies. Confiscated private property would be returned to its previous owners. Attendees were very excited at the news. One old guy stood up and said with tears in his eyes: Thank heavens! I can finally die under my own roof. But local officials, including the commune Party secretary, pulled long faces and remained sullen throughout my speech. After the meeting was over, the Party secretary pulled me aside and said, There's nothing to give back to the peasants. Over the past two years, people have grabbed and stolen most of the public assets. They even smashed the big rice container in the public kitchen as a protest. I can't blame them because they are hungry. It's hopeless. I criticized him for being too pessimistic about the future. He defended himself by saying: As a Communist Party official, I have tried to do my work. But this is truly a tough situation. More and more people are dying of starvation. Do you know that people in this region are turning into cannibals?

His remarks came as a shock. I probed further. The Party secretary looked around and then whispered to me: My daughter is married to a guy at a village on the other side of the mountain. She ran back home last week, telling me that many little girls in her village have been killed and eaten.

I couldn't believe what I was hearing. If what he said was true, I needed to report the information back to the county as soon as possible. So I sent a fellow team member back to headquarters. I borrowed a bicycle and went directly to the village that the Party secretary had mentioned. I briefed Comrade Liu, the head of the work team there. He was totally in the dark about what was going on in the village.

In the week that followed, the county conducted a thorough investigation and revealed a terrible scandal involving cannibalism at the Fifth Production Division. That division encompassed 82 families, with a population of 491. Between December 1959 and November 1960, peasants had killed and eaten 48 female children under the age of seven, which represented 90 percent of the female children in that age group. About 80 percent of the families were involved in cannibalism.

Wang Jiefang was an accountant at the Fifth Production Division. He was the first one to witness cannibalism. During the investigation, he told us that starvation occurred at his village in December 1959 when the communal kitchen had run out of food and began to serve wild vegetable soup or plain hot water. With food running out, villagers began to search for other alternative means. They wandered all over the mountain, eating anything they could get—leaves, roots of grass, wild vegetables, mushrooms, and worms. Many people accidentally swallowed some poisonous plants and died. As people became more and more desperate, they turned to their fellow human beings.

It was a different story for village officials. They had embezzled the grain and secretly cooked and ate the food several times a week at the communal kitchen after midnight. When confronted by the guilt-ridden security chief who was invited to the midnight meals, the village chief said, Ordinary villagers can collapse from hunger, but not the Party officials. If anything happens to us, the revolution would lose its backbone. After stuffing themselves with embezzled food, those hypocritical officials would patrol the village, making sure that nobody was violating the policies and no smoke came out of individual home chimneys.

Wang and another village security guard were on duty on a clear moonlit night. While patrolling the village, they noticed wisps of smoke coming out of Mo Erwa's house. Wang was quite surprised because Mo Erwa was quite an honest peasant who had never done anything illegal before. He and his wife had seven kids. Two of them had already died of starvation. So Wang and the guard decided to find out if Mo Erwa had stolen food from somewhere.

Mo Erwa's house had both a big front yard and a backyard, fenced in by tall dry cornstalks. So Wang and the security guard crept along and hid behind the fence. They saw Mo Erwa's wife sitting at the front porch. Apparently, she was on the lookout for patrolling officials. Wang and the guards walked stealthily around to the back, where there was a door leading to the kitchen. Wang said he could see a small kerosene light glowing feebly in the dark. So he and the guard kicked the back door open and burst in. Wang raised his flashlight and yelled, Don't move. Mo Erwa and his kids were scared. They blew off the kerosene light and began running around in the dark, like rats. In the process, someone kicked over a big boiling pot on the ground. Then the whole room steamed up and smelled of greasy meat. Wang yelled again: Don't move. Otherwise I'm going to shoot. His threat worked. When Mo Erwa and the kids calmed down, Wang struck a match and re-lit the kerosene light. He realized that Mo Erwa had dug a hole in the kitchen floor and was using it as a makeshift stove. The pot lay upside down and chunks of meat lay scattered on the floor. Wang asked: Where did you get the meat from? Mo Erwa answered calmly: We just boiled our three-year-old daughter. The guard didn't believe what he had just heard. He picked up one piece from the floor and examined it under the flashlight. Before the guard had a chance to find out, Mo Erwa snatched it from the guard and stuffed it into his mouth. Then all the kids followed his example and dashed down to the floor to grab the remaining morsels. Despite Wang's yells and threats, the family devoured all the meat within minutes. Wang and the guard finally subdued Mo Erwa, tied his hands behind his back, and then dragged him to the village chief's office.

The next day, the village chief sent several guys over to investigate. They found a small bag of bones and the little girl's skull, which had been buried in the backyard. The village chief was so disgusted by the atrocity he ordered two militiamen to lash Mo Erwa fifty times. Mo Erwa screamed and his whole family knelt outside the interrogation room, appealing for mercy. According to Mo Erwa, the family didn't have anything to feed the little girl. Lack of food had stunted her growth. So they just killed her. The village chief interrupted Mo Erwa by saying: Do you know that killing and eating your daughter is a capital crime? Mo Erwa argued back: She was going to die of starvation anyway. It was better for us to sacrifice her to save the rest of the family. We just hope she would reincarnate into something else in the next life. It's too hard to be a human being.

After the lashing, the village chief convened a meeting with several other officials. They decided to keep it quiet for fear that the incident could cost them their jobs. So two days later, Mo Erwa was released, but his story soon spread fast among the villagers. They took it as a sign of approval from the government and more families began to follow suit. Since boys were traditionally favored over girls, young girls were targeted. Some families ruthlessly murdered and ate their own daughters. Others would exchange their children with neighbors. Since a child could only last them for a couple of days, some, including Mo Erwa, began to kidnap children from other villages. Booby traps, which were used for wolves, were employed to capture kids.

By the time we found out, the practice had spread to other villages.

LIAO: Did you report the results of the investigation to the provincial government?

ZHENG: I wrote a lengthy report and hand-delivered it to the county chief. I was hoping that the government could take legal measures to stop the killing of children and halt the spread of cannibalism in the region. I also recommended that the county chief bring those cases to the attention of the provincial government and ask for the badly needed food subsidies. But the chief sighed after reading my report: What can the provinical government do? The central government has already delivered food subsidies, thirty-five kilograms of rice and corn per family for the whole year. The whole country is experiencing hardship. He was right. The newspapers carried photos of Chairman Mao wearing patched jackets and pants. He had cultivated a small garden in front of his house to grow vegetables. Liu Shaoqi, the president at that time, went to the Beijing suburbs to pick wild berries to supplement his food ration.

LIAO: Don't you think that was just for show? Chairman Mao and other senior leaders should be held responsible for the famine.

ZHENG: I don't blame Chairman Mao. Local officials, such as Li Jin-
quan, the Party secretary of the Southwest Regional Bureau, should
take full responsibility for the disasters in our province. He hid the
truth from the Central Party Committee. He forced peasants to turn
over all their grain to the central government, despite the fact that people were starving to death. He told the central government that
Sichuan Province had wonderful climate conditions and an oversupply
of grain. He even offered to help out other provinces while people in
his region were dying of starvation.

At Dongyang Commune, and in all the rural areas of Sichuan,
peasants ate a type of white clay called Guanyin Mud. I tried it once.
The stuff tasted sweet and metallic. The clay was considered precious
because it helped soothe the sense of extreme hunger. Some ate too
much and the mud got stuck inside the intestines. Then hunger turned
into painful cramps. I constantly saw people writhing on the ground
with severe stomach pain from the clay. The most effective laxatives
were raw vegetable oil or castor oil, which cleared out the mud but also
killed people with uncontrolled diarrhea.

In those years, the lives of ordinary people were worthless. Those
in power had access to food. They didn't have to eat white clay or kill
their daughters. But poor families had to resort to extreme means to
survive.

LIAO: How did you finally stop the practice of cannibalism in the region?

ZHENG: Three months after our investigation, Mo Erwa was caught
again. He had kidnapped and killed two boys from a nearby village with
booby traps. This time, the county had to take action. The local militiamen arrested Mo Erwa and put him on trial. He was sentenced to
death. The county held a public execution with the hope of intimidating villagers and preventing more cases of cannibalism. Before the
local militiaman shot him, Mo Erwa screamed loudly: I'm innocent. I
was hungry. His cries brought tears to the eyes of the local militiamen.
They couldn't pull the trigger. Eventually, the county had to get the
police to finish the job.

LIAO: What happened later on?

ZHENG: In the spring of 1961, there was still no relief from the famine. I went back again to Dongyang Commune as head of a four-man work team. I wasn't doing too well either. My legs were all swollen. I was literally wobbling all day long. We ate lots of corn soup with wild vegetables and grass. I was quite young at that time and pulled through. Also, I could indulge myself with a couple of nice hearty meals each time I returned to the county government to attend my monthly meetings. There was enough food for officials at the county cafeteria.

LIAO: People in the city were much better off than those in the rural areas.

ZHENG: Urban residents were guaranteed a monthly ration. The government called on urban residents to donate food and money to peasants in the rural areas. But it was too little to make a dent. In my region, a second wave of cannibalism began. Luckily, none of the cases involved killing children. People simply cut flesh off those who had died of starvation.

LIAO: Did you arrest more people to stop the practice?

ZHENG: Legally, it fell into a gray area because those people didn't kill anyone. It was hard to prosecute. Leaving moral and ethical issues out, we had to admit that eating human flesh was a better alternative than eating white clay. It was easy to digest, even though we were told by medical personnel that one could catch all sorts of disease from consuming a dead person's flesh. People were desperate and didn't care what diseases they could catch. When a relative died, the flesh would be cut off for the living.

　　When that occurred, we really didn't have any legal justifications to arrest people. We simply turned a blind eye. Well, there were many villagers who resisted eating human flesh. One time, I went to visit several families in a big courtyard. Four villagers were lying on top of wooden doors taken from their houses. They were lying on their stomachs, with their legs spread apart. Several others were pouring tung oil into their rear ends to loosen them up. One guy explained to me that initially, they had tried to force people to drink the tung oil, but it smelled and tasted really bad. Many had thrown up, and it was hard to get it into the intestines. So they decided to do it from the other end. I recommended that they use vegetable oil, which was less poisonous. Those folks looked at me strangely and said: Do you know that we have never seen any vegetable oil for over two years? It's true that tung oil is tough on the intestines. But as long as we can get the clay out of our system, a little damage to the intestines is worth it. I couldn't stay and watch the operation. Before I walked out, one guy opened his eyes and said to me: Tell the government that we have never touched human flesh. We would rather die than commit a crime like that.

I didn't know how to answer him. Looking back, you have to admit that Chinese peasants are the most kind and obedient. They never thought of rebelling against those who had brought them so much suffering. I bet the idea had never occurred to them.

LIAO: Even if they had had the idea, they wouldn't have gotten far. The Party controlled the guns. Chairman Mao wasn't afraid of people rebelling against him. He could crush them like bugs.

ZHENG: The Party was worried about peasant rebellion. That was the reason they sent the work team to the rural areas. We were like the firefighters, trying to put out fires of discontent among peasants.

LIAO: Did you suceed?

ZHENG: We did. Aside from handling cases of cannibalism, our main job was to ease the Party's extreme policies and help peasants survive. There was a popular saying among officials at that time: "No matter whether it was a white cat or a black cat, if it catches the mouse, it is a good cat." We would do whatever it took to save lives. The communal cafeteria was disbanded. Villagers were allowed to get their cooking utensils back. Brick stoves were rebuilt at each individual home so that peasants could cook their own meals. In the old days, the government subsidies were distributed to the commune, and commune officials would normally embezzle some and redistribute the rest to each individual production division. Then the production division would take some and then allocate the subsidies to each village communal kitchen. By the time the subsidized food landed in the bowl of each villager, there was only a tiny amount left. We streamlined the process by distributing the emergency food aid directly to the villagers. The daily ration was half a kilo per person. Members of the work team stood by the warehouse and made sure nobody was stealing the food aid. We also allocated a tiny plot of land for each family so they could grow some vegetables and crops for their own keep. Of course, that *ziliudi,* or "land for self-keep" system, came under fire during the Cultural Revolution as a capitalistic practice.

LIAO: Well, the "capitalist" policies did save lives during the famine, didn't it?

ZHENG: Yes. The situation gradually improved. In the summer of 1962, starvation pretty much stopped. Prior to 1962, we were under a lot of pressure to find food for peasants. We thought about food day and night and came up with many creative ways. For example, we gathered all the dry corn, wheat, and rice stalks, ground them into powder, and boiled them for a long time to extract starch. Then we used the starch to make pancakes. They tasted pretty good. We also sent people to collect urine. We then poured the urine into a big container and mixed it with garbage. After a week, there would be a layer of green algae floating on top of the mess. We scraped the thin layer out, added some water and sugar, and drank it. It didn't taste bad at all.

LIAO: I have to say that you guys were dedicated Party officials. By the way, I read an article recently, saying that during the three-year famine, peasants in a village rounded up former landlords, rich peasants, and other counterrevolutionaries, slaughtered them, boiled their bodies in an open-air cauldron, and then ate the flesh. People then shouted and screamed in celebration of what they called "triumph in class struggle." Did you witness anything like that?

ZHENG: No. I strongly question the accuracy of the story. Cannibalism was driven by hunger, not by hatred. It is true that the landowning class was attacked in several political campaigns, but I'm not aware of any incident like what you have just mentioned. There was a commonly accepted moral standard in the rural areas that eating human flesh was wrong, even though it was the flesh of a counterrevolutionary. Moreover, cannibalistic activities were carried out secretly because people knew that if they were caught, they would have been punished by the people's government. Cannibalism occurred when our government couldn't feed its people. It's unfortunate that we lost more people in peacetime than during the war. The Party made some serious mistakes. Half a century has passed, yet the leadership still hasn't offered an official explanation to people. It's sad.

THE FORMER LANDOWNER

For his entire life, my grandfather never ventured out of his hometown. He was a former landowner in Sichuan's Heiping region. The land he had purchased over the years made him rich before the Communist takeover in 1949, but it also became the source of endless misery and trouble. In 1950, when Chairman Mao initiated the reforms of distributing land to the poor and classifying landowners as the enemy of the people, my grandfather lost all his property and was the target of many of Mao's political campaigns.

I always wanted to find out about his life, but never had the opportunity. He passed away in 1988 at the age of eighty-four.

A fellow writer of mine, Zhou Mingyue, presented an opportunity for me to make it up. His grandfather, Zhou Shude, was also a former landowner. Recently, I visited him at a village in northern Sichuan. At the age of eighty-nine, the senior Zhou was lucid and articulate.

—ɯ—

LIAO YIWU: Sir, at your age, what's your biggest wish?

ZHOU SHUDE: I don't have any big wish. I have turned into a lonely old man. I have raised three sons and three daughters. None of them is living with me now. They all have promising careers somewhere else.

LIAO: Your house is a little run-down. Why can't your children give you some money to fix it?

ZHOU: Mingyue's father has asked me many times; he says he will cover my living expenses, to go live with my second daughter in Panjiagou. But if I go, who is going to take care of this ancestral headquarters? On top of that, I would have to forfeit my resident registration card and would no longer be considered a member of Zhou Village. When that happens, the government could assign my land to someone else. This place looks shabby now, but when it was new, it was a beautiful court-yard house with a left wing, right wing, a main hall, an annex room, and a servants quarters. My grandpa had purchased the property and passed it on to my father. In 1934, my father died of exhaustion from overwork. In his will, he divided all of his land and this house, and left equal parts for my elder brother and me.

My brother, Zhou Shugui, was the black sheep of the family. He's been dead for many years, but I still can't forgive him to this day. I'm not done with him. Someday, I'm going to settle the score with him, even if it means I have to follow him to hell. Anyway, after he got his inheritance, he would go visit the city a couple of times a month, eating and drinking at nice restaurants, and visiting prostitutes. Even worse, he became hooked on opium. Young guys like you probably don't know what it's like to be an opium addict. It means your whole life is ruined. Stacks of cash can be smoked away just like that. That was the case with my brother. Within a few years, he sold his land and then his house to feed his habit. You know what? He even pawned his wife. When his wife found out, she jumped into a nearby pond to commit suicide, but was stopped by relatives. That still didn't awaken his con-science. Finally, his wife went to the Zhou clan leader, begging him to grant her a divorce.

The clan leader sent a village security guard to my brother's house, dragged him out, and tied him to a big tree in the middle of the village. He was left there for a week, getting soaked in the rain and baked in the sun. That was our way of detoxification. However, minutes after he was untied from the tree, he dashed into my house, begging for money to buy opium. After I said no, he smacked his head on the ground, slapped himself on the face, and threw himself at the wall. Seeing that I wasn't moved by those tricks, he began to threaten me, saying that he would burn our ancestral shrine if I refused to give him money. Dis-heartened as I was, I decided to grant him his wish, provided that he would agree in writing to sever blood relations with me. He couldn't care less. He put his fingerprint on the agreement, snatched the ten sil-ver dollars that I gave him, and disappeared. Our clan leader was a very kindhearted man. Out of desperation, he called all the Zhou family members together and officially declared that my brother, Zhou Shugui, was a disgrace and would be forever expelled from our clan. If ever he was seen coming into the village, the leader would issue an order to have his legs broken.

To redeem my family's reputation, I worked very hard, rising early and going to bed late. I took up the salt-trading business while my wife, who was six months pregnant, worked in the field with hired farmers. I vowed to buy back the property sold away by my brother. While it was hard to earn money, it was equally difficult to keep it. By 1937, I managed to pay off all the debts that my brother had owed and invited my sister-in-law and her children back to our house. They lived in the right wing. It was one big happy family again. Everyone contributed in his or her own way. Both people and livestock were healthy. Our life was finally set on the right track. Before I went to bed every night, I lit a candle and burned incense, thanking my ancestors and asking for their blessings.

Unfortunately, our good life didn't last long. The Communists came. In 1950, the local county government sent a Land Reform work team. I was branded a member of the exploiting class. Our clan leader and the former village security chief were both classified as "evil landowners." After being paraded in the county in a series of public denunciation meetings, both of them were executed. My wife and I were grouped together with a bunch of other landowners or rich farmers, and shuffled to the village square to witness the execution. Aiya, it was very traumatic. I was educated at a private school, and was well versed in Confucianism. I was kind to others. I had never harmed anyone or harbored any ill feelings toward others. However, my fellow villagers, who used to be polite and respectful, had suddenly changed, as if they had all donned different facial masks. At the "speak bitterness meetings," two of my hired farmers accused me of exploiting them by forcing them to work in the cold winter days and randomly deducting their pay. I didn't agree with their accusations because I was working along with them in the field. Also, even under Communism, we still need to work the fields in wintertime, don't we? Those two traitors! I used to treat them so generously. They even led the government work team to my house and reviewed the inventories of my land, property, and livestock. They annulled all my land titles, land leasing, and property rental agreements. They confiscated everything I owned.

Of course, the world around me suddenly changed: rich people ended up suffering and the poor became the masters. It was hard to accept it at first.

The thing that hurt me the most was my brother. That bastard! He squandered all of his wealth on drugs and became a street beggar. Then the world changed. As a poor street person, he was made a master of the land, and rose to the top. As for me, the rich landowner, I became the enemy of the people and sank to the bottom. Overnight, my brother turned into a devout Communist supporter. He denounced me at a public speak bitterness meeting, slapped me on the face, and scolded me for oppressing him and treating him like a pig and a dog. He accused me of illegally taking his land, and abducting his wife and children. What a liar! Heaven knows I didn't deserve the treatment. Everyone in the village knew that I helped support his wife and raise his children. But when my brother was spewing out those lies, there wasn't a single person who stood up and spoke on my behalf. I was mad as hell and couldn't breathe. Soon I passed out right on the spot. By the time I regained consciousness several days later, I noticed several strangers had moved into my courtyard house. All my family members were kicked out into the small annex room. My brother occupied the three large rooms in the right wing. With the help of the Communists, he now possessed a house, which was mine, a plot of land, which I used to own, and a family, which I had supported. Who would have guessed that an opium addict could have been rewarded with such wealth!

Each time I saw him walk around in the courtyard, I was full of anger. As time went by, I got used to it and accepted my fate. Sometimes, when we bumped into each other, he would mock me in private: Little brother, you worked like an ox for your whole life. Have you managed to keep our ancestral fortunes intact? I would answer: I'm the former landowner, and you are the poor revolutionary peasant. I'm the enemy of the people. You and I should draw a clear line. We don't belong to the same class. He would say: Fuck it. If it hadn't been for opium, both of us would have been classified as landowners. We would have been executed by now.

LIAO: Your big brother wanted to make sure that you could appreciate what he had done for the family. How did you manage to get through that period of your life?

ZHOU: Mine wasn't the only family that had lost everything. There were
thousands of people who had been branded as landowners and counterrevolutionaries. All of those people had been deprived of their
wealth and had broken families. It was a change of dynasty and someone was bound to suffer. In those days, I kept telling my wife: The most
important thing is that we are both alive. We have a future ahead of us.
I told her not to commit suicide or do anything stupid. Since my children were all grown-ups, I told them they could either sever their ties
with us or they could leave for faraway places. It was up to them.

There is a Chinese saying which goes: "All misfortunes originate in
your big mouth." So I kept my mouth shut and nobody came to bother
me. In the old days, they installed a loudspeaker in this courtyard.
Each time, there was a speak bitterness meeting, the loudspeaker
would be turned on. Our names would be called. About twenty of us
"bad elements" would be ordered to gather in front of the podium. We
would stand there, with our heads down. Over ten militiamen would
watch us. Sometimes, at small-scale meetings, we would be asked to
sit down. See this tiny stool over here. I had it made in the year of the
Land Reform for those public meetings. It's still sturdy. Its surface has
become as slippery and shiny as a piece of stone slate. If it was a large-
scale political meeting that involved the whole county, we had to walk
five to ten kilometers in a single file to the county headquarters. At
those meetings, the attendees could number over ten thousand. All the
leaders would sit in the first two rows on the stage. Then, over a hundred bad guys like me would stand in front of the stage facing the
crowd. The meeting could last for many hours.

Sometimes we had to stay out for three consecutive days for different public gatherings. We would get up before dawn, cook some rice,
and try to eat as much as we could. It would be a whole day event. We
wouldn't be able to come home until late in the evening. Getting
through those long meetings could be tough. It was very easy for me to
fall asleep. That happened a couple of times. The militiamen beat me
up pretty badly. I was in my forties then. Years of hard labor, such as
carrying heavy sacks of salt on my back, made me pretty strong. The
tough punishment and the long hours of standing at those public meetings didn't bother me much. But as time went by, my back started to go
because the militiamen forced me to bend down very deeply. I never
complained or disobeyed. At the end of the Land Reform movement,

the leader of the work team came to talk with me. He complimented me for being cooperative with the government. I was all smiles and bowed to him. In my heart, I felt as if someone had been stabbing me with a blunt knife.

By the 1970s, those political campaigns were running out of steam. County-level public meetings were no longer in fashion and decreased in frequency. People's hostility toward former landowners was somehow softened. Gradually, my fellow villagers began to renew their friendship with me since everyone in the village was in one way or another related by blood. We all shared the same family name Zhou. So as the saying goes, fortune can leave you, but your health, your family, and true friends are indispensable.

LIAO: When I was a kid, our school always invited poor peasants to our speak bitterness meetings. The intent was to urge young students to forget the "bitter past" under the Nationalist government and to cherish the "happiness" under Communism. At those meetings, we were obligated to eat rotten food so we could get an idea of the kind of food that poor peasants used to consume in pre-Communist days. One day, we went to visit the mansion of a big former landowner who had been executed by the government during the Land Reform movement. The mansion was converted into a museum. There were many exhibits showing how the landowner had exploited his farmers and how he had tortured those who couldn't afford to pay back debts. We were shocked by his brutality. After that, we hated all landowners. After hearing your stories, I get the impression that the landowners were pretty nice people. Do you mean to say that the Land Reform movement was a mistake?

ZHOU: You are a smart person and can decide for yourself. Let bygones be bygones. The government rehabilitated my name in 1979. I no longer carry the "evil landowner" label. I'm grateful to Deng Xiaoping for his economic reform policies. The Party realized its mistakes and was not afraid to correct them. I was given the second chance to be a respectful human being. I guess I need to correct myself here. I didn't mean to say that the Party realized its mistakes and was not afraid to redress them. I should say I am not afraid to redress my own mistakes. Nowadays, my life as an ordinary peasant is much better than that of a landowner before 1949. We have electricity and TV. We have plenty of meat and you can eat however much you want. This was never possible in the old days. We could only afford to eat meat once a week. My grandson, Mingyue, told me that even prisoners can eat meat twice a week. Both my grandfather and my father were country bumpkins. They worked in the fields along with our hired farmers. Sometimes, they overworked the ox that pulled the plows. When the animal began to cough blood, humans took over the plows. That was how we accumulated wealth. Not like today. Young men and women leave the village empty-handed and migrate to big cities to look for jobs. In a couple of years, they come home with money. It's magic. They can build new houses and buy lots of stuff. If we apply the same classification standards used during the Land Reform, half of the villagers today would be called rich landowners. My son is a teacher in a big city. My grandson, Mingyue, has graduated from a university, and I heard he has a doctorate degree or something. In the old days, having an advanced degree was very rare in this part of the country. My private tutor used to tell me that the scholar Hu Shi grew up here. He had a doctoral degree in the early 1900s. The emperor met him in person and sought advice from him. Just imagine how scholarly and knowledgeable my grandson is. I assume the Communist leaders also consult him frequently. Who knows!

As for my past, I have forgiven everything and moved on. Like an ancient Chinese saying goes: "Experiencing the most difficult hardships makes one the toughest of all human beings." As an old fart myself, I have nothing to regret or to be bitter about. I simply see my past sufferings as something that I have endured on behalf of my children and grandchildren. At the beginning of the Land Reform, my fellow villagers made up lies, saying that I had kept a secret ledger, jotting down every piece of injustice that others had done to me with the intent of settling scores with my enemies in the future. They even linked me with the bad things that happened within the Communist Party headquarters in Beijing. When senior Communist leaders, such as Liu Shaoqi, Lin Biao, and the Gang of Four were purged, the local government called me "the filial descendant and loyal follower" of those disgraced Party leaders. When we talk about it today, it sounds like a ridiculous charge. But in those days they really meant it. For example, during the Cultural Revolution, there was a slogan which read "Down with Zhou Shude, the loyal descendant of Liu Shaoqi." I didn't know who Liu Shaoqi was at that time, never mind that I was related to him. If I do get the chance to claim a royal relative, I want to be related to Deng Xiaoping because he helped reverse my verdict. I don't have to be his descendant. But if he wanted me to be his slave, I'm all for it. Anyhow, as time went by, I cared less and less about what other people said about me. That was fate and I accepted it.

LIAO: From your story so far, I can tell you are quite contented with life. That probably explains your longevity.

ZHOU: I'm turning eighty-nine this year. I've long become tired of life. What can I do? The more I want to die, the further away I am from death. The pine coffin that lies in the main hall was made for me over twenty years ago. As you know, in China, old people like to have their coffin made before they die. It's an auspicious thing to do. Several feng shui masters have visited this house and they were full of praises for this location. The annex room, located in the southeast corner, captures all the good feng shui. That was probably why my fortune could turn around after years of suffering. The upcoming good fortune should not fall on an old fart like me. It should follow my children and grandchildren. After he graduated from high school in the mid-1970s, my grandson, Mingyue, was denied the opportunity to join the army or to find a job in the city because of me. In 1979, after the government took away my label, Mingyue was allowed to enter college. The other grandchildren of mine are also doing pretty well. At the moment, my great-grandchildren are already in elementary schools.

LIAO: I'm sure you will live to be a hundred.

ZHOU: Why do I want to? I'm the only one left with this courtyard house. The rest have either died or moved out. I must have taken all the luck of longevity from the other members of this family. After I was kicked out of the main section of the house, none of the new occupants lived past fifty. Can you believe that? My brother, Zhou Shugui, died in the famine of 1960. So did my wife. My brother deserved to die. Oh well, since he is dead now, I guess I should show some respect.

LIAO: You should live with your children or grandchildren so they can take care of you.

ZHOU: At the invitation of Mingyue's father, I lived in the city for two months. My son is a respected high school teacher. He lived in a high-rise on the school campus. I was so bored that I soon became ill. I felt like a pigeon trapped in a cage. I couldn't walk around the building freely to get fresh air because each time I was down on the street, a bunch of high school students would follow me and poke fun at me. They treated me like some kind of antique or exotic animal.

One day, I was getting some sun by a basketball court. It was warm. So I unzipped my pants and began to catch fleas on my underwear. Suddenly, I heard some loud screaming. If this had been in the countryside, nobody would give a damn about such a trivial thing. But it was a big deal in the city. How dare Mr. Zhou's father unzip his pants in public? It totally embarrassed my son. There was another thing that drove my daughter-in-law nuts. She couldn't stand it when I smoked tobacco in the house. I was forced to smoke on the balcony. There are too many rules in the big cities. On the street, you have to pay to take a dump at a public toilet. In the rural areas here, you can take a pee or dump anywhere you want. It doesn't matter where you relieve yourself around here because all the crap will be gone the next day. The wild dogs will have eaten it all.

I have been pretty mad at Mingyue and several of my grandchildren. Those youngsters have been bugging their parents about demolishing this courtyard house. Well, you can't really call this a courtyard house. The other three sides have all collapsed. This side where I live is OK, but the beams have been corroded by white ants. In the evenings, I can sometimes hear squeaking on the roof. One of these days, the roof will collapse. However, the stone and rock foundation is still pretty solid. Look at that stone lion statue in front of the house. Over the past many years, the head of the lion has become shiny because I touch it all the time for good luck. This house has been around for over a hundred years. Those youngsters don't understand the fact that once we move, it means the end of my life.

LIAO: I didn't realize that after years of getting bullied for being an "evil landowner," you are still quite stubborn.

ZHOU: That's right. The thing that I hate the most is to be manipulated by other people. When my grandchildren come to visit me, they are too afraid to live here for fear of fleas. I have cats. Those animals love to play in my bed and sleep by me. I'm old and my body is cold all the time. In the evenings, those cats offer lots of warmth. I always talk with them, telling them stuff that would be of interest to people in my generation. You never know, cats could be the reincarnation of people who have died.

LIAO (laughing): You don't sound like a former landowner. You sound like an old monk who is now taking care of an old temple.

ZHOU: Speaking of this old temple, I don't think I can take care of it for too long. According to Chinese tradition, if a person passes away at an advanced age, it's considered an auspicious thing. His friends and relatives would snatch the stuff used by the deceased and offer it to younger people as a gift so they could rub off the luck of long life. I'm not even dead yet, but my friends and relatives in this village use all kinds of excuses to come visit me and steal my stuff—bamboo shelves, cricket cages, straw raincoat, and straw hats. They have even grabbed my bowls and chopsticks.

LIAO: You still have a long way to go. Your grandson Mingyue and I are hoping that you could someday move to the city. There are many senior people in the city. You can practice tai chi, go fishing, or raise dogs and cats.

ZHOU: Where should I put my coffin if I move to the city?

LIAO: You won't need a coffin. In the city, people are cremated after they die.

ZHOU: Burn me into ashes? That won't work for me. Cremation will make my reincarnation impossible. To tell you the truth, I have already chosen the place for my burial, next to Mingyue's grandma. I have already had a hole dug for me. It's a good location and the feng shui master has seen it. It's located right on the tail end of the Phoenix Mountain. There is an old saying that goes: "Good fortune lies at the head of the dragon and the tail of the phoenix." It will bring good luck for my descendants. I have lived a full life. I feel as if it was worth being labeled a landowner. I have suffered to redeem the sins of my children and have created future happiness for them. I heard that we will soon be allowed to sell and buy land again. Aiya, there will be more landowners and rich people than before. Things just move in cycles.

THE YI DISTRICT CHIEF'S WIFE

The Yi ethnic group, with a population of over seven million, is one of the fifty-five minorities in China today. Most Yi people live in the southwestern provinces of Sichuan, Yunnan, Guizhou, and Guangxi, farming and raising livestock. Before 1949, the Yi people were stratified into four different castes, with Nuohuo, meaning Black Yi, as the ruling class. The other ranks were considered Black Yi's subordinates. According to a Chinese government report, the rank of Nuohuo was determined by blood lineage, and used to make up 7 percent of the total Yi population, but owned 60 to 70 percent of the arable land. In the early 1950s, the government sent work teams to the Yi region and launched the Land Reform movement to end what the Communists called "oppression and exploitation" by the Nuohuo class.

In December of 2005, I visited a Yi village in Yunnan. My guide introduced me to Zhang Meizhi, a Nuohuo and the wife of a former district chief. Zhang was eighty-four years old, but in good spirits. When I arrived at her house, she stood up from her chair, her back hunched but her wrinkled face beaming with a smile. I sat down with Zhang and her two children— daughter Yang Sixian, 59, and son Yang Siyi, 57.

—⚍—

LIAO YIWU: I passed by a big traditional courtyard house that stood tall and imposing in the middle of the village. My guide told me the house belongs to your family. When was the last time you lived there?

ZHANG MEIZHI: In the early 1950s. After the Land Reform movement started, the newly founded Poor Peasants Revolutionary Committee forced us to move into a cowshed.

LIAO: Could you tell me what happened? The Land Reform movement affected the lives of millions of people. However, that part of history is gradually fading from people's memories. All the history books say that the Land Reform movement enabled the Communist Party to change China's unequal system of land ownership. However, there is no mention of the brutal fact that over two million people were executed at random.

ZHANG: I don't know if my story will help young people learn history. But, on a personal level, I lost over ten family members in that chaotic period.

LIAO: Let's start from the beginning. How many people were there in your family?

ZHANG: I had quite a large family. On my husband's side, he had two brothers. The eldest one used to be a well-known political figure in the region. He left home at an early age and attended the Yunnan Provincial Military Academy. In 1935, at the age of twenty-five, the governor of Yunnan appointed him to be the chief of Deqin County. As you know, for someone who grew up in a remote and isolated region like Zehei, becoming a county chief was a big deal.

In the old days, Deqin was overrun with triads and gangsters. They colluded with local officials to bully the innocent. After he assumed office, the eldest brother took tough measures and cleaned up the area in no time. He gained quite a reputation for himself. The Nationalist government even awarded him a medal for his good work. He was a strong believer in the old government under Chiang Kai-shek, and there was no way he would have switched his loyalty to Chairman Mao's Communist government. Luckily, he had died before Mao's army came. Otherwise he would have been tortured and executed. The second brother served as a sheriff in the Sayingpan region. My husband followed in the footsteps of two of his brothers' and served as the Yongshan district chief. In my family, I had two siblings. My brother, Zhang Yinxin, became the chief of Zehei Township. I had a sister who was married to a local landlord.

In 1952, when I turned thirty-one, a work team from Deqin County arrived in our region to mobilize local peasants to join the Land Reform campaign. Peasants were encouraged to speak out against the landlords and former government officials and confiscate their property. A week later, the work team arrested my husband and my brother. They locked the two of them up in the Zehei Elementary School for a few days and then transferred them to a county jail.

LIAO: What happened to you and the rest of the family?

ZHANG: During the first couple of weeks, the work team left us alone. One day in September, however, several militiamen showed up at my house. They said I had to join my husband and brother at a speak bitterness meeting and to hear my fellow villagers tell stories of their sufferings under my family's oppression. They tied my hands behind my back and then escorted me to the playground. When I got there, I saw many villagers had already gathered there. They were shouting slogans. The militiamen ordered me to stand in front of the crowd, side by side with a dozen former landlords or rich peasants. The stage was about ten meters away, right behind us. I turned around and saw my husband and my brother. They were kneeling on the ground, their arms and legs tied up with thick ropes and their mouths gagged with rags. A narrow black bamboo slate stuck out from the back of their collars. In the old days, I had seen criminals who had those bamboo slates in place before being sent to the execution grounds. I immediately realized what was going to happen. And I started to cry.

Soon the meeting began. Two militiamen pushed our heads down. One Communist official in military uniform went on the stage and shouted slogans: "Death to our class enemy! Long live the victory of the Land Reform!" The whole crowd raised their right arms and followed in unison. Then, after the shouting died down, the official declared through the microphone: These two class enemies on the stage have been sentenced to death by the village committee. The execution will be carried out immediately. His words drew a wave of loud cheers. Then the loudspeaker started to blast revolutionary songs. The militiamen pushed my husband and my brother off the stage. My group was ordered to follow them to the execution ground by a river. A large crowd walked behind us. After we arrived, the militiamen put me about two or three meters away from my husband and made me watch. Then two guys shoved my husband and my brother down on their knees, pulled the bamboo slates out from inside their collars, pointed a rifle at their chests, and then *bang, bang,* fired two shots. The sound of the gunshots was so deafening. My brother was a big guy. After he was shot, his body tilted a little but didn't fall immediately. A second militiaman stepped up and fired two more shots at his chest. Blood spewed out and splashed all over. The guy was startled by the blood. He kicked my brother's body really hard, wiped the blood off his arms, and cursed loudly. Then I saw my brother slump to the ground, next to my husband. He and my husband lay on the ground, head to head. Blood oozed out of their chests. Under the bright sunshine, their faces looked calm, as if they were whispering to each other. Two militiamen grabbed my hair and made sure that I saw the whole process. I tried to close my eyes. But my torturer propped my eyes open with his fingers. Tears ran down my cheeks. I tried to tell myself to be brave. But I couldn't. I just screamed and then passed out.

Someone poured cold water on me. I woke up and saw two militiamen prodding open the mouths of my husband and my brother with knives. So I yelled: What are you trying to do? One guy kicked me and said: Shut up. We are going to cut their tongues out. I screamed with my hoarse voice, Take my tongue if you want. Please keep their body parts intact. One militiaman hit my head with the butt of a rifle and knocked me unconscious again.

LIAO: Why did the militiamen want to cut out the victims' tongues? Was it some sort of execution ritual?

ZHANG: No. I was told later that a leader in our village wanted the human tongue to treat his illness. The leader had been bitten on the thigh by a dog. The wounded area became infected and wouldn't heal. Local doctors prescribed all sorts of herbal remedies and none of them worked. Then a feng shui master recommended cutting human tongues into pieces, drying them in the sun, and grinding them into powder to spread on the infected areas. The feng shui master said the powder had been very effective.

LIAO: Did it work?

ZHANG: No, it didn't. He had probably caught rabies, but in those days, nobody knew what was going on. There was no Western doctor in the village. The tongues didn't heal his wounds. Instead, his health got worse. He soon died. The local government held a big memorial service and made that bastard a revolutionary martyr.

After the execution, they dumped the bodies of my husband and brother at my house. I washed the blood off them and sent one of my children to tell my parents in a nearby village. That evening, three of my relatives came, took our door off, stacked the bodies on top, and carried them to a location up on the mountain. Since it was dark, they couldn't see well. They simply dug two shallow holes and buried them in a hurry. A couple of days later, when I went up there to check the tombs, I saw their bodies had been dug up by wolves. All that was left was a pile of bones.

LIAO: Can I take a look at the court verdict against your husband and your brother?

ZHANG: My family never received any court papers. In those days, the work team acted like members of the triad. If they decided that someone deserved the death sentence, they simply called a public condemnation meeting and then had the person executed on the spot. Over thirty people were killed like that in this region. We never heard about things such as court rulings in the 1950s. People's lives were at the mercy of the local officials.

LIAO: Those practices were very common in other parts of China too. It was a very tragic and brutal era.

ZHANG: My family tragedy was far from over. During the next two years, I lost more family members—my niece's husband, who had served in the Nationalist government, was also executed. In despair, my niece lost her mind and choked her three children to death with ropes. She then gulped down two bottles of rat poison and killed herself. My husband's second brother, the sheriff, and his two sons were shot to death at similar public speak bitterness sessions. My mother was branded as the lazy wife of a rich landlord. The militiamen dragged her through the street during a parade. Her body couldn't take the torture. She died shortly after. My father was locked up inside a warehouse where he was beaten constantly. One day, when the militiamen were asleep, he hanged himself from the ceiling with his belt. I had a brother who was executed at the age of twenty, a week after he got married.

LIAO: You probably know I also grew up in a landlord's family. My grandpa was also badly tortured during the Land Reform movement . . .

ZHANG (sobbing): I know we were not alone. Why did the government murder so many people? What crimes had we committed to deserve this? After all these years, I'm still haunted. In the middle of the night, I constantly wake up from nightmares and shake with fear.

LIAO: Could you tell me how you managed to survive those horrible years?

ZHANG: Following the execution of my husband and brother, the militiamen came again to get me. They locked me up for over forty days. Whenever there was a public speak bitterness meeting, the militiamen would drag me out in front of the podium, with hands tied behind my back and my head down. I had to carry a big cardboard sign on my neck. The cardboard sign said "Wife of the Evil Landlord." I would be asked to confess the crimes of my husband. I was an ordinary woman who had spent most of my time at home with the kids; how was I supposed to know what crimes my husband had committed? I simply read a prepared statement drafted by the work team. Also, they confiscated all of my property. They accused me of hiding money and dug holes all over the dirt floor of the house to look for it.

While I was away at the detention center, nobody was home taking care of my kids. My youngest daughter died of starvation. She was only two years old.

LIAO: How many children did you have?

ZHANG: I had seven children, four boys and three daughters. The first two were my stepchildren. By the way, I was nineteen years younger than my husband. His first wife had died. When the Communists came, my elder stepson, Yang Siyuan, had turned nineteen and was a student at a county college. After I was detained, the village committee accused him of harboring evil intentions of killing Communist soldiers. Good heavens! He was a bookish young man too timid to even touch a gun, never mind kill people. You know, in those days, there was no way for us to defend ourselves. He simply ran off and hid inside the mountain for two years. My second stepson, Yang Sipu, was barely sixteen. A neighbor reported to the authorities that Sipu had written anti–Land Reform slogans on the wall of a latrine. Since our neighbor belonged to the Poor Peasants Revolutionary Committee, the authority believed everything he had said about my son. My poor Sipu was sentenced to seven years in jail.

At the beginning, my two stepsons had taken care of their little brothers and sisters, who were between the ages of ten and two. Then, after the eldest one escaped and the second one was imprisoned, the rest of my kids simply went out begging and searched for food in the field or in trash cans.

My eldest son's escape made the village committee really mad. The village chief sentenced him to death in his absence. He put my stepson on the most-wanted list and posted his picture everywhere. He said that my stepson had gone up the mountain to join the triad and collaborate with the Nationalist forces in the hope of overthrowing the local government. Then the committee vented all their anger at me. It was during the rainy season. There was water everywhere. My torturers forced me to kneel in a water puddle on broken bricks and pieces of charcoal. It felt very painful initially, then both of my knees became numb. Look at the scars on my knees now. Even today, I still feel the pain here. One time, they hung me from the ceiling, pulled my hair, and slapped my face with shoes. They even pulled several of my teeth out. Can you see? I don't have many left.

LIAO: Where did your eldest son go?

ZHANG: I thought he had run off to some faraway place. When I was released and got home, my third son whispered to me, I know where my big brother is hiding. It turned out that my eldest son was hiding inside an old vegetable cellar on the other side of the hill, not too far from us. He stayed in the cellar during the daytime and came out to look for food in the field at night.

Several months after his disappearance, the momentum for Land Reform gradually weakened. The most wanted posters of my son were torn down. People seemed to forget about him. The militiamen still dragged me to speak bitterness meetings and denounced me for the same crimes again and again. I became accustomed to the humiliation. During the day, my family was ordered to grow buckwheat on a small piece of land on the far side of the mountain. So I used the opportunity to dig a small cellar in the far corner of the field next to a big tree. My younger sons and I moved a stone slab on top of the entrance, spread a thick layer of soil on top and planted buckwheat seeds. When the buckwheat grew out, nobody could tell there was a cellar under there. We also planted lots of bamboo nearby and drilled holes inside the bamboo trunks so they could all serve as ventilators for the cellar. When it was finished, we secretly moved my eldest son in there.

LIAO: That sounds like a pretty risky and complicated project.

ZHANG: Well, we had to come up with some clever ideas. Otherwise, we wouldn't have survived. Every day, I would strap some extra food, such as steamed buckwheat buns, boiled potatoes, or corncobs, on my children's legs. After we got to the field, we would slip the food down to him. For two years, my son almost forgot how the sun rose or set. He lived like a worm. The cellar was damp. He got skin sores all over. Initially, he wore his clothes. Later on, he didn't even bother and wore nothing. As time went by, he had almost turned into a ghost. He had shoulder-length hair. His arms and legs were covered with inch-long gray hair, like mildew on a piece of rotten tofu. Once in a while, as the buckwheat stalks were waist-deep, I would wait until dark. When I had made sure nobody was around, I would open up the cellar. He would poke his head out. I hugged him and combed his long gray hair, which was overrun with lice. Each time I saw him, I would burst out crying. He would look around and cover my mouth with his hands.

 He was always hungry for food. Each time, even before I had the chance to bring the food out, he would desperately grab my pockets and ask for it. Then, he would wolf the potatoes or corn bread down. He would always choke. When that happened, he would straighten his neck like a snake to allow the food to slip down. Then, after he finished all the food, he would jump out of the cellar like a monkey, and plunge his head down into an irrigation trench nearby to drink water. One time, as he was drinking, he suddenly heard something. He immediately jumped right back into the cellar. His hearing was sharp like a dog's.

I never dared to stay with him long for fear that the village militiamen could check up on my house at night. Before I left, I would whisper to him: Siyuan, Ma needs to go. I will come back later. He would nod his head, and whimper: "Ah—ah." He could hardly talk like a human being. After I walked out of the buckwheat field, I turned around and saw he was still watching me. One day, I waved my hands, asking him to go down the cellar. But he mistakenly thought I was giving him a "danger" signal. He jumped around and disappeared. He was literally like those savage creatures that scientists said they had discovered in the rain forest here.

LIAO: Have you ever seen the famous movie *The White-Haired Girl*? As you know, in the movie, a poor girl was raped by an evil landlord. Her dad was beaten to death because he couldn't pay back a debt. She ran away and ended up living on the mountain like a savage. Over time, lack of nutrition turned the girl into a white-haired woman. Eventually, Chairman Mao's army came to her rescue and executed the landlord. That propaganda movie motivated generations of Chinese to join Mao's revolutionary campaigns against the evil, ruthless landlord class in China. He Jingzhi, who wrote the story, was promoted to be the deputy director of China's Propaganda Ministry. Who would have thought that your family had the experience in reverse?

ZHANG: The movie presented such a warped view of people who owned land. In those years, I used to think to myself: As long as the Communists were in power, my stepson would never have the chance to see the light of the day.

LIAO: Did your stepson get caught?

ZHANG: By the fall of 1954, my stepson had stayed inside the cellar for over two years. My third son had turned twelve. He was very close to his eldest stepbrother and would constantly sneak up to the field to meet him. At the beginning, their meetings would last a couple of hours. Then, gradually, he started to visit often and stay there longer. I became really worried. I tried to discourage my third son from going there too often. I said it would mean death if his brother was discovered. He promised that he would not visit again. But, when I wasn't home, he continued with his secret visits. It was harvest-time. Everyone was busy in the field. The militiamen somewhat relaxed their control over their class enemies. Because of that, I became a little complacent and didn't monitor my third son as closely as I should have.

That little devil also became bold. In late October, he stayed with his stepbrother for over three weeks. I was worried to death and went up there to bring him home, but he didn't want to leave. My stepson begged me: Please let him stay with me for a couple of more days. If it hadn't been for my little brother, I wouldn't know how to speak any-more. I will try to teach my little brother how to read and write here. He is a very smart kid. I sighed and thought to myself: My third son had been deprived of fatherly love at a young age. His eldest brother was like a father. If he wanted to be close to Siyuan, how could I be so cruel? So I yielded to their wish.

For the next week, several of my kids took turns smuggling food up to the mountain. Then, in the evenings, I started to have nightmares of the blood-tainted bodies of my husband and brother again. I woke up many times in a cold sweat. I sensed that something ominous was going to happen. My premonition was right. Two days later, two village militiamen showed up at my door for a regular inspection. One guy noticed the absence of my third son and questioned me. I lied and said he had gone to visit a relative in the morning.

He slapped me hard on the face: You sneaky wife of a landlord. Why didn't you report to us? Which relative did he go visit? He must have gone to carry out counterrevolutionary activities.

The village immediately reported the information about my missing son to the county. Officials there issued an order to put my family under the supervision of my revolutionary neighbors. During the day two people followed me to the field, and at night they tied me and my kids together with a long rope in one bed. So there was no way we could go see and deliver food to the two brothers.

Later on, my eldest son told me that they had waited for four days, without anything to eat and drink. They knew something had gone wrong and didn't dare to come out. At one time, they had to drink their own urine. On the fifth day, they couldn't take it anymore.

They climbed out. Since it was right after harvesttime, all the buckwheat stalks had been burned. There was nowhere to hide. They crept around like mice. They got some water from a ditch and dug out several big sweet potatoes in a field nearby. They survived on the food for a couple of more days. After that, they were made bold by their success. They got out again and entered another field to steal sweet potatoes. Little did they know the militiamen had posted guards there. As the two of them were sitting stark naked, munching on their food, the guards jumped out and aimed their guns at them. But my stepson's look startled one of the guards. He began to scream, "Ghost, ghost!" As the two guards were shaking with fear, my two children jumped up and tried to run away. The guards fired shots at them. The first bullet hit my stepson's shoulder and he fell. His younger brother was scared and lost control. He threw himself over his elder brother. Then my stepson said the militiamen fired the second, third, and fourth shots. The bullets hit his younger brother in the back and then the head.

By the time the militiamen realized that they were safe, they walked up and saw that my twelve-year-old son's body had been turned into a bloody mess. They pulled my stepson out from underneath the body and forced him to carry his brother's body all the way to the office of the village chief. News of my son's capture spread fast. Soon many people got up and crowded around the chief's courtyard. People wanted to get a glimpse of the "savage man." It was like a circus. They dumped my younger son's body in front of my house. Then they shackled my stepson's legs, tied his arms, and locked him up in the village warehouse.

The next day, people around the whole region had heard that a counterrevolutionary savage man had been captured. On the third day, a countywide public meeting was held. Amid the noises of gongs and drums, my stepson was paraded onto the stage. The rest of my family was forced to stand next to him. His skin was pale; his long gray hair had reached his waist. Several of his teeth were protruding out of his mouth. Even his siblings were a little scared and embarrassed by his grotesque look. I felt so sorry and sad. People yelled and threw rocks at him. Many wanted to get closer to touch him. Since he had been in the dark for so long, he wasn't used to the light. He became blind for over a week before his eyesight was restored.

LIAO: I remember you mentioned that your stepson had been sentenced to death in his absence.

ZHANG: By that time, the Land Reform campaign had pretty much ended. I guess the leaders in Beijing must have realized they had killed too many people. They ordered village leaders to go easy and reduce the number of their random executions. As a result of the relaxed political environment, the village committee resentenced my stepson to life imprisonment. He was sent to a prison in the provincial capital of Kunming. Before he left, I went to see him. He kept telling me: I killed my brother. I owe my life to my brother. We hugged each other and cried. My stepson ended up spending thirty years behind bars. In the early 1980s, when the government reversed his verdict, he was already in his fifties. After his release, he got a job at a machinery factory next to the prison.

In 1984, my daughter Sixian took a long-distance bus and went to Kunming to see her stepbrother. When her brother was taken away, Sixian was only a little girl. By the time of their reunion, she was already in her mid-thirties and had three kids. Sixian brought her infant son with her. Look at this picture. It was taken the second day after my two children got together. He was still wearing his work overalls, and carried his little nephew. He was smiling. It was so rare to see him smile.

Before my stepson ran off to hide in the cellar, he had a girlfriend. Actually, they had gotten engaged a year before. That poor girl never married anyone else. After my stepson was released, she officially moved in with him and they lived together for another twenty years. They never had any kids. Three years ago, my stepson died of kidney failure. My daughter-in-law moved back home with us. She doesn't want to talk to anyone about her past or her late husband.

LIAO: How do you feel about all this now?

ZHANG: After so many deaths and so much suffering, my heart has become numb. I can't believe how I have managed to live to be eighty-four. That's quite a miracle. I guess the suffering has made my body and mind tougher. During the past fifty-some years, I was implicated in countless political campaigns. They put me through all sorts of tortures. I thought of killing myself many times. I hated myself for bringing disasters on my children. As you know, because of me and my family, my children were not able to finish high school. They were denied job opportunities in the city. I grew up in a family with generations of educated people. We had a glorious family history. I used to keep a record of my family history. The Poor Peasants Revolutionary Committee dug it out and burned it. My house was so thoroughly searched that there was no place for a mouse to hide.

LIAO: Do you harbor hatred against those who tortured you in the past?

ZHANG: I know the Land Reform was an inevitable trend of the time and there was no way for ordinary people to avoid it. I don't blame anyone. Of course, I dare not blame the Party and Chairman Mao. Even though the government has never officially apologized or reversed their verdict against my family, I'm trying to make peace with the past. By the way, I have been converted into a Christian. I found comfort in God. God has taught us forgiveness. Right now, fortune has started to smile on my family again. My children didn't get to receive formal education. But my grandchildren have turned things around. Several of them have been able to attend universities since Deng Xiaoping came to power. Three of them are now in Kunming and have gotten good jobs. Two came back and have taken up important positions in the county. Those two are now famous in the region for being intelligent and capable, just like their grandparents in the past. The descendants of my torturers constantly come to visit me with gifts and flattering words. Rather than calling me "the wife of the evil landlord," they now address me as "the Respectable Grandma." One guy was here last week and kept calling me grandma. He said: Grandma, you have good karma and enjoy such longevity. I almost puked. This guy's grandmother used to beat me up. But unfortunately, she died during the famine of the 1960s. For some reason, that made me feel really sad. That poor woman! She was five years younger than me.

LIAO: Do you think those who persecuted you in the past will tell their children about the past?

ZHANG: I doubt it. Do you think murderers would brag to their children about their "heroic" past? Even the Communist Party now seldom mentions its past and encourages people to move forward. We are moving forward. Last year, one of my grandchildren, the one who is a senior government official here, held a banquet in the dilapidated courtyard of my old house. We prepared over ten tables and invited all the former landlords who had shared a similar fate. The majority of them had passed away. Their descendants came. We also invited some former revolutionaries who showed great humanity during the many political campaigns. I specifically asked my daughter to invite our former tenant and helper, Mr. Sun, to sit at the head table, next to me. During the Land Reform campaign, the work team members repeatedly told him to denounce us publicly and beat us. But he just sat there, refusing orders. He was persecuted for not drawing a clear line against the landlord class. On that day, I personally thanked him in front of everyone, and kept putting food on his plate. I told my grandchildren to take care of his family and donate money to support his granddaughter's education.

That banquet became the topic of the village. Many people weren't invited. They simply watched on the side. The younger generation had no idea what that meant. But the older ones certainly knew. We even lit firecrackers and prayed for good luck. We used the occasion to claim our family name back and to appease the sad spirits of my murdered relatives. After the banquet, I called my college-educated grandchildren together and asked: Was it too showy? They said, There is no need to worry, Grandma. Let bygones be bygones. Our family has finally seen a new day.

THE VILLAGE TEACHER

Sixty-nine-year-old Huang Zhiyuan was a friend of my father's. He grew up in Chengdu, and left home in 1965 for a teaching job at a small village in the mountainous region of Yanting County. In 1984, he became tired of the tough rural life, quit his job, and moved his whole family back to Chendgu. Without a hukou, *or a city residential permit, he had a hard time finding a regular job and lived in constant fear of being caught by police. In recent years, as the government gradually phases out the* hukou *system, Huang's life is changing for the better. He now owns a grocery store and the business is doing fairly well. He visited my family recently. I asked him about his former life as a village schoolteacher.*

—ɯɯ—

LIAO YIWU: How did you end up teaching at a rural school far away from home?

HUANG ZHIYUAN: I entered college in 1961 and graduated in 1965, right before the Cultural Revolution. At that time, we were not allowed to choose our future jobs. The decision was made by the university. Since my family ran a small business before the Communist takeover and we were not classifed as the proletariat, I wasn't eligible for a work assignment in provincial government or large state enterprises based in the city. Young people in that era were quite gullible and obedient, especially those of us with questionable family backgrounds. When I heard that the Party entrusted me with the task of using my knowledge and skills to help make a difference in the poor countryside, I accepted with gratitude. I saw my new job assignment as a chance to redeem and cleanse my tainted family history. At the graduation ceremony, I said in a speech that if the Party wanted me to block enemy gunfire with my body, I would dash forward without hesitation. Just to show you how fanatical we were.

LIAO: Your remarks certainly echoed young people's ideals of that era. By the way, as a city guy, it must have been quite a challenge to settle in Yanting.

HUANG: At the beginning, I was quite excited. I felt like I was starting a new chapter in life. My destination was Shanya High School, which was affiliated with Shanya People's Commune in Yanting. So I bid goodbye to my parents, tucked my graduation speech inside the breast pocket of my Mao jacket, and boarded a long-distance bus with two classmates of mine.

About seven hours later, I woke up from a nap and began to see totally different scenery. The bus bounced along on the rutted country road. I had never seen such a shabby road before. It was like in a World War II movie. Around dusk, the bus broke down. The driver got off and checked the engine. He couldn't fix it. So he sent a fellow passenger who was from that area to inform the commune leaders that some city students had arrived. The guy literally ran for over fifteen kilometers to relay the message. About two hours later, a tractor rumbled into our view. It had been sent by the county government. We anxiously jumped on with our luggage. As the tractor lurched forward, I could see the steep cliffs hanging over our head. The lonely moon was high up in the sky. Occasionally, we would encounter a huge piece of rock sticking out, blocking half of the road. The tractor would slow down and scrape past it carefully. Thank heavens, the commune was not too far. Otherwise, I would have suffered a heart attack before I got there.

After the tractor dropped us off near the center of the Shanya Commune, we suddenly found ourselves alone. It was pitch-dark. Electricity was still an inaccessible modern luxury. Mr. Wang, who came to pick us up, said people still used kerosene lamps. There was but one street, with shops on both sides. In the distance, we could see flickering lights coming from one shop. We were told it was the local blacksmith's. The occasional banging and clanking from the shop made the surrounding area seem eerily quiet. It was like walking on the moon.

Like a tour guide, Mr. Wang began to tell us stories about the blacksmith's shop. It was originally a Buddhist temple. Next to the temple was a small hill of rocks. A statue of the Buddha sat on the top. The statue was about eight stories high. For the past hundred years, worshippers had flocked in from hundreds of kilometers away to pay tribute. The village of Shanya was built around that temple. Gradually, as the population grew, the village expanded into a township. After the Communist takeover in 1949, local officials called on people to eliminate any superstitious or religious practices. They converted the temple into a blacksmith's shop. At the time when we arrived, the statue of Buddha was completely neglected, but the temple, or the blacksmith's shop, had become quite busy and prosperous. During planting and harvesting season, the shop would stay open until midnight. Farm tools that needed to be fixed piled up like a small hill.

Anyhow, after we passed the blacksmith's shop, we were right there in front of the commune office compound. The Shanya Commune Party secretary came out to greet us and welcomed us into the commune. One official brought out the kerosene and gas lamps, and within minutes, the conference room was brightly lit. Then the cook came in, carrying our dinners on a huge tray—two plates of sweet potatoes and five huge porcelain bowls filled to the brim with corn porridge. Pickled vegetables floated on the top.

The Party secretary raved about the food, which featured three treasures of Shanya: corn, pickled vegetables, and sweet potatoes. The sweet potato, normally stored in a cellar, was the local staple food for half of the year. Since sweet potatoes can cause heartburn, locals ate them with pickled vegetables; pickled Napa cabbage and bok choy balance the unpleasant effect of the potatoes. Later on, I found out that Yanting tops the nation in the number of stomach cancer cases. Medical experts believe it is directly linked to the traditional diet of sweet potatoes and pickled vegetables.

LIAO: On the night of your arrival, the local folks were really genuine and nice.

HUANG: They were flattered by the fact that urban youths were willing to work in isolated areas like theirs. Before we left for the school, the Party secretary said: The mountains are high over here. Life is tough. Changing the world is not as easy as scenes in a movie. Please be prepared to bear hardship.

LIAO: How was the school over there?

HUANG: It wasn't bad. We had more than thirty teachers and half of them had college degrees. We even had veteran teachers who had taught in colleges for many years. They were sent down there in the late 1950s because they had been convicted as Rightists. Despite the fact that we were all graduates of top universities in China, no one complained or felt that we were overqualified to teach at a poor rural school. People were truly passionate about building a new Communist society.

The Shanya High School was started by a local scholar at the end of the Qing dynasty, around 1910. The classroom building and the auditorium took on some of the Western architectural styles. The courtyard houses, which served as dorms for both students and teachers, were built in a traditional Chinese manner with arched eaves. The buildings survived the war against Japan and the civil war against the Nationalists. Not far from the school was a pond with tranquil green water. The pond was hemmed in by mountains and was used for irrigation and as an outdoor swimming pool. There was a big orchard next to the school. The commune put the orchard under the jurisdiction of the school principal, who instructed students and teachers to work on fruit trees in their spare time.

LIAO: You started teaching at the time of the Cultural Revolution, when students in cities were busier beating up their teachers than learning science and history. What about Shanya?

HUANG: Chairman Mao did a great job in spreading the revolution. We were soon caught up in the movement. Initially, I was asked to teach Chinese and math. Soon, all that was permitted to be taught was the chairman's Little Red Book. Chairman Mao's quotes were treated like the words of God. We had to read them three times a day and check out our daily behavior against his teachings. Unfortunately, his quotes were not enough to empower the students to solve problems in math, chemistry, or physics. But nobody dared to say anything. I knew a teacher who specialized in Chinese literature. He liked to teach a classic essay, "The Admiring Qualities of a Pine Tree," written by a well-known Chinese general. However, when that general lost favor with Mao, that teacher was labeled a counterrevolutionary.

You probably remember a movie released in 1975 about a Maoist agricultural university. There was a scene relating to students taking a college entrance exam. A student applicant, who was an illiterate blacksmith, failed the exams. But a Communist official examined the hands of the blacksmith and said: These are the hands of a proletariat. The calluses on his hands are enough to make him a qualified candidate for the university. Of course, the student was admitted. That movie triggered strong reaction from students in my school. Many believed that they no longer needed to study for college. For farm kids, working and playing in the field was more fun than learning math and physics.

The headmaster, who was raised in a farmer's family, was a practical man. With the revolution going on, he was very glad to change the curriculum, half a day learning Chairman Mao's teachings in classrooms and the other half farming in the field, where he took the lead by carrying buckets of manure on shoulder poles to the field. Students and teachers all followed his example. During the harvesting season, students worked in the field full-time.

The playground in front of the classroom building was turned into a big grinding platform, with horses and donkeys pulling rolling stones to grind and help separate the wheat from the husks. Peasants even moved their windmills over. It was quite a scene. If students were planning a basketball or football match, they had to coordinate with the production team beforehand.

Anyway, of my twenty years of service there, only five were spent in actual teaching. We didn't start our regular curricula until the late 1970s, when Deng Xiaoping came to power. The nationwide college entrance exam was resumed. Initially, a teacher had to teach all subjects. Later on, when the government required all schools to follow a more challenging curriculum, the school decided to divide the teachers into various groups based on their expertise. I began to focus on physics.

LIAO: At the onset of the Cultural Revolution, many urban students formed all sorts of Red Guard organizations and rebelled against authorities. What was it like in Shanya?

HUANG: It was the same as everywhere else. Students at Shanya High School were divided into two groups: the Young Rebels and the Old

Loyalists. Both claimed they were the real defenders of Chairman Mao. The only difference is that the Old Loyalists group also defended the commune leadership, whereas the Young Rebels wanted to kick the leaders out of the office. The two groups engaged in serious armed conflict. The peasants also established their own revolutionary organization, the Red Brigade of Revolutionary Peasants. The peasants' group was more practical. They sided with the Old Loyalist faction and wanted some order. As a result, peasants also got into fights with the Young Rebels group. One day, the Young Rebels blew whistles and gathered everyone on the playground, announcing their decision to ban peasants from using the school playground to grind "capitalistic" grain. The students claimed that the playground was the place for Red Guards to conduct revolutionary military exercises. They also prohibited the use of the auditorium as a grain warehouse, saying that the auditorium was the hall for people to practice the revolutionary dances, not to store corn and wheat. Those decisions were devastating to the peasants. Thousands of them got together and staged a demonstration in front of the school. They uttered their angry curses and surrounded the school for several days. The students clutched Chairman Mao's Little Red Book to their hearts, and sang, nonstop, revolutionary songs such as "It Is Heroic to Make Sacrifices" or "If Necessary, We'll Call on the Sun and the Moon to Make a Better World."

I have to say that folks in the countryside were honest and simple people. They had no intention of hurting the students. Meanwhile, those students, who were articulate and literate, used quotes from Chairman Mao to engage in verbal war. Peasants were not their match at all, but they didn't want to give in. The confrontation lasted several days. Eventually, the commune government, with leaders installed by the Young Rebels, intervened. They dispatched two special representatives to the commune and issued an order to the peasants: If you dare to attack those young revolutionary rebels, all of you will be labeled as counterrevolutionaries. With those threats from the commune, the peasants gradually dispersed like defeated dogs.

LIAO: Even though your school was so far away from the political centers, you certainly didn't miss any of the "fun" from the Cultural Revolution.

HUANG: One might think isolated regions like Shanya could be spared. It was equally bad. Remember the famous statue of the Buddha I mentioned earlier? The Red Guards blew the statue into pieces with dynamite. Villagers were really scared, believing that disasters were going to befall them. But two years had passed and nothing happened. On the contrary, the blacksmith's shop, which had been converted from a temple, became so prosperous that it expanded into a farm equipment factory, employing ten blacksmiths. In 1968, when the Young Rebels group was locked in a fight with the local peasants, the blacksmiths sided with the peasants and supported the old commune leadership. The Young Rebels called the farm equipment factory a counterrevolutionary citadel. They would organize a huge rally once a week in front of the factory entrance, singing revolutionary songs and shouting slogans. The blacksmiths would stop what they were doing, line up near the factory gate, and stare at those Red Guards with hostility. Their dark, shiny, and bare-muscled arms and the hammers in their hands were quite intimidating.

To the students, the blacksmiths were scarier than those legendary man-eating monsters in old Chinese horror stories. Not long after the peasant–Red Guard conflict started, the head of the Young Rebels, Red Plum Zhang, disappeared without a trace. Students suspected that those blacksmiths had murdered her. Several hundred Red Guards showed up at the factory demanding answers. Some were even armed with guns that they had obtained from the County Public Security Bureau. They surrounded the factory for half a day. The blacksmiths were really mad. They dashed out of the wrought-iron gate and swung their hammers at the Red Guards. Many were hurt. A couple of guys were hit on the head and blood spewed out. It was horrible. Out of desperation, the Red Guards, who outnumbered the blacksmiths, fired several shots to the sky to scare the blacksmiths. They eventually got into the factory and destroyed many machines. One Red Guard shot at a blacksmith and blew one of his ears off. In the end, the Red Guards never found Zhang, nor could they find any evidence against the blacksmiths.

LIAO: What happened to the commune Party secretary?

HUANG: Our Party secretary was a nice and honest man. That was the reason why the peasants and blacksmiths had defended and protected him. He came from a family with three generations of blacksmiths. Even after he was promoted to be the commune Party secretary, he would still sneak back into the farm equipment factory now and then, and pick up his old trade. Soon after we met him, he was labeled a "capitalist road taker" and was publicly humiliated and denounced. One day, the blacksmiths snatched him away from a public denunciation meeting. They hid him inside the factory for over two years. Eventually, when the Red Guards took over the factory, they captured him, moved him to our school campus, and locked him up in the same room as the former school principal. Every day, he and other deposed leaders were forced to run barefoot on the school playground in rain or snow. While they were running, their captors would order them to shout slogans or randomly ask them to stop, or run faster, without any warning. Many of them ended up falling head over heels, and had bruises all over their bodies. One day, the Party secretary couldn't take the torture anymore. He threw a blacksmith's temper tantrum and resisted orders from the Red Guards. The poor guy was beaten up so severely that he became incontinent. The Red Guards still wouldn't let up. Every morning, they would grab him and drag him all the way to a statue of Chairman Mao, forcing him to confess to Mao about his "crimes." He refused to talk and, later, he bit off the tip of his tongue. He died a couple of months later.

There were many sad stories like these. Many years after his death, I still remember vividly how he was the night when I arrived in Shanya: his hair was parted on the side, and he looked like those warm and caring Communist characters in old Chinese movies.

In 1969, as chaos began to spread all over China, the central government issued another edict, calling on all Red Guard factions to unite and form revolutionary alliances. The famous quote from Mao at that time was "Learn from workers and peasants." With that mantra, workers and peasants entered schools and began to help manage the students. Let me tell you, the wind suddenly changed. In Shanya, Red Guard leaders were denounced as gangsters. They were paraded around the commune and humiliated in public meetings. With their leaders gone, the students were easily put under control and their arrogance evaporated. The campus was once again in the hands of local peasants. The playground soon became the harvesting backyard. Several classrooms were turned into pens for pigs or chickens. When school started in the fall, no student registered. Not surprisingly, the peasants, who were given the authority to run our school, encouraged students to do more farmwork. If any faculty ignored their instructions, the peasants would knock on their doors and insist on talking with them until they agreed to obey orders.

LIAO: You have told me a lot about the Cultural Revolution. How hard was it for you to live there?

HUANG: It was tough. In the sixties and seventies, hunger was a daily struggle.

We were put on a ration system. Every adult was given 13.5 kilograms of food per month. It was certainly not enough. To improve the nutritional intake, many of us would get up at midnight to catch frogs in the rice paddies, and boil them. They tasted really fresh.

Many of my students lived on campus because their villages were pretty far away. They brought food from home. The staple food was normally rice with vegetable soup, without meat at all. As a result, many students suffered from malnutrition.

Luckily, there was a cook for teachers. He cooked awful food. Nobody dared to complain because asking for nicely prepared food was not a revolutionary thing to do. Once a week, we could have meat. On Sundays, before dinner, a crowd would gather outside the canteen. Bowls were laid out on the big table and everyone would wait for the cook to dish out the meat. When he did it, all eyes would be focused on the ladle. If someone lingered a little longer, hoping to get some extra morsels, others would immediately boo him away. After getting our share, we would instinctively turn the meat pieces around as if to make sure they were real. Then we would carefully bite a small piece at a time so it could last a little longer.

Because of the gnawing hunger, I developed such an obsession with food. I met my wife because of food. She was brought up in the local village there and used to work in the noodle shop. Each time I went to buy noodles, she would sneak some extra into my bowl. Her bribes really worked. Soon we started dating and then we got married. After the marriage, she began to complain about my food obsession and even my eating habits. She complained that I made too much noise when slurping on noodles. She would say, People can hear you a kilometer away.

LIAO: You were a college graduate and she was an uneducated country girl. How did you end up with her?

HUANG: In those days, college graduates or intellectuals were trampled down as stinky bourgeois. Many people tried to stay away from me for fear of getting into political trouble. I was in my thirties and no girl wanted me. By contrast, she was a well-known beauty in the village and was not short of suitors. We dated secretly for over a year before we made it public. When her dad found out about our relationship, he strongly objected to it. He said his daughter was like a rose planted in the cow's dung. But like the old saying goes: "People with the same stomach make good husbands and wives."

LIAO: Why did you leave Shanya?

HUANG: The older I got, the more homesick I became. So in 1984, after twenty years of teaching in Shanya, I quit my job and came home. I was forty-five at that time. Because of my resignation, I lost my government pension. When I returned to Chengdu, I found myself without a city *hukou*; no government agency or schools could hire me. So I became an illegal resident for many years. I took on odd hard-labor jobs to make ends meet. I worked as a porter for at least five years. Then, I drove a flatbed tricycle.

The ones who really suffered were my wife and two kids. My kids couldn't enter any schools. My wife had to pick up some odd jobs. The most unbearable thing is that police constantly visited homes to check on people's *hukou*. We constantly had to be on the run. It's ironic that this is the city of my birth and I wound up being an illegal alien.

LIAO: Have you read the novels by Li Rui, a writer in Shanxi Province? Peasants in Li's novels love and worship the land they grow up on. Despite the extreme poverty, they choose to stay and make changes there.

HUANG: That was pure propaganda crap. In every regime or dynasty, there are writers who like to fabricate stories to ingratiate themselves with the rulers. Since peasants seldom read novels, whatever you write about them, they won't know.

China's remote mountainous regions are hopeless. No matter how much money you invest there, the returns become as intangible as moonlight in water. In many areas, where trees have been cut, the water has become polluted and undrinkable. Under Mao, you couldn't go anywhere without a residential permit. So people were tied to their land, poor and ignorant. Under Deng Xiaoping, the rules are becoming flexible. Those muddy-legged peasants are running faster than us. They go to faraway places in droves to search for better opportunities. Look at Chengdu—there are so many migrant workers. I have bumped into a couple of my former students from Shanya. Some of them are running businesses; others are working at odd jobs. No matter what they do and how well they do, they share one common aspiration: to get the hell out of the countryside.

Speaking of my former students, let me tell you a story. One day, when I was driving my flatbed tricycle near the Mozi Bridge area, I ran into the city police. They cornered me and confiscated my tricycle because I didn't have a permit. I squatted by the side of the road in complete despair. At that moment, someone tapped me on the shoulder. I turned around, and saw a chunky young man who addressed me as "Teacher Huang." I had long forgotten that I had been a teacher. I had no idea who he was.

The chunky guy pulled me into a nightclub nearby. When we started talking, I realized that he was the second son of the commune Party secretary in Shanya. I had been his head teacher for three years. He graduated from junior high in 1980 and was transferred to a different school. He gave me his business card. It said he was a nightclub manager.

The Party secretary's son became nostalgic about the past. He invited me for a couple of drinks and then called his contact at the police station, asking the police to return the confiscated tricycle. That guy certainly had lots of connections. He could drink, too. Not long after we started, he downed a bottle of red wine and was a little tipsy. He offered to get me a girl for what he called "entertainment." That almost scared the hell out of me. He said to me: Teacher Huang, you are a city guy and my dad was a country bumpkin. Both of you ended up with a similar fate: he was killed by the Red Guards and you ended up on the street. Life is so unfair. As your former student, I have to show you how to enjoy life.

I shook my head hard and told him that in China, we teachers keep our dignity. You students should respect teachers. How could you pull your teacher into a muddy hole like this? He laughed. You were my teacher in school. Outside school, we are friends. Do you remember that you used to offer me all sorts of special treatment? After my dad died, you always let me use your office to do my homework and you shared food with me. It's time for me to pay you back today. I said, I understand your kindness, but moral values are important to me. Your father's spirit would agree that— He burst out laughing and interrupted me: Forget about my father. When a person dies, he is like a flame that has been put out. Before I even had the chance to argue, two young women came up to me, snuggled against me, and offered me a drink. I became so embarrassed that this old face of mine began to blush. When my former student saw my awkwardness, he got up and said: Take your time. I will go get you a prettier one. I want to change the outlook of your generation.

When I finally got rid of the two women and left the room, I saw a crowd gathering at the other end of the corridor, blocking the passageway. I managed to squeeze to the front and found that my former student was beating up a young woman. He grabbed her hair, punched her, and kicked her with his feet and knees. The woman curled up in a fetal position, her body shaking and her face bleeding. Several onlookers tried to stop my former student, but he had the genes of a blacksmith and nobody could subdue him. Sensing that he could kill her, I went up and tried to stop him. But I ended up getting punched in the face.

When he saw the blood coming out of my nose, my former student began to realize that he had hit the wrong person. Sobriety returned somewhat. He explained to me: When I asked this bitch to service you, she thought you are too old for her. No shit. She has slept with hundreds of men and she still thinks she has a fresh pussy. I couldn't bear to hear him talk like that and left right away.

Later on, I didn't even go ask for my tricycle, for fear that the Party secretary's son could find me. One day, I was reading the *Huaxi Metropolis Daily* and found a report in the social news section about how my former student had been charged with beating up a young woman and forcing her into prostitution. When he was interviewed in the detention center, he was quoted as saying: My former teacher took care of me when I was kid. Now it's time to pay him back. I don't regret staying at the detention center because I did it for him.

LIAO: I have never seen such a loyal student as him.

HUANG: If his father knew about this, he would be turning over in his grave.

LIAO: Have you been back to that school?

HUANG: No. I heard that the Shanya High School has been closed. The classroom buildings have been demolished and the playground is piled with dirt. The school is now turned into farmland. My guess is that the school lacked financial resources and couldn't get qualified teachers to work there. Times have changed. College graduates are no longer as idealistic as we were. They are all looking for high-paying jobs with international companies. Sometimes, I don't know who is right, Old Mao or Old Deng. Is it good to open China's door to the West or is it good to keep it shut?

THE MORTICIAN

There is a funeral home on Chengdu's Qunzhong Road. Next to the funeral home is a big teahouse, with a run-down façade. The business at the teahouse is fairly good. About 80 percent of its clients are senior citizens. It was inside the teahouse that I recently met the seventy-one-year-old Zhang Daoling, a senior mortician at the funeral home.

—⚏—

LIAO YIWU: Master Zhang, how long have you been in this business?

ZHANG DAOLING: Over forty years. I'm about to retire. I was one of founding members of this funeral home. I started out here in 1957, when I graduated from the local art school. It was the time of the anti-Rightist campaign. Many educated folks had been purged for speaking out against the Communist Party. So people were quite nervous. When my school assigned me this job, I took it right away. If I had refused, I would have easily been labeled a Rightist for disobeying Party orders. When I first started out here, we had about ten staff members. In those days, people seldom used funeral homes. All burial services and rituals were conducted in their own private homes or villages. Most of the dead people were sent to our funeral home by police who had picked them up on the street. They were either murder victims or people killed in traffic accidents. Starting in the mid-1950s, Chairman Mao and other senior Chinese leaders began to encourage citizens to change the traditional practice of burial to cremation because there was simply not enough space for cemeteries. Our funeral home added the cremation service. But the concept of cremation was something that people found hard to accept. As a result, we didn't have much to do at work. My supervisor assigned me the job of designing a bulletin board to publicize Chairman Mao's political teachings. As you know, the Party was launching one political campaign after another. Lots of propaganda materials came in. I had to read them and then publicize them via the bulletin board.

LIAO: I assume the extra assignment kept you fairly busy.

ZHANG: Yes. Following the anti-Rightist campaign in 1957, Chairman Mao launched the Great Leap Forward movement in 1958. In this neighborhood, some young people stormed into the funeral home, urging us to convert the cremation furnace into one that could produce iron and steel. Their reason was that we didn't use the furnace that much and that we needed to make contributions to Chairman Mao's great plan. The funeral home director tried to explain to them that the two types of furnaces were designed differently. The neighbors didn't believe a word he said. They claimed that if a furnace had the capability to cremate a human body, it could be easily converted into one that could melt scraps of metal. When the funeral director refused their demand, they turned him over to the police and had him arrested for obstructing Mao's Great Leap Forward. After our director was taken away, the neighbors moved chunks of ore and coal into the courtyard. Luckily, the county chief heard about it; he rushed over and stopped the mob from destroying the furnace. As a compromise, the county chief allowed the neighbors to build a new furnace in our courtyard. As you can imagine, the quiet and spooky funeral home was turned into a mini smoke-filled noisy factory. I was quite caught up in the movement. I rushed in and out of the funeral home like crazy, collecting every piece of metal I could find from bicycles to cooking utensils. I had almost forgotten that my real job was as a beautician at the funeral home. Oh well, in the next few months, we produced quite a few chunks of useless, low-quality iron. It was a total disaster. The only good thing that came out of that crazy campaign was that I met my current wife. She was in the Communist Youth League and was assigned to the funeral home to help out with our steel production.

LIAO: When did the funeral business officially take off?

ZHANG: It was in the famine of 1960. About twenty to thirty thousand people died of starvation in this county alone. The large number of deaths made it impossible to conduct burial services for each individual. People didn't even have the time and strength to prepare a coffin. All they did was to wrap up the dead in a straw mat and dump the bodies in here for cremation. In the second half of 1960, we were so overwhelmed here that I had to work overtime. The furnace operated quite differently then. We needed to carry the body and push it into the furnace. Sometimes, if the power button didn't work as planned, the flames would start before we had fully adjusted the body in the furnace. Often, we would end up having the leftover ashes blown all over our faces. We looked like we had just murdered the person. But nowadays everything is automatic. You press a button; the body is sent down to the furnace on a conveyor belt.

LIAO: I thought you were a beautician. Why did you have to arrange the actual cremation?

ZHANG: All the dead folks sent over to our funeral home were famine victims. Their relatives couldn't afford extra makeup services. Initially, we could still do a little something to make them look better. In the spring of 1961, food shortages got worse. As more bodies poured in, I didn't even have time to do any makeup. In that year, thousands of people roamed the mountain like locusts, desperately searching for things that were edible—tree bark, grass roots, wild vegetables, even bugs. Unfortunately, all the mountaintops had been deforested to feed the furnaces for iron and steel production. There wasn't much available for people to eat. While walking around to look for food, many people simply dropped dead. The public security guards would force the prisoners—former landlords, rich peasants, Rightists—to climb up the mountain and pick up dead bodies. Those poor prisoners were also hungry. They staged a strike. If they didn't get a steamed wheat bun, they refused to go. When the guards punched them with the butts of their guns, the prisoners still wouldn't budge. Then the county sheriff came up with an innovative body-collecting idea. He used a long rope, tying several dead bodies together and then had some young people drag them down from the mountain. It did save us a lot of energy.

LIAO: Were you affected by the famine?

ZHANG: Luckily, state employees were guaranteed a fixed monthly ration of food. Since the funeral home played an important role in preventing the spread of disease caused by dead bodies, the county government made sure that the furnace ran properly and employees were fed. At the beginning of 1962, signs of cannibalism appeared. The bodies brought back from the mountain were mostly dismembered. The flesh around the thighs, the shoulders, the backs, and the buttocks was all gone. Local government leaders ordered us to keep quiet and get rid of the bodies right away. The public security officials patrolled the mountains at night, ambushed a couple of cannibals, and sent them to jail. Do you know why they wanted to eat human flesh? Many people were suffering from constipation after swallowing a combination of wild grass and white clay to appease the gnawing hunger. Their stomachs became very bloated. Then some herbal doctors told them that human flesh was an effective laxative. They wanted the relief badly.

LIAO: I remember the famine very clearly. I suffered from edema and almost died from it. Let's switch to another topic. What happened to you later? Did you ever switch professions?

ZHANG: Nope. After the famine was over, the funeral business went back to the normal workload. In subsequent years, burial was banned in many places, and more and more people began to accept the practice of cremation. As a result, the funeral home was expanded to include a special hall for memorial services and a makeup room. Makeup procedures varied according to the social status of the dead. For government officials or the more educated folks, we were asked to do a more elaborate makeover for the wake. For ordinary folks in the rural areas, their families didn't even request a wake or a memorial service. All they did was to have a private viewing so relatives could say goodbye. In that case, makeup was very simple: I would wash the face of the deceased, comb the hair, stuff some cotton into the mouth, and apply lipstick and some powder on the cheeks.

LIAO: That was it?

ZHANG: Yes. Sometimes makeup jobs can be challenging. According to Chinese tradition, when a person passes away, the family sets up a wake at home, with his or her body on display for three days. On many occasions, when the body was brought in for a memorial service and cremation, the arms and legs had already become very stiff, the cheeks all sunken and the face blue. If the death had occurred in the summer, the deceased would start to smell. It took a lot of work to make the dead look presentable. The hardest job is to treat violent murder victims. It needs skill and patience to make a ghastly looking face into a normal smiling one.

LIAO: This is a profession for the brave.

ZHANG: Can't say I'm that brave. In many ways, I'm like a doctor who dissects the body. After a while, you just become too desensitized to feel anything. Many writers have written spooky ghost stories about the mortuary. I have worked here for many years, and have not encountered any ghost as described in those books. One time, some guys played a practical joke on me. In the middle of the night, they removed a body that I had worked on and put it against my door. Later on, when I got up and opened the door to use the outhouse, that sucker bumped right into my face, its mouth hitting mine. It scared the hell out of me. Luckily, I soon recognized the body and quickly got myself back together again. I held the dead body, slapped its face twice, and carried it back to the funeral home. After it was all done, I went back to sleep. I didn't really feel anything afterward except my mouth tasted of formaldehyde for several days.

LIAO: When you told the story, my hair almost stood on end. But you talked as if this were something funny.

ZHANG: I was used to it. During the Cultural Revolution when factions of the Red Guards began to engage in gunfights, they made quite a mess in the area. Every couple of days, dead bodies wrapped in red flags would be wheeled in. The Red Guards would force me at gunpoint to clean and embalm the bodies of their comrades. When I dipped some of the bodies into the sink to wash them, the water would immediately turn red. After the wash, I would carefully cover the holes and cuts on the bodies with adhesive plasters. Then, I would change them into the Red Guard uniforms—green army jacket and red armbands. One time, a Red Guard leader was stabbed in the heart by his opponent. When his comrades brought his body into the mortuary a couple days later, his teeth were still clenched, and his eyeballs almost bulged through the sockets. In the end, I had to use a pair of pliers to pull down his eyelids to cover them.

LIAO: Didn't realize you had to use those mechanical tools.

ZHANG: We had to. It was quite a challenge to open his mouth. After I pried it open with a knife, a bunch of maggots crawled out. It turned out that his tongue had rotted. I was so grossed out. I covered my mouth and dashed out for some fresh air. A few minutes later, I pulled myself together and returned. I brushed his teeth, and pumped bottles and bottles of formaldehyde into his stomach. It was like washing a toilet bowl. After I worked on it for a whole afternoon, that angry, distorted face was finally turned into a friendly one, with the smile that everyone remembered. The Red Guards were really touched by my work and my perfectionist attitude. They put a Red Guard armband on my arm and shouted slogans based on Chairman Mao's quotes, "Learn from the workers" and "Serving the people." They even made me an honorary member of their group.

LIAO: I'm very touched too. I assume that the majority of people coming to pay tribute to the deceased are overcome with grief. After the funeral is over, very few can remember you, a magician who could turn a rotten piece of flesh into a miraculously human-looking body. We seldom read about people like you.

ZHANG: Even if journalists write wonderful things about us, people still don't want to be in this profession. Last year, I bought a new house and moved into a new neighborhood. I was completely cut off from my old friends and from things I was familiar with. The only advantage is that none of my new neighbors knows what I do. Once my son's girlfriend found out about my profession; she vowed never to visit my house again. I heard that she was so scared that she wouldn't stop washing her hands after shaking hands with me. Luckily, my son was really close to me and the incident with his girlfriend didn't affect our relationship. After all, what's to be afraid of? Sooner or later, everyone is going to die. But when people are alive, I guess they don't want to be reminded of death. I understand that perfectly. When I work on those dead bodies, I don't even associate them with death. I block it out of my mind completely. It is just a job.

LIAO: Does it mean that you have transcended human emotions?

ZHANG: Pretty much. There was only one time that I became really emotionally attached. A little girl was killed in a traffic accident. When they brought her to the funeral home, half of her head was gone. I touched her hands and arms, and sadness overcame me. After my assistant bathed her, I asked to be left alone so I could reconstruct her head and face. I filled the back of her head with silicone gel, and covered the gel with a piece of someone else's skin that had been soaked in formaldehyde. I carefully washed and combed her hair, braiding it into a thick pigtail. After I applied some makeup to her face and her lips, I put a white dress on her. She looked radiant, with a sweet smile, as if she were alive. I specifically put on some French mascara. Her eyes looked beautiful. At the memorial service, all the attendees were shocked to see the beautiful angel lying there. They cried and took turns hugging her. I was observing from the corner. I was secretly praying, hoping her parents could allow her to stay in the mortuary one more night so I could look at her alone, bringing some flowers or toys to her. But they quickly wheeled her into the crematorium after the memorial service. All that work lasted for over an hour. Beauty doesn't last. It's bound to be destroyed.

LIAO: Don't be too sad, Master Zhang. Beauty leaves its imprints in the mind. Throughout history, there have been many beautiful moments that can never be recovered, but you and I know that they existed. For example, you know about the epic story of *Farewell, My Concubine*. About two thousand years ago, General Xiang Yu's troops were trapped by his enemy inside a small southern town. The night before his last battle for life, he sat in his camp with his beloved concubine Yu Ji and sang: "My strength could pull mountains, my spirit could conquer the world. Yet so unlucky am I that my horse just refuses to gallop! What can I do if my horse denies me even a trot? Oh my dear Yu Ji, what would you have me do?" To which Yu Ji replied, after performing a final dance in front of him: "The Han have invaded us. Chu's songs surround us. My lord's spirit is depleted. Why then should I still live?" She cut her own throat with his sword. Grief-stricken, Xiang Yu fought his way to the Wu River. After all his men had fallen, he took his own life. People took this tragic story and imbued it with new feeling, imagination, and meaning. The concubine, a rare, unimaginable beauty, perished from the world, just like the little girl you talked about. But her story passes on from generation to generation.

ZHANG: You writers make things sound so poetic. You have very good memories. Even though I only understand half of what you just said, I know you are complimenting my work. Throughout my career, nobody has used those poetic words to praise me. I have spent most of my life in that funeral home. What am I going to do after I retire? I don't know how to play cards or chess. I don't like to chat with people. All I know about is dead people.

LIAO: You can raise a cat or a dog or go fishing. People can have different hobbies.

ZHANG: I'm too afraid to feel attached to anyone or anything. Cats and dogs are like human beings. After you live with them long enough, you begin to feel attached, and one day, when you have to part with them forever, you will feel sad. So many nice people and good-looking people die each day. I work on their bodies, hoping to temporarily preserve and enhance their beauty before they are gone forever. It's tough. The scariest part of life is not death, but the loss that comes with death. When I look around me, I notice that I can't afford to lose stuff anymore.

My former boss died at the beginning of this year. He was not even seventy yet. I did the makeup for him. This guy had one hobby when he was alive. He collected all sorts of wedding invitations when he was young. After he turned fifty, he began to collect obituaries. His whole room was filled with his collections. He used to say that all obituaries sounded the same and that we Chinese people lack imagination in the use of language.

LIAO: That was kind of eccentric.

ZHANG: Well, he wanted his own obituary to be imaginative and unique. So he began to compose his own when he was still alive. He had printed a couple hundred copies and stored them in a drawer, along with his bank accounts and his will. After he died, his friends located those copies and showed one to Old Wang, the new Party secretary at the funeral home. Old Wang, who was going to preside over the memorial service, read it aloud to several people during the rehearsal. Nobody could understand what the obituary was about. It was so archaic.

LIAO: I assume he must have used an ancient style of liturgy.

ZHANG: Perhaps. They sounded like haiku. I didn't know half of the characters. They were handwritten, and I assume that he must have read it hundreds of times before he died, hoping those could be the last words he left for this world. Unfortunately, the new Party secretary didn't think his obituary reflected the revolutionary spirit of the new era. So he composed a new one filled with modern political jargon. It was written in a style and language that our past director had despised. He could be turning over in his grave. Oh well, what can you do? This is China. You don't have much control when you are alive. When you die, you won't have control over your own obituary either.

THE NEIGHBORHOOD COMMITTEE DIRECTOR

Since 1954, the government has set up a system of neighborhood committees on a nationwide basis to extend security and control beyond what could be provided by the police. Each committee usually consists of between three and seven full-time cadres, augmented by unpaid local residents, such as housewives and retirees. Over the past fifty years, neighborhood committees have served as a primary means for disseminating propaganda, mediating disputes, controlling troublemakers, and spying on any possible violations of the government's one-child policies.

I spent my teenage years in Jinguang District, which is one of the oldest slums in Chengdu. Located in a remote corner of the city, the area has been overlooked by developers. Old run-down apartment buildings are still squatting there, like ugly Dumpsters. The seventy-nine-year-old Mi Daxi was my neighborhood committee director for many years. He was quite an idol of mine in my childhood days.

—m—

LIAO YIWU: I'm looking for Director Mi of the neighborhood committee.

MI DAXI: That's me. By the way, I'm no longer the director. I'm retired. I'm here today to help out my daughter. She is out running some errands. What's your name? Do you have an ID card or a recommendation letter from your company?

LIAO: Do you recognize me? I used to live on the second floor. I'm the son of Teacher Liao.

MI: You have changed a lot. I can hardly recognize you. Where are you making the big bucks nowadays?

LIAO: It's very refreshing to hear a diehard Communist like you talk about money.

MI: Times have changed. Everyone talks about money and nobody cares about Communism anymore.

LIAO: I guess so. In the old days, I remember, your office used to be located in a beautiful building on the main street here. This current office looks kind of shabby, doesn't it? Anyway, which year did you join the neighborhood committee?

MI: It was about forty years ago. When I first started at the neighborhood committee, I was not even forty yet. I had suffered injuries on my right hand while working at the local machinery factory. They put me on disability leave and assigned me a part-time job at this neighborhood committee. At the beginning, I was pretty depressed because working at a factory was a very popular profession in the 1960s. Mao called workers "the pioneers of the Communist revolution." I couldn't see myself working with a bunch of gossipy mothers and grandmothers who staffed the neighborhood committees here. The local officials offered me encouragement and support. They told me that controlling every household in the neighborhood was an important task. We had to watch out for bad elements that could pose a threat to our Communist rule. They even honored me by electing me to be a delegate to the District People's Congress, the local legislative body. So, after a while, I began to like it.

The old neighborhood committee building belonged to a rich capitalist. He had owned a textile factory before the revolution in 1949. All of his children had escaped overseas. He and his wife were left behind because they didn't want to live in a foreign country. In the early 1950s, the government took over his factory and converted it into a state asset. The capitalist lost his job and simply stayed home, idling around all day long. At the beginning of the Cultural Revolution, the passion of the Red Guards was almost palpable. They were ready to kill or beat up any counterrevolutionaries. That capitalist knew very well that he could be the next target. So, one day, when Mr. Wang, the local police chief, and I walked into his house, that guy immediately offered to move out of his house. He said he had committed crimes by exploiting workers in his factory. After years of receiving Communist education, he had reformed himself and wanted to start a new chapter in life. He called the house a symbol of his family's shameful past. His only request was for a smaller apartment so he and his wife could have a place to sleep. Mr. Wang was a no-nonsense guy. He took out his pen and wrote a letter, ordering the local housing authority to arrange a small run-down apartment for the capitalist. So the neighborhood committee moved into the big house.

LIAO: How could you take over other people's property like that?

MI: In that era, Chairman Mao's words were the supreme law. To tell you the truth, after we converted his living quarters into an office, his old neighbors applauded the decision unanimously. That capitalist and his wife used to live in that huge courtyard house with over ten rooms while his neighbors were crammed inside tiny run-down apartments. We kept asking ourselves: What was so special about him? Anyway, his decision to move out had also saved the house from being burned down by the young Red Guard rebels.

LIAO: What happened to the house later on?

MI: During the Cultural Revolution, people in the neighborhood were all divided into different factions. Each faction believed that they were more revolutionary than the others. There were gunfights every night. The neighborhood committee office served temporarily as the headquarters for one of the powerful factions. A couple of years later, the provincial Communist Party dissolved the warring factions. The house was then occupied by a local government agency. It wasn't until the mid-1970s that the neighborhood committee was allowed to move back in again.

LIAO: Is the neighborhood committee part of the city government?

MI: It's a pseudo-government organization. I will say it's at the bottom level on the city government organizational chart. The local public security bureau is a bona fide government agency. Right now, only one policeman has been assigned to our neighborhood. So the committee ends up being the eyes and ears of the police.

LIAO: Did you get a regular salary when you were the director?

MI: I got a monthly stipend. Do you consider that salary? Let me tell you, that menial job was the hardest thing in the world. We made sure all the Party policies were being communicated to every household, and we were obligated to report to authorities what people were doing. If a woman violated the one-child policy and became pregnant with her second child, we had to talk with her and persuade her to have an abortion. If she refused, we would have to report her to her work unit. She could end up losing her job. If a couple got into a fight or a young person didn't want to pay money to support his ailing parents, we would be called on to mediate and resolve the family crisis. Of course, priorities shifted all the time. For example, thieves and gang members are now as rampant as rats. Without the help of the neighborhood committee, the public security bureau would have a hard time cracking down on them.

LIAO: I see. Could you tell me how the neighborhood committee ended up in this shabby office here?

MI: In the late 1970s and 1980s, China started the "open door" policy. Overnight, having a relative overseas became a fashionable thing. The government rolled out its red carpet for overseas Chinese, hoping that they would invest in China. That capitalist I mentioned earlier had two sons who returned from America in 1985. They were very shrewd people. When they first walked into the courtyard, they bowed to us three times, expressing their gratitude to the Chinese government, the Communist Party, and the neighbors for "taking care" of their house. They even presented a banner to show their gratitude.

LIAO: You and the local Communist Party took their house illegally. Were they really serious about "thanking" you?

MI: That was American capitalistic bullshit. It was a diplomatic way to kick us out of the house. We had no other alternatives but to get out. The minute we moved out, the two guys put the house up for sale. It was the eighties. China's economy was not as developed as it is today. The majority of the people here lived on meager salaries and there weren't any rich people around. So the house ended up on the market for a long time. Then those two bastards contacted the city, offering to sell the house to the government at a hefty price of 300,000 yuan [US$36,000]. That was so evil. If it had been in Mao's era, the revolutionary neighbors would have stepped out and slapped them in the face. Oh well, times had changed. The government showed lots of mercy toward those two American bastards and decided to buy it. They hoped the kind gesture could help heal the wounds of the capitalist who had been traumatized during the Cultural Revolution and help lure his children back from the U.S. You know what? Those two bastards had already been brainwashed by the U.S. imperialists. They took the money and left. They even complained that we had trashed their home.

LIAO: But I think buying the house might be a good deal for the government. Considering the real estate market here, don't you think that house is worth at least two million yuan [US$240,000] now?

MI: The house was demolished. It was really a shame. I'm not wasting any regrets over the house. I just hated the fact that the money had gone into the pockets of those two bastards. In the 1980s, 300,000 yuan was worth a lot. We could have used that money to build ten elementary schools for children in poor regions. The street where the house used to be was close to the main thoroughfare. The whole block was demolished to give way to a new shopping mall. Those who lived in that area were lucky because they were able to relocate to new houses in nicer areas.

But this area here is on an isolated corner. It's a ghetto. Several developers have come, but have not seen any potential for development. Those who get stuck here will be stuck here forever. Some older folks still come to the committee out of habit, thinking that we could somehow help them relocate to a new area. This is not the Mao era. What do they expect us to do?

LIAO: People like you are still considered the backbone of the government.

MI: But who is my backbone?

LIAO: Don't be so pessimistic. Nowadays, people are no longer enthused about Communist revolutions the way they used to be in the 1960s and

1970s. But your services are still needed. In this area, there are all kinds of migrants floating around. If anything happens, such as robberies or gang fights, the public security officers wouldn't even know where to start their investigation without your help. From your little shabby office here, you can see clearly which family is playing mah-jongg and engaged in gambling, which apartment has been rented out, who the visitors are, and which young couples are moving in together before they get married, etc. As a kid, I remember gang members were afraid of you because you were connected with the local public security bureau. Before police decided to send anyone to the reeducation camp, they would consult with you first.

MI: They still consult with me now. But under most circumstances, the public security bureau no longer sends kids to reeducation camps. They simply levy a heavy fine. Not long ago, my daughter led the public security officers to search an apartment building, and they found ten guys who had migrated here from the rural areas. None of them had any city resident permits. Some were caught gambling. Others were found watching porno tapes together. The officers rounded them up and put them in a suburban detention center. Several days later, they paid a fine and were released.

LIAO: I don't think you can arrest or detain people simply because they don't have a resident permit, or simply because they watch porn.

MI: You have the wrong ideas in your brain. To me, it is a crime to watch pornography because it leads to sex crimes. In the old days, people were jailed for reading a handwritten manuscript of a love story. Remember the kid who lived next door to you? He was circulating the handwritten book *The Yearning Heart of a Young Woman,* which was a very popular love story published underground in the 1970s. One of his classmates reported him to the police. I led the police to his room and we found the evidence. The police hung a black cardboard sign around his neck and paraded him around the neighborhood for circulating lurid materials to young people. He spent three years in a reeducation camp.

LIAO: That was during the Mao era. Just think about it: those kids were your neighbors. Why would you want to ruin their future simply because they were reading a love story? If you go to the shopping malls nowadays, you can get all sorts of magazines and books on love and sex at the newsstands.

MI: You can have too much sympathy for bad people. I can tell who is a good person and who is a bad person by simply looking at him. In the old days, there was a North Korean movie called *The Invisible Battlefield*. The movie told a story about how counterrevolutionaries were trying to overthrow the Communist government in North Korea. I was very touched by the movie. I proposed that all neighborhood committee members should see the movie, and become vigilant. The movie was a good education for us. We decided to mobilize all the people in the neighborhood, so they could report to us any suspicious activities. Before the 1980s, each time we received a tip, we would conduct large-scale searches of individual homes.

LIAO: I remember that. In 1975, my uncle was released from prison. He was among the last batch of POWs to receive amnesty from the government. After he got home, you led the police to our apartment. My uncle was taken away and detained overnight.

MI: Well, your uncle fought on the side of the Nationalists during the civil war. He was categorized as a class enemy. It was our job to be vigilant. Oh well, I had to apologize for the detention. He turned out to be a nice man. Over the past forty years, that was probably the only mistake I ever made. At present, the government has beefed up its crackdown on crime. Since last year, there have been several large-scale police roundups. But the neighborhood committees are no longer playing a critical role as they used to.

LIAO: Is it good or bad?

MI: Well, what do you think? We have been treated as a symbol of the past. My feelings are hurt.

LIAO: I personally think that the neighborhood committee was given too much power in the Mao era. Nowadays, we need to rule society with law. You guys cannot just search people's homes at random. Like everyone else in China, people at the neighborhood committee should find something else to keep them busy.

MI: We are trying to reinvent ourselves. Last summer, the government provided funding and authorized the neighborhood committee to open a teahouse, which turned out to be a very successful venture. My original idea was to make the teahouse a venue to publicize government policies. In the old days, all the neighbors gathered together every Wednesday afternoon to sit in the open air to study Mao's works and read Party newspapers. I figured the old mandatory study sessions no longer worked. But we could use the teahouse to get folks in the neighborhood to come in and sip tea while reading the Party papers. It was like killing two birds with one stone. Also, the teahouse could create a couple of jobs for those unemployed youth. But this teahouse venture turned into a monster. Nobody wanted to hear me read the newspapers. Not only that, they even booed me off the podium several times. So my daughter told me to be more flexible and stop preaching Communism. We then invited some Sichuan opera singers to perform at the teahouse. Old folks loved it, but young people hated it. They used all sorts of means to sabotage it. One evening, soon after the operas started, a young guy called the local TV station to come investigate noise pollution in the teahouse. The journalist filed a news report that totally distorted the truth about us. It was just so hard to please everyone. In the end, our customers decided to take matters into their own hands. They converted the teahouse into a mah-jongg parlor. Soon it became so popular that we ran out of mah-jongg tables. People simply brought tables from their own homes, and installed a couple more lightbulbs in the teahouse. It was really shameful. They turned the teahouse into a gambling parlor. They recommended that I charge a fee per table.

LIAO: You must have made lots of money from it. As the Chinese saying goes, "When the fortune of God wants to come in, you cannot stop it!"

MI: I'm an old-time Communist who has received years of orthodox education from the Party. How can I lead my people astray to something evil?

LIAO: Don't you think it's an overreaction on your part? Playing mah-jongg is a popular pastime for people in China. You cannot call mah-jongg players evildoers, can you? Besides, all the teahouses in this city run mah-jongg games.

MI: Many folks spent all night here playing mah-jongg. If they won, they would go piss away the money in expensive restaurants and whore-houses. When they lost, they started stealing. I really regretted what I had created, but it was too late to close down. Even my daughter dis-suaded me from complaining. One time, the old hunchback who lives on the fifth floor of that building gambled away ten thousand yuan [US$1,220] just in one night. He became so crazy. He went home and drank some DDT to commit suicide. Luckily, his wife found out and sent him to the hospital. Otherwise, he would be dead by now. After this incident, I went to the police and reported the gambling activities at my teahouse. They eventually raided the place. Many people swore at me behind my back. As a result, I resigned from the neighborhood committee. Right now, the government has appointed my daughter to be in charge.

LIAO: But I get the impression that you are still in charge.

MI: No, not really. My daughter is the real boss. She is in her fifties now. She loves to practice tai chi, do folk dancing with other retired women in the neighborhood, and hang out with people. Her temperament is more suitable for this job.

LIAO: Now that the teahouse has been closed down by police, what are you going to do next?

MI: I had an electrician install a loudspeaker on the rooftop of this office building and set up a mini radio station so I can broadcast news three times a day. Actually, the neighborhood committee ran the radio station for over ten years. Before the 1980s, most residents didn't have TV at home and they couldn't afford to subscribe to newspapers. Therefore, that radio station was very popular. I even hired a professional radio announcer, who would read excerpts from the newspapers or party documents. We also aired revolutionary music, such as "East Is Red."

Our radio program was quite professional and could compete with the big radio station in Beijing. When TV reached the homes of everyone here, nobody cared about radio anymore. But now, I have started again.

LIAO: Let me take a look at your mini radio station. The whole wall is filled with portraits and flags. I can see you still keep the big pictures of Karl Marx, Friedrich Engels, Vladimir Lenin, Joseph Stalin, and Mao Zedong—the world's well-known Communist leaders. I remember seeing them on this wall when I was a kid. They do look like antiques to me.

MI: I have had them for over thirty years.

LIAO: They are quite authentic then. This room is too small for these "great men." You make it seem as though you worship these famous Communists every day.

MI: Well, I can't do that. If we want to set up an altar for them, there are specific rules. You cannot treat the pictures of these great men the same way you do pictures of movie stars. You cannot tilt them, or put them in separate places. There are five equally great men, and they have to line up on the same wall. Otherwise it would be a political mistake.

LIAO: Director Mi, your office looks like a museum of the Mao era. Time seems to have stopped here. I will try to find another time to read every one of those flags and see what is written on them.

MI: Those flags were awarded to me for my contributions to the revolution. Chairman Mao used to teach us: "Don't sit on your accolades. One needs to continue with the good revolutionary work." It's too bad nobody will continue with the Communist revolutionary work today. The work of the neighborhood committee is getting harder and harder. Look, since I relaunched this radio broadcast early this year, I couldn't find any young person to commit to this community radio station. Several old folks in the neighborhood are now taking turns doing the broadcasting. Since we are old and can't see properly, we constantly make mistakes. We have to shorten the radio broadcast time. We read newspaper excerpts and the weather forecast, play music, and air some personal commentaries.

LIAO: What kind of personal commentaries?

MI: For example, in the morning, after we finish the opening music, someone will go on the air to remind folks about morning rush hour traffic and ask residents to take care when they cross the street. He will then talk about the importance of eating breakfast and on how to prevent low blood sugar. He also urges those young people who have been laid off to cheer up and not give up on life. In the evenings, another guy will go on the air, telling residents to close their windows and lock their doors before going to bed. He will offer tips on how to prevent carbon monoxide poisoning, and give the phone numbers for the fire or police department.

LIAO: This is truly like a big Communist family.

MI: Each time I enter this room and become surrounded by these past accolades, my youthful energy comes back.

LIAO: You are still young at heart, but your mind is living in the old days.

THE FORMER RED GUARD

*For many people in China today, the Cultural Revolution con-
jures up images of young students dressed in green army jackets,
wearing red armbands, waving copies of Mao's Little Red Book
and chanting "Long live Chairman Mao!" Known to the world
as "Red Guards," those young rebels raided schools and government agencies, intent on beating up their teachers, intellectuals, and government officials whom they believed were straying
from Mao's revolutionary line. Between 1966 and 1976, the
upheaval led to the deaths of millions of Chinese citizens.*

*Liu Weidong joined a Red Guard group when he was a
high school student in Zhongjiang County, Sichuan Province.
He now lives in Chengdu.*

—⚋—

LIAO YIWU: When did you become a Red Guard?

LIU WEIDONG: I think it was in the summer of 1966. That was the year
when Chairman Mao launched "the Great Proletariat Cultural Revolution." It was his view that the Communist revolution, which had taken
over China in 1949, was starting to lose its impetus. Many Party
bureaucrats focused too much on developing China's economy and
were deviating from socialism. More important, Mao, who was then
seventy-three years old, believed that his senior colleagues were trying
to seize power from him. So he enlisted the support of college and high
school students, who immediately rallied around him.

LIAO: According to history books, many radical students began to turn
on their teachers, administrators, and Party officials, attacking them for
spreading capitalist and bourgeois ideas. In Beijing, students began to
wear armbands, calling themselves the "Red Guards"—the defenders
of Chairman Mao and vanguards of the new revolution.

LIU: Yes. The concept of the Red Guards spread quickly around the country. Students in Sichuan caught on very fast.

LIAO: There were many factions within the Red Guard organization in Sichuan. Which faction did you join?

LIU: I joined the Army of Revolutionary Rebels group, a county-level Red Guard faction. All the nationally famous Red Guard organizations were based in big cities such as Beijing and Shanghai. At the county level, the Red Guards were merely a group of young rebellious hicks. But the Army of Revolutionary Rebels was an exception. We were precocious politically, even though most of us were suffering from malnutrition and looked much smaller than our ages.

LIAO: Compared with today's high school students who are more obsessed with MP3 players and pop music than with the Communist revolution, you guys were really precocious.

LIU: We had no choice. If you didn't pledge to support Chairman Mao, you would be accused of going against history. As you know, our parents who had gone through previous political campaigns all told us that the only way to survive in China was to listen to the Party. So, within a few weeks after the Cultural Revolution started, we were all mobilized. We didn't need to register or get approval to form a Red Guard organization. We would just get our buddies together, come up with a revolutionary name, and have it carved on a rubber or wooden stamp. Then we would go buy some red armbands, get a big red flag, and declare ourselves a Red Guard group. In Lanting County, over a hundred Red Guard organizations were formed within a week.

LIAO: With so many Red Guard groups, which government agency was supervising them?

LIU: None. The county Communist Party branch had already been taken over by the Red Guards. Prominent government officials were locked up as "capitalist roaders." Then all the Red Guard groups coordinated what we called a ten-thousand-person meeting to publicly denounce them as enemies of the people. The meeting was held at a high school playground. Every Red Guard group displayed its own red flag in front of the stage. It was quite festive. Before the meeting started, a contingent of counterrevolutionaries was herded onto the stage. Those enemies included the county chief, the Party secretary, the director of the County Cultural Bureau, the principal of the largest county high school, former landlords, Rightists, and several of our teachers. The Red Guards forced them to wear white paper dunce caps and to hang a black cardboard sign around their necks. They lined up in front of the podium, with their heads down, arms tied at the back. One after another, students went up to the podium, condemning those counterrevolutionaries for representing the Four Old Elements of society. The public condemnations lasted about four to five hours. After the meeting, Red Guards paraded those counterrevolutionaries on the main thoroughfare. Onlookers shouted slogans such as "Down with those who take capitalist roads! Defend Chairman Mao and the Communist revolution." Some spat on their former officials and teachers. Kids threw stones or chased them around with bamboo whips. I noticed that most of the counterrevolutionaries had bloody faces.

In that era, our passion for the revolution and our admiration for Chairman Mao were equally matched by our hatred for those whom we believed went against Mao.

LIAO: Didn't realize persecuting people could give you guys such a high.

LIU: Oh yes. In previous political campaigns, the purges were carried out under the supervision of local Communist Party officials. It was different during the Cultural Revolution. Ordinary folks turned around en masse and began to target those in power. Red Guards beat up whoever they felt were counterrevolutionaries, without worrying about any consequences. It was like catching a pickpocket on the street. Every onlooker wants to get a piece of the action, slapping or kicking the thief. The person who kicked the hardest would get the most applause. That was exactly what happened during the Cultural Revolution.

I also played a role during the ten-thousand-person meeting. My job was to stand behind Mr. Bai, our former school principal. Each time the audience shouted revolutionary slogans, another Red Guard and I would kick Mr. Bai, grab his gray hair, and push his head down farther as a sign of deep repentance. We tied a piece of metal string around his neck, with a big chunk of stone hanging at the other end. I could see the metal string cut into his flesh. Even so, we were still not satisfied and constantly searched for new ways of torturing him. Several days later, he could no longer take it. He had been moaning all day long. At night, he asked permission to use the latrine. I escorted him there and waited outside. Twenty minutes had passed; he didn't come out. So I went in. He wasn't in there. I became really nervous and immediately reported the incident to the Red Guard headquarters. They sent a dozen Red Guards over and we searched all over the latrine and there was no sign of him. While we were discussing whether to put out a most-wanted poster on the street, we heard noises coming from a well outside the latrine. One guy got a very long bamboo stick, and reached down, trying to figure out what was happening. The stick wasn't long enough and it didn't work. So the commander of my Red Guard group ordered me to go down the well myself to check it out.

With a rope tied to my waist I slipped down the side of the well. About ten meters down, I switched the flashlight on and searched the water below. There, I saw a body floating, with its face down. My hair stood on end. My ears were ringing. My body was shaking. I wanted to climb up right away. But if I didn't get the body, I knew I was going to be in big trouble. I composed myself a little bit and called the people from above. They threw down another rope with a hook. I grabbed the hook, attached it to the shirt collar of the dead body, and climbed up as fast as I could. Then people on the ground began to pull the other rope. Halfway up, the shirt collar broke and the body plummeted back into the water like a heavy deepwater bomb. The commander ordered me to go down a second time. After I pulled the body out, we found out it was Mr. Bai. His body was covered with bruises. There was a belt tied to his neck. He seemed to have been choked to death, rather than drowned. Poor Mr. Bai! He was born into a family of rich and conservative intellectuals in the 1940s, when China was still ruled by the Nationalists. While he was in college, he joined the underground Communist Party. After graduation, he went to teach at high schools in the rural areas. He used teaching as a cover to mobilize peasants to rebel against the Nationalist government. After the Communist takeover, he was appointed the principal of a high school in our county. Many times, he turned down promotions and opportunities to work in big cities. When the Cultural Revolution started, we accused him of forcing students to learn Western science and technology.

News of Mr. Bai's death spread fast. It was a mystery, and nobody knew how he managed to sneak out of the latrine and end up down in the well. I was there guarding the latrine. How could he try to kill himself by hanging and then jump into the well? Could it be that he was murdered? Someone must have choked him to death and then threw him into the well. But what was the motive? He was already declared the enemy of the people, and had been punished with severe beatings. Why would anyone bother to kill him?

LIAO: Mr. Bai disappeared "under your watchful eye"? Didn't the police interrogate you?

LIU: Not really. All they did was ask me to write down what I had seen. They quickly reached a conclusion: suicide to escape punishment. In those days, it was very common to see students beat their teachers to death. So, if an accused capitalist was tortured to death, nobody cared. There was another school principal, who was elected as a model Communist leader before the Cultural Revolution. He was a famous horticulturist. He planted many fruit trees inside the school campus and converted the school into an orchard. He had students go to classes in the morning, and assigned them to work in the orchard in the afternoon. For a while, he was a celebrity in the area. People from all over the country came to visit his school. In 1967, his students smashed the farming tools and accused him of being a capitalist, because he had sold the fruits at the local market to fund his school. They locked him up in a classroom. Each time there was a public meeting, he would be the target for condemnation. After the Red Guards got tired of torturing him at public meetings, they forced him to run around the rice paddies every day. That went on for about six months. One day, while he was running, he plunged right into the rice paddies and never got up. He died of exhaustion. The Red Guards were really mad that he had been sent to hell so fast. They pulled his body out and dragged it over to the school auditorium. There, they had another public denunciation meeting before they reported his death to the county. In those days, many of the Public Security Bureaus were paralyzed. Nobody was in charge. Nobody dared to question the case. If they had, they would have been accused of siding with the enemy. It was a lawless society. The words of Chairman Mao were the ultimate law of the land.

It was a crazy time. Even elementary school students were mobilized to rebel against their teachers. Some girls grabbed their female teachers and shaved half of their hair off, calling it the "Yin and Yang" hairstyle. On the street, you would constantly see children carrying Chairman Mao's Little Red Book and a red sword made of wood. They would stop adults on the street, asking them to recite Chairman Mao's quotations. If they made one mistake, the children would stab their back with the wooden sword, and force them to start from the beginning. If they continued to make mistakes, children would report them to the Red Guards, and that person could be charged with "forgetting Chairman Mao's words." If the adult became defensive and refused to admit guilt, he or she could end up getting slapped in the face.

LIAO: I remember that. Looking back, those Red Guards were really like the Nazis. The Cultural Revolution reminds me of the killing of Jews during World War II or the purges under Joseph Stalin in the Soviet Union.

LIU: That's an exaggerated statement. Initially, many of those "capitalists" were beaten up because they wouldn't admit their guilt and attempted to argue with us. As time went by, they became very obedient. If you accused them of being a spy, they would nod their heads and agree with everything you said. So the beatings became less severe. Then we moved our targets to something else. We began to declare war against the old religious temples, which Chairman Mao called "feudalistic and superstitious strongholds." Lanting was a small county, but there were many Buddhist temples, filled with statues and art objects. We first burned scriptures, books, and paintings. Then we used hammers to smash the smaller statues. With large statues, we borrowed rock drills to bore holes in their bodies, and then we smashed their heads off. There was a huge Buddhist statue carved on the cliff of a mountain. We went up there, trying to get rid of it with rock drills but couldn't reach it. One guy managed to get some explosives. That sucker ended up blown into pieces. After the statue was gone, we painted in red a big slogan on the rocks nearby: "Long Live the Great Proletariat Cultural Revolution. Long Live Chairman Mao."

There were also lots of funny tales during that time. Some junior monks in a monastery decided to form a Red Guard rebel group. They tore off their *kasayas* and donned Mao jackets. With their shaved heads, those monks looked very comical. Our group even sent some representatives over to show moral support. The monks dragged the abbot out of the temple, pulling the prayer beads from around his neck, and then replaced the beads with a black cardboard sign. They paraded the abbot and several nuns on the street and had a public denunciation meeting. One monk went up to the podium and accused the abbot of spending too much time reading Buddhist scriptures. They recommended that the abbot should read the revolutionary works of Chairman Mao. Another monk said he once purchased a picture of Chairman Mao from the store and wanted to put it up in the main prayer hall. But the abbot rejected his request by saying that Chairman Mao was not a god, just an ordinary human being. While the young monk was recounting this episode, tears welled up in his eyes. He walked up to the abbot and slapped him in the face. He then raised his arm, shouting: Down with the abbot, the filial descendant of China's leading capitalists. He then turned around to the nuns and shouted: Sister Liu [the senior nun in the temple] is the capitalist's concubine. Down with Buddha, the representative of feudalistic superstitions.

LIAO: That was ridiculous. Didn't you ever think that you guys had gone too far?

LIU: I was born into a family of blue-collar workers. The Cultural Revolution offered me the opportunity to finally trample on those elite. It was glorious. I couldn't get enough of it. My youth, my dream, and my passion were all associated with the Cultural Revolution. The most exciting moment in those days was to see Chairman Mao in person, when he greeted millions of Red Guards in Beijing's Tiananmen Square.

LIAO: Tell me how you ended up going to Beijing to see Chairman Mao.

LIU: Between 1966 and 1967, Red Guard organizations around the country started a nationwide movement to travel and spread Mao's words to the masses. The final destination for the Red Guards would be in Beijing so we could get a glimpse of our Great Leader. My friends and I formed a "Long March Red Guard Touring Group." We walked hundreds of kilometers to the city of Chengdu. All the hotels in the city had opened up to us. The city had even turned the theaters into youth hostels because there weren't enough hotels to accommodate all the Red Guards. Since we were one of the earliest groups, we managed to get into a nice hotel. All we had to do was to show our Red Guard badges and we could eat and live for free. During the day, we would go out to the local market to buy or swap pins and badges of Chairman Mao. By the way, at the height of the Cultural Revolution, every region and every company designed and produced its own Chairman Mao pins and badges. They became collector's items.

Not long after, we all became bored with Chengdu and decided to board the train for Beijing. When we showed up at the station, the Beijing-bound trains were quite full. My buddies and I climbed in through the windows. Each car was dangerously packed: people lay on the baggage racks or under the seats; many simply stood back-to-back in the aisles. It was hard to breathe. Despite the hard conditions, none of us wanted to get off. It was already September. We had heard that Chairman Mao would greet the Red Guards one more time that year. There was no way we would miss it.

The train finally moved haltingly, but half an hour later, it stopped. Then it moved again. There was no schedule to follow and the train just took its time. Each time the train stopped, the heat inside the cars would become unbearable. But we didn't dare to drink water because there was no access to toilets, which were filled with people who couldn't find a space. We could only use the toilet when the train pulled into a station. Many girls ended up peeing in their pants. When guys couldn't hold it, some simply squeezed close to the window, took out their stuff, and then aimed at the outside. During those desperate moments, everyone was so understanding.

Believe it or not, we were on the train for over forty-eight hours before we finally arrived in Beijing.

We slept inside a classroom at an elementary school. On the night before Chairman Mao's appearance, we were so excited that we couldn't sleep. At about 3 a.m., we put on our green Red Guard jackets and walked for about eight kilometers toward Tiananmen Square. By the time we got there, the main road had already been cordoned off by police. We had to walk around and follow the crowd to another entrance. Tiananmen Square, which is about 440,000 square meters, was fully packed with Red Guards. I looked around and saw a sea of green uniforms and red flags, which were waving in the early morning breezes. Everyone felt so proud, anticipating the most exciting moment to come.

We stood in the square from early morning until noon. Finally Mao emerged in the tower over the Gate of Heavenly Peace. Instantly, the square became alive with the deafening sounds of slogan shouting. We waved red flags and the Little Red Book, crying and chanting, "Long live Chairman Mao." Mao took off his green army cap and waved it in his hand. Through the microphone, he shouted back, "Long live the people." You wouldn't believe the excitement that the Great Leader had generated. We felt the Great Leader and the people were one. We stayed in Tiananmen Square for several hours under the hot sun, jumping and screaming. Our adrenaline was running high. Many of us lost our voices and couldn't talk for several days afterward. We were so euphoric, happy, and blissful.

LIAO: Do you still have the same euphoric feeling you had then?

LIU: No, but I still cherish those memories. I will never forget them. We were so pure and innocent.

LIAO: What do you mean you were pure and innocent? Beating up your teachers, smashing ancient relics, and engaging in armed fights among the various Red Guard groups, those were not the doings of pure and innocent people.

LIU: We were fighting for our beliefs. We were defending Chairman Mao and the Communist revolution. Anyone who obstructed the revolution deserved to be punished. Today, most people no longer have any spiritual aims. Money is everything and people are killing one another for money. Women sell their bodies for money. Corrupt officials sacrifice their principles and violate laws for money. A son can strangle a mother to death to get her money. Money corrupts the soul of this country. Where are the Communist ideals and beliefs? Oh well, my generation was so passionate about Communism. We gave up schooling to engage in the revolution. Later on, when Chairman Mao encouraged high school graduates to settle down in the countryside to receive reeducation from peasants, we followed Mao's holy words, bid goodbye to our parents in the city, and left without any hesitation. In other parts of the world, people in their teens and early twenties were learning science, technology, arts, and literature in colleges. In China, we wasted our younger days plowing and planting in the rice paddies. Now that the Mao era is long gone, people of my generation have become a bunch of useless simpletons. Those capitalists, who used to be the target for persecution, are now ruling the world. The Chinese government calls itself a socialist country, but it has gone full-blown capitalistic. As I have told you, since people like me didn't get to go to college when we were young, we have become the first ones to be laid off. Compared with many of my fellow Red Guards who are still stuck in the countryside, poor and neglected, I'm pretty lucky. At least I have managed to move back to the city.

LIAO: What's your status now?

LIU: The company I work for used to be state-owned. It's been insolvent for years, but the government subsidized it. With the current market reform, the government has abandoned state enterprises. My company is on the verge of bankruptcy. Half of the people in my company have been laid off. I work in the human resources department and have managed to stay on. But life is just going downhill day by day. I've been told that a private developer has expressed an interest in buying the company, demolishing the old factory buildings, and building luxury residential houses. Who knows what will happen next. I don't even dare to think about it. Oh well, so far, my life has been a total failure and a waste. I'm already forty-nine. If I lose my job, I can't see myself starting all over again. It's too difficult.

   During the Cultural Revolution, I remember we felt we were invincible and aspired to save the whole world with Communism. I would never have imagined that I could end up like this half a century later. I can't even save myself.

THE COUNTERREVOLUTIONARY

There used to be more than twenty political prisoners locked up inside a prison in northern Sichuan. All of the prisoners were participants in the student democracy movement of 1989. They were charged with "propagating and instigating counterrevolutionary activities." Their sentences ranged from two to twelve years.

Wan Baocheng, who was then thirty-five years old, came from what we call a "red family" because his father was a senior official and had fought with Chairman Mao during the war against the Nationalists in the 1940s. From the way he talked and behaved, one could hardly tell that Wan had a distinguished parent and that he used to be a powerful official himself. During that special time in 1989 when the whole country woke up to the call of democracy, he became an enemy of the Party.

This interview took place in February of 1993 when I was locked up in the same jail with Wan. He was released in 1994.

LIAO YIWU: Among all those who have been locked up here since the 1989 student democracy movement, you held the highest position within the government. Is that right?

WAN BAOCHENG: I guess so. Before I landed in here, I was the deputy director of the largest government-owned bank in Sichuan. I was the best of the crop in my field. I used to be an expert on the government's economic policies. Each time the government issued a new policy, I would study it very diligently. I was also a keen reader of the Communist Party official newspaper—*People's Daily.* It was the basic training for a government official. I followed the Communist Party line at all times and avoided making mistakes.

LIAO: How did a distinguished government official and businessman like you end up here?

WAN: In May of 1989, I happened to be in Beijing on a business trip. My assignment there was to collect an overdue loan payment. We had planned to send a clerk to do the collection, but the students' pro-democracy demonstrations were at full throttle. The whole country was in chaos. As a measure of prudence, I decided to go myself.

LIAO: Why did your bank issue a loan to someone way out in Beijing?

WAN: The company was headquartered in Beijing and had opened up a branch in Sichuan. Then the branch was closed and all the assets were transferred back to its headquarters. Anyhow, I took the train to Beijing at the end of May. It was such bad timing. As you remember, the student demonstrations started in April to commemorate the passing of the former Communist Party secretary Hu Yaobang. Then the demonstrations turned into protests against government corruption and a call for democracy. By the end of May, when the government refused to engage in a dialogue with protesters, the movement spread all over the country. More students poured into Beijing.

    The minute I walked out of the train station, which was fairly close to Tiananmen Square, I could feel the tension. People from all walks of life joined the students and the whole city was paralyzed. Since the government media blocked out news relating to the demonstrations, rumors that people heard through the grapevine were getting more and more dramatic. One minute, you heard someone say that the air force had been mobilized and would parachute troops into Tiananmen Square for the crackdown. Another minute, you heard that a pro-student general, supported by several senior Chinese leaders, had started a coup.

    My mind was pretty much all set, and I didn't believe any of those rumors. My father used to serve in the Communist troops under Mao and he pledged full loyalty to the Party. Somehow, I must have inherited some of the loyalty genes from him. People around me were all in a frenzy, but I chose to stay calm and focus on my work.

    I went directly to the company's headquarters. The building was empty. There was one person at the reception desk. She told me that the managers and staff had gone to Tiananmen Square, waving banners and flags to show support for the students. So I left and checked into a hotel near Cuiwei Road in downtown Beijing. My room was on the second floor, with the window facing a busy intersection. I could see residents and students march by under my window. Before dusk, I went downstairs and watched people gather in small groups, exchanging the latest news and rumors. Someone standing on a wooden box said about thirty thousand soldiers would enter the city to keep order. Another one in the audience argued that there would be twenty thousand. Anyway, things around the hotel didn't quiet down until after midnight.

I stayed inside my room reading work-related material. The next day, I went back to the company again and couldn't find anyone. So I decided to postpone my trip back for another two days. On the night of June 3, 1989, I could see that the street outside my window was getting more and more crowded. The hotel was eerily empty because all the staff members had left to join the students in the street. Someone was standing on the stairs of the front entrance, and was delivering a speech on how to set up roadblocks to stop tanks from entering the city. The crowd got denser by the hour. I had never seen people so passionately involved since the Cultural Revolution. But for me, nothing changed my long-standing support for the government. I continued to be nonchalant and even went to bed earlier than usual.

Later that night, the commotion outside the hotel became louder. I got up, closed my window, and went back to bed. I kept reminding myself that I was a government official and shouldn't join the mob outside. So I took a sleeping pill and soon I was out cold.

I was awakened by loud gunshots outside. I remember going to the window, and I saw soldiers shooting and tanks rolling in the street. Like I have said, I had never seen anything like that in my whole life. During the Cultural Revolution, when different factions of the Red Guards were fighting against each other, some gunfights were involved. But this was nothing like that. On that night, the ones carrying guns on the street were our own soldiers. They shouldn't shoot at innocent citizens. Their guns should have been aimed at our enemies outside China. I wanted to check to see what was going on, but I was still under the influence of the pill. My head was heavy. I soon fell asleep again.

At about ten in the morning, a loud knock on the door woke me up.

It was the cleaning lady. She walked in and started to scream: Sir, how could you sleep under such conditions? Look at your window. I looked in the direction of her finger, and saw the window had been hit by a stray bullet and glass was shattered all over the floor. Thank heaven I hadn't stood by the window long that night. Otherwise I would have been shot dead. The cleaning lady told me that a guy on the tenth floor had reached his head out to yell at the soldiers on the street. He was hit by a bullet and died. When I heard this story, blood rose to my head. I couldn't be an outsider anymore.

LIAO: So you changed your views about the student movement.

WAN: Yes. I looked out of my window and saw the wreckage on the street. I saw hundreds of helmet-wearing soldiers patrolling the street. Every couple of minutes, there would be a tank rumbling by. A young civilian guy was running on the street. The soldiers ordered him to stop. I could tell that the guy was scared. He stopped for a few moments, but then started running to escape. One soldier raised his gun and shot at him from behind. The guy fell forward, and then plopped down, motionless. It was like in one of those war movies. I don't think my dad, who fought in the Chinese civil war, had witnessed such horrible scenes before—a soldier killing an unarmed civilian.

I was stunned. The cleaning lady pulled me from the window and asked me to go back to bed. She warned me: The soldiers have become crazy. If you get hit by a stray bullet, it will be your tough luck. Nobody is taking responsibility.

Well, I didn't care. During the next few days, I showed up on the street and talked with those who had witnessed the government brutality on the night of June 4. I visited two hospitals and saw students and residents who had been wounded by bullets. However, when I turned on the TV in the evenings, there was no mention of the massacre. The official version was that the Chinese soldiers had defended the capital from a small handful of "hooligans" and that nobody was killed. To me as an economist, the most important thing was honesty. I felt the urge to write. I jotted down everything I had seen and heard. In the past, I had only written numerous accounting reports or office memos. Overnight, I became a different kind of writer. My pen was flying. Sometimes I wrote with total outrage, and other times with tears streaming down my cheeks.

Within a week, I finally finished the draft of my article. It was seven pages long. I corrected some grammatical errors and rewrote some passages. Since we didn't have computers then, I had to hand-copy the draft neatly on fresh paper. I called my article "An Eyewitness Account of June 4." Before I left Beijing, I secretly went to a store and Xeroxed one hundred copies.

On the train back from Beijing, I began to distribute the article to my fellow passengers. It was about a week after the government crackdown. All the student leaders had been placed on the government's most-wanted list. Police were on heightened alert and constantly searched the train cars for former leaders who were on the run. I was very cautious. Luckily, many people pitched in to help. By the time the train pulled into my hometown station, I had given away all the copies.

Life became normal again. I took a couple of days off and then resumed my work at the bank, as if nothing had happened. In the back of my mind though, I was nervous.

In the following month, every employee at the bank was forced to condemn the student movement and to pledge support for the Party. Many people who were privately outraged at the government massacre had to show compliance in public. Protesting against the government was like throwing an egg against a big rock—a futile attempt with big personal loss. Everyone was supposed to read articles from the *People's Daily* and toe the Party line. At staff meetings, I also voiced my support for the government's decision. As the deputy director of the bank, I had to take the lead in the brainwash movement. At the end of the month, since no employee at my bank claimed any involvement in local demonstrations, we all ended up with a handsome bonus. I knew that many people had joined the demonstrations, but nobody reported on the others.

As time went by, I almost forgot about what I had done in Beijing, but the police didn't. Two months later, I think it was in August, my director called me into his office. When I walked in, I saw two other strangers in there too. My director said, Mr. Wan, please confess everything you did in Beijing. His words sent cold chills down my spine. Almost instinctively, I pretended to be dumb: Director, you know very well what I have done. Upon hearing this, my director's face turned red and he said: Unfortunately, we don't know what you have done.

Later on, I found out that the police had obtained the article from several passengers who had helped with the police search. They had been following me for quite some time. After I was detained, many people refused to believe that, as a shrewd official, I could have been involved in something like that. At a briefing to the city council regarding my case, the municipal Party secretary even defended me by saying: It's impossible. He was born into a revolutionary family. His father and I joined the Communist army in the same year. Mr. Wan Junior is also a good Communist. He was admitted to the Party at the age of eighteen. He grew up under my nose and has always been a good boy and an excellent banker. It can't be true. The Party secretary even pleaded: This kid is a rising star. Please don't make the wrong charges and ruin his career.

The police, becoming impatient with the defensive remarks of my family and friends, invited my relatives to an office and showed them my article and the testimonies from the hotel staff and passengers on the train. Everyone was shocked. Embarrassed by the good things he had said about me, the Party secretary signed my arrest warrant.

Faced with the evidence, I had no choice but to confess. Luckily, I didn't have an accomplice and my case was relatively simple. But instead of admitting any wrongdoing, I openly declared that what I had written in the article was true. That was when the shit hit the fan. My dad's former colleagues—I mean those who held important positions in the city, my boss at the bank, and even leaders at the Public Security Bureau—came to the detention center to reason with me, and to persuade me to retract my statement. They advised me to plead guilty by claiming that some evil people had forced me to make up shameless lies to slander and sabotage the reputation of soldiers guarding Tiananmen Square.

I told both the interrogators and my dad's friends: As a Party member, I swear to Chairman Mao that everything I wrote is true. One interrogator banged on the desk and said: You are no longer a Communist Party member. They have expelled you. But if you admit your crime and be cooperative, we will reduce your sentence. I wouldn't budge: As a Communist Party official, honesty is something I live by. The interrogator was furious: Mr. Wan, don't be so fucking arrogant. You used to be the deputy director of the city's largest bank. That was your past. Right now you are nothing. I didn't buy his attitude: I'm not a corrupt official. Don't you dare speak to me like that! He replied in a cynical tone: You would have been lucky if you had been involved in a corruption case. At least your dad could use his connection to bail you out. You could still go home and live a normal life. In China, you know as well as I do, once you get involved in a political case, your whole life is done. Don't you understand? I snapped back: Since this is a serious political case, I can't admit any wrongdoing. Otherwise, it will be like dumping shit all over my head.

Nobody could change my mind. In the end, they notified my dad. I was told that he trembled with fury. He cursed me and let out a loud scream: That little short-lived bastard. He then collapsed onto the floor. My siblings took him to a hospital nearby and the doctor said he had suffered a stroke. He was partially paralyzed, but his mind was very lucid. So the police decided to bring my old man out to the detention center to see me. Using my dad as a bargaining chip totally destroyed my last piece of confidence. When police wheeled him into the detention center courtyard, I was heartbroken. He was a healthy person before I left. Now he was in a wheelchair. It was just . . . too much for me to bear. I threw myself at his feet and burst into tears. As you know, I'm the only boy in the family. He had pinned all his hopes on me. He named me after the Baocheng Railroad, China's first cross-province railway, which opened up in 1957. He was hoping that my future could be as developed as the railroad. When I was growing up, I tried to live up to his expectations, and I did very well in school. He used to tell people that I was the best thing that had ever happened to him. He could never have imagined visiting his son in prison.

When police saw me crying like that, they began to think that their game plan was working. One guy, who was the police chief, helped me to my feet and said: If you admit your crime, we will be able to reduce your sentence. You can spend more time with your dad, taking care of him. You can continue to work hard at the bank to make up for your crimes. There were many innocent people like you who have been deceived by the counterrevolutionaries. People and the government will forgive your past. I hope you can return to the bosom of the Communist Party and the Chinese people. My father kept nodding while the police chief delivered his lecture. The old man even summoned enough strength to raise his hand and said, Do what the Party tells you to.

I became really agitated. I raised my voice and said: Dad, you know very well what kind of person I am. One of the things that I have learned from you is to be honest, and never lie or cheat. What I have written is all true. Innocent people were killed in Beijing.

He interrupted me and gave me a nasty look: You only witness what you are allowed to see. So what if you witnessed the killing? Those counterrevolutionaries deserved to die. We fought hard with Chairman Mao and have made China red. We can't easily give up. We can't allow the former Nationalist government or the American imperialists to destroy Communism in China. I think you have sat your butt on the wrong chair. You have moved to the enemy camp. You have slacked off on your political studies and have been corrupted by Western thinking. It's very dangerous. You should accept the punishment. You are my son and you should listen to me.

Seeing that my dad was sweating profusely, I couldn't bear to argue with him anymore. The police felt very relieved and asked me to record an "I plead guilty" message in front of my dad. I did.

LIAO: You didn't raise any hell after your dad left, did you?

WAN: I finally decided to compromise and admit that "my action had jeopardized the reputation of our country and the Communist Party." But I didn't accept the charges that I had made up stories and spread rumors. Those charges were such insults to my character. Do you remember that poor Chinese guy on American TV? Following the government crackdown, that guy told an American reporter on camera that there was blood all over Tiananmen Square and that thousands of people had been killed. He had exaggerated, of course. After the interview was aired in the U.S., the Chinese government was furious and put this guy on the government's most-wanted list. A week later, he was caught and was sentenced to ten years in prison. I'm not that guy. I didn't exaggerate or lie. Anyway, my case is not over yet. Someday, when the official verdict on Tiananmen Square is reversed, I'm going to sue the government for wrongful imprisonment.

LIAO: You've been sentenced to four years in prison, right?

WAN: Yes, four years. It could have been worse. During the final court hearing, the judge said that my sentence was reduced due to my cooperative attitude. That was such baloney. Before I got here, I had never encountered any counterrevolutionaries. I'm now locked up with over twenty counterrevolutionaries who were involved in the June 4 student movement. All of them are just ordinary folks: teachers, college students, workers, migrant workers, a deputy county village chief, a tax collector, a journalist, and some unemployed youngsters. There is a student from a technical high school who was not even eighteen when he was arrested. Everyone is so kind, not only to one another, but also to animals.

Let me tell you a story. One morning, a pigeon suddenly fell from the sky to the ground. I was the first one to discover the poor thing. Initially, the pigeon haltingly stretched its wings and attempted to fly again. But, seconds later, it plunged like a piece of stone to the courtyard ground. We all dashed out and carefully picked it up. Luckily, the ground was covered by a layer of snow, which saved the life of that poor thing. But its wings and legs were broken. This small accident glued all the inmates together and kept us busy for quite some time. We took turns caring for that little pigeon. One guy made a cast out of a bamboo shoot and attached it to the pigeon's leg. Another inmate stole some antibiotic ointment and cotton swabs from the prison clinic to treat its wounds. My new friend, Little Yang, got some uncooked rice from the prison kitchen, chewed the rice in his mouth to make a pulp, and then fed it to the pigeon. At first, the pigeon wouldn't take anything. Little Yang and Old Lei pried its beak open and gently fed it down its throat. During the next few days, we dug up worms, and saved rice, beans, and corn from our own ration to feed the bird. We divided our group into five nursing teams. During the daytime, when we labored away in the field, we hid the pigeon inside a mosquito net over an upper-level bunk bed. We put a small bowl of rice on the bed and placed a piece of newspaper under the pigeon to catch its droppings. Generally speaking, political prisoners were treated slightly better than ordinary criminals. Guards seldom checked our cells. After two weeks, the pigeon was fully recovered. It became restless and was ready to say goodbye. Everyone felt very sad. At the same time, we all envied the pigeon's ability to fly to a free world outside.

The time finally came. The pigeon fluttered its wings, turned around and around on the ground, and kept cooing to us. It was such a smart bird. Lao Lei had an idea: Why don't we use this pigeon to send a message to the outside world?

Everyone thought it was a great idea. We found a pen and a piece of paper. Lao Lei wrote a message on our behalf: We are the twenty-three political prisoners. We are in jail because of our involvement in the

June 4 student movement. We aim to overthrow the totalitarian system and bring democracy to China. That's our aspiration. We hope people outside don't forget about us and about our fight for democracy.

We tied the paper to the leg of the pigeon and held a farewell ceremony in the courtyard. We named the pigeon our "messenger for democracy" and released it. The pigeon circled above our heads and then up to the sky. A few minutes later, for some unknown reason, the bird came back, circled around, and flew in the direction of the correctional officers' dorm building.

Everyone was so carried away and nobody saw the little movement at the end as anything unusual. Afterward, we would look at the clock on the wall, trying to figure out where the pigeon was at that very moment. Lao Lei wondered if the one we saved could be a special messenger from Hong Kong or Taiwan. Little Yang totally believed it. He said it was highly possible. The pigeon from the free world deliberately landed in this prison to carry a message of hope to us. I nodded in agreement. Inside this hopeless prison, it was better to have something to believe in. Hope made time pass fast.

LIAO: You guys attached too much symbolic meaning to an ordinary pigeon. The world is so big. I wonder where the pigeon finally landed.

WAN: Be patient, I haven't finished the story yet. The next morning, our courtyard was suddenly surrounded by armed police with machine guns. Prison officers ransacked our beds and our clothes. All kinds of paper products—books, poems or essays written on toilet paper, journals—were taken away. Then several officers came in to hold individual talks with each one of us. They wanted to investigate what they called the "pigeon incident."

LIAO: What happened? Did the pigeon get shot down by the police?

WAN: It turns out the pigeon was a pet raised by one of the prison officers. When the pigeon dropped to the courtyard, the guard thought it might have been killed. Then, two weeks later, his pet miraculously returned, with a note tied to its leg. The officer immediately reported it to his boss. They were thrilled by the precious intelligence his pet had gathered.

LIAO: You guys saved a spy pigeon!

WAN: Our hope was dashed in seconds. Several of us were locked up in solitary confinement for two days. Luckily, they didn't find any hard evidence. But, after that incident, our whole group was separated. I'm now staying with murderers, rapists, and drug dealers. While doing physical labor outside, each political prisoner has been assigned two or three guards. Life is getting very miserable.

LIAO: What are you planning to do after you get out of here?

WAN: I don't think they will allow me to go back to work in the government bank anymore. The government will never give a counterrevolutionary an opportunity to be financially successful. I don't know what I will do. Maybe I should become a professional democracy advocate. I guess I'm supposed to be a piece of stone, being used to pave the way for bigger things to happen in China. If that's my fate, I accept it, even if it means sacrificing my life.

THE TIANANMEN FATHER

In early 2005, when I was visiting Beijing, I finally had the chance to meet Professor Ding Zilin. She founded the Tiananmen Mothers, a group of more than 150 courageous families who lost relatives on June 4, 1989, when fully armed soldiers and military tanks rolled into Beijing and crushed the student pro-democracy movement. Professor Ding's only child, a seventeen-year-old high school student, was killed by a soldier's bullet on a street west of Tiananmen Square as he confronted the troops, trying to persuade them to stop using force against unarmed students.

In the past nineteen years, I have heard many heroic stories about Professor Ding, who refused to be silenced by the Chinese government. Following the massacre, she was the first to step forward and talk to the Western media about her son's death. Despite constant police harassment, house arrests, and detention, she has never ceased to gather information about other Tiananmen victims and to raise funds from overseas to help victims' families. She has never stopped challenging the government claim that the pro-democracy movement was a "counterrevolutionary riot" and that soldiers never opened fire on citizens.

On that visit, Professor Ding told me about her upcoming book, Looking for the June 4 Victims, *which has documented the names and stories of those who were killed in the bloody crackdown. As I was leaving, she handed me a card and encouraged me to contact Wu Dingfu, a fellow Sichuanese who lost a son in the massacre.*

Since Ding's book contained only a small paragraph about Wu's son, I was curious to find out more. After I returned to Chengdu, I made a phone call to Wu, who lives in Xinjing Township, not far from me. When he learned that Professor Ding was my friend, he became very enthusiastic and immediately invited me over for a visit.

On the morning of May 19, 2005, I left Chengdu on a shabby intercity bus. Three hours later, I arrived in Xinjing

Township. A tricycle cabdriver took me to the Janing Apartment Complex. I found Building A, Unit 4, and stepped into the dark hallway. A man was standing near the stairway on the second floor. He had a big prominent nose. "You must be Liao Yiwu," he said. I nodded. As I followed him through a door on the right, I heard footsteps behind. I turned around and saw a gray-haired woman. She was Wu's wife. "I was out waiting for you. We must have missed each other," she said apologetically.

The living room was that of a family going downhill. The walls were bare and the furniture old. A large black-and-white picture on top of a desk caught my eye. It was a picture of a young man. That youthful and perpetual smile beaming from his face and the eyes behind the glasses triggered in me a flood of sad memories of that turbulent time. As I was lost in thought, Wu handed me a cup of tea and said, "That was my son, Guofeng, when he was a freshman in college . . ."

—⁂—

LIAO YIWU: You probably know that the purpose of my visit is to talk with you in detail about what happened to your son and the rest of your family during and after June 4. You are not afraid to revisit this painful and sensitive topic, are you?

WU DINGFU: Not at all. After my son died, all hopes for my family were gone. I'm not afraid of being interviewed. Where do you want me to start?

LIAO: Why don't we go in chronological order and start with Guofeng as a kid.

WU: OK, I will try. I have three children. The eldest is a daughter. Guofeng, who was born in 1968, was the second. He had a younger brother. Three generations of the family were born and raised in Xinjing. Ours has always been a working-class family. I was born in 1942. When I was growing up, I experienced the most turbulent years in Chinese history—the resistance war against Japan and the civil war between the Nationalists and the Communists. My family was quite poor and I constantly suffered hunger as a kid. I started school late and didn't finish junior high school until 1960. My family couldn't afford to pay for my education anymore. So I dropped out of school and got a job as a requisition clerk at a small factory. My wife was born in 1944 and was also raised in a similarly poor family. She didn't finish high school either. After we were married, she stayed at home as a housewife.

LIAO: So the whole family depended on your salary.

WU: Yes. In the 1970s, my monthly salary was thirty yuan [US$4]. Guofeng's mother would pick up some odd jobs such as sewing buttons or lock-stitching shirt or pants borders for tailors. So between the two of us, we made about forty yuan per month. We had to use that money to raise three children. It was under Chairman Mao. Nobody dared to run any small business for extra cash. Life was hard but we took comfort in the fact that our second child, Guofeng, was really smart. He really made us proud. His grandparents doted on him, treating him like a shiny pearl in the palm of their hands. His grandpa was a tricycle driver, but he had taught himself how to read and write. He became fairly well educated. In his spare time, he would come babysit Guofeng and teach him how to write Chinese characters. Under his grandpa's tutelage, Guofeng excelled in elementary school. He was always at the top of his class and earned lots of honors. Even at an early age, we could tell that he was made for big things in the future.

LIAO: I guess poor kids are more motivated to excel.

WU: Due to our family's dire financial situation, I persuaded Guofeng to apply to a technical school after he graduated from junior high. He could learn some practical skills at the technical school and get a good steady job, an iron rice bowl. In those years, getting into college was very competitive. Only 2 to 3 percent of the high school graduates could get the opportunity. My eldest finished junior high school and could easily have gotten into a technical school. But we bowed to her wish and let her complete senior high school and take the national college entrance exam. Guess what? She didn't make the list. Since the whole town was filled with high school graduates like her, it was hard to get a job. For several years, she just idled around the house. So I didn't want the same thing to happen to Guofeng. But Guofeng was a smart-ass. He made a nice promise to me, then he secretly took the senior high school entrance exams. Since he had gotten very high scores, he was accepted. By the time I found out, the rice was already cooked—too late for me to intervene.

So I accepted reality. I decided to tighten my belt and do everything I could to support him. Luckily, in the 1980s, China was changing. People were allowed to start their own businesses. Guofeng's mother set up a stall in front of our house, selling small groceries to subsidize our income. I did the household chores after work and took care of the children. I soon forgave Guofeng because he continued to remain at the top of his class.

The last year of senior high was critical. Several months before the college entrance exam, all students had to attend intensive exam-preparation classes. Many of my neighbors' kids began to give up every type of extracurricular activity and stayed up very late at night to prepare for the seven tests that made up the exam. But Guofeng continued with his usual routine and looked quite relaxed. I got worried and constantly pestered him: Passing the exam is your only way out. Otherwise, with your nerdy looks, no factory will want to hire you. Each time he heard my nagging, he would adjust the glasses on the bridge of his nose and say: No worry, old man. I know what I'm doing. I still didn't trust him. I went to see his teacher. He laughed and repeated the same thing: There is nothing to worry about. Your kid does very well. Make sure he gets enough rest so he can be ready for the exam.

LIAO: You were more nervous than he was.

WU: My generation had been tossed around so much by Chairman Mao's political campaigns. Our lives were all ruined and wasted. We pinned all our hopes on our children. That's why we could be overly pushy and desperate. A couple of weeks later, the three-day national college entrance exam began. It was in the summer of 1986, and hot as hell. On the first morning, I put him on the back of my bicycle and pedaled him to the testing center. After he walked in, I joined hundreds of other parents and waited patiently outside. Not long after, several students were carried out of the classrooms on stretchers because they had passed out. I was so relieved that my son had survived the initial tension. At lunchtime, when his mother put the specially prepared meat dishes on the table, I asked how he did. He simply said, in his usual laid-back kind of way: Not too good. Good heavens! I was expecting a more upbeat answer. Oh well, I didn't want to say anything that could affect his concentration on the rest of his exams. So I simply told him to take a nap and get ready for the afternoon test. I waited outside in the afternoon, all sweaty. When he came out later, he repeated the same thing: Not too good. My heart sank like a big piece of rock. That night, I lost sleep. In the next three days, my nerves were stretched to the limit. I felt like I was going to have a heart attack.

LIAO: Didn't you have to go to work?

WU: I had asked for three days off. My boss was very understanding. The whole nation focused its attention on the exam because it was so critical for a child's future. At the end of the third day, when he came out, I couldn't hold it anymore: Tell me what has happened? He finally smiled: Old man, I don't mean to brag. If I fail, 95 percent of the students won't even have a chance. I was stunned, but felt so relieved. He then asked for some cash: My classmates and I have decided to treat ourselves for our hard work. We are going to take turns hosting parties at our homes. I immediately offered him one hundred yuan [US$13], which was a lot of money then. To tell you the truth, I had never been that generous in my whole life. But I was so carried away.

Two weeks after the exam, the test results were publicized: he got the highest score in the whole Xinjing Township, averaging 91.5 in seven subjects. As you can imagine, my whole family was overjoyed. Neighbors and relatives from afar came to congratulate us. It was such an honor. Then the authorities did a political background check and he passed. Soon, an acceptance letter arrived from People's University in Beijing. I held the letter and burst out crying. Like I said, generations of my family had been working class. He was the first one in the Wu family to be a local champion in the national exam and to be enrolled in a prestigious university in the capital city. I sincerely believed that my family's fortune was finally changing for the better.

The day he left Xinjing, my factory sent a special car and drove him to the train station in Chengdu. The station was fully packed and we had to wait for several hours. Seeing that we were very sad, he tried to cheer us up and told us not to worry about him. He was really different from those spoiled rich kids.

LIAO: Was this in the fall of 1986?

WU: Yes. He turned eighteen that year and he was admitted to the industrial economic management department. Look at this group picture. He and his dorm mates had it taken when they first moved in. Guofeng was a very independent kid. He got along with his classmates well and quickly adjusted to big-city life in Beijing. He was elected deputy class leader.

We sent him one hundred yuan every month to cover his food and other necessities. As society became more and more open, his mother's grocery business was taking off. Our life was getting better. In his second year, he began to date a girl from another department at the same university. She came from the northeastern city of Changchun. Both of her parents were medical professors. Initially, we objected to it, for fear that his relationship with that girl could jeopardize his studies. But Guofeng was stubborn and he wouldn't listen to us. In the summer, he asked for more money, saying that he was accompanying his girlfriend to Changchun to meet her parents. So we did send him money.

LIAO: The girl in this picture is quite pretty. Looks like they were madly in love!

WU: The girl was quite politically active. She soon became a Communist Party member. Guofeng brought her back to Xinjing in their sophomore year. When we saw they were so happy together, we became more supportive. We could see that they were a good match. Of course, after Guofeng died, she was still very young and naturally made other choices. Since People's University offered her a teaching job after graduation, she was under a lot of pressure to remain silent about June 4. I totally understand it. I choose not to talk too much about her so we don't get her into trouble.

LIAO: I understand.

WU: Anyhow, things worked out smoothly for Guofeng. He was energetic and full of hope for the future. Of course, he was the only hope of our family. Then, in April of 1986, he sent a three-page letter home, telling us about the death of Party secretary Hu Yaobang—

LIAO: It should be in April of 1989.

WU: You are right. I'm sorry. It was in 1989, 1989! That was the longest letter he had ever written. The letter was filled with excitement. He used very poetic language when he described the memorial service in Tiananmen Square, the demonstrations on the street, the slogan shouting, and the eulogies. He said all his classmates and teachers were involved. I immediately wrote him back and reminded him to focus on his studies and stay out of politics.

LIAO: That was a very typical response of Chinese parents.

WU: We were not educated enough to advise him. But we knew instinctively that he could face terrible consequences if he opposed the totalitarian government. My generation went through many political campaigns. We've seen them all. One minute, the Party seems to relax its political control. Once you let down your guard, they come out to get you. They've played this trick for years. The Communist leaders change their face like the April weather. I guess living with the fear of persecution made us jaded and overcautious. Guofeng lived in Beijing and was at the center of everything. He was hot-blooded and wouldn't listen to our advice. We wrote back four or five times and I couldn't get him to change his mind. In one of his letters, he asked for one thousand yuan [US$130]. I bowed to his request and sent him the money over a period of two months.

LIAO: That was a big sum of money. Why did he need so much money?

WU: He told me he had lost his bicycle. He also needed the money to cover his books and food. I was so concerned about him. I sort of spoiled him a little bit.

LIAO: Was he up to something with that money?

WU: I was completely in the dark. I became so worried, but the only way to reach him was through letters. I knew that he and other students were pursuing the right path for China and it was hard to turn him around. But I kept warning him. In my letters, I wrote: The Communist Party is brutal. They have persecuted thousands of people to death in the past and have never even bothered to apologize or make compensation. Guofeng, you have been blessed with the good karma brought about by the hard work of generations of the Wu family. You were born at the right time, in the post-Mao era. You have the opportunity to enter college. If you study hard, you will have a promising future. You will change the miserable fortune of our family. Don't ruin it.

Oh well, Guofeng was still the young cub, quite inexperienced. Of course, he wouldn't listen to my advice. In the end, he didn't want to get into any arguments with me. He simply stopped writing. Later on, after his death, we found out that he had purchased a camera with that money. He told his classmates that he wanted to record history and leave some valuable snapshots for future generations.

LIAO: He was quite visionary.

WU: We were in a state of feverish fear, like ants crawling on a hot tin pan. After work, I came home and stared at the TV all night long. Initially, the government media called the student demonstrations a patriotic movement. Then, on April 26, the *People's Daily* newspaper carried an editorial, calling the movement a riot. Those bastards! Then, in late April and May, there were more protests against the editorial in the *People's Daily*, followed by a hunger strike. Students knelt in front of the Great Hall of the People to present their petition to the senior leaders. Then Premier Li Peng hosted a dialogue with student leaders. After that, the government imposed martial law . . . I couldn't take it anymore, I wanted to travel to Beijing to get my son back. Finally, on May 31, I received a telegram from Guofeng, saying that he was ready to come home but didn't have money for train fare. At that time, I didn't know he had bought the camera. I began to wonder where he had spent the money. Despite my doubts, I sent him another two hundred yuan [US$26] and waited for him to come home. I calmed down a little bit. Two days passed and he hadn't arrived. Then, the political situation in Beijing changed dramatically. The troops had been ordered to crack down on the student protesters. I tried to put a positive spin on the crackdown. The government probably used tanks to scare students. Well, I thought to myself, chasing them back to campus wasn't a bad idea.

In the next few days, I became more worried. The stress had led to a partial paralysis on my face. I had to see an acupuncture doctor every day. On June 8, I was feeling better and sat outside, relaxing in the sun. Then two strangers showed up. They were sent by the Xinjing Township government. I was told that an official wanted to see me. So I got up and followed them to the township government building. After we entered the building, I was led to an office. A guy who looked like a senior official said without any introductions or greeting: Wu Dingfu, do you know that your son was involved in the counterrevolutionary riot in Beijing?

His words scared the daylights out of me. I just automatically blurted out a question: What are you saying?

The official cleared his throat and said slowly: We want to notify you that your son, Wu Guofeng, has died.

My mind went blank. I could hear myself saying: Can't be true, can't be true.

The official answered in a stern tone: We just received a telegram from the authorities in Beijing. Your son is dead.

My body slumped to the floor, like a soft noodle. I tried to support myself against the chair: What, what telegram? Could you give me some more details?

The official said bluntly: We don't know any details. We have decided to purchase for you two train tickets. The deputy Party secretary will accompany you to Beijing to handle the cremation and help bring your son's ashes home.

I said: OK. Then, I began to shake uncontrollably, which was followed by cold sweats. I tried to stand up, but collapsed. Two people helped me to my chair. I rested a few minutes and then struggled to stand up and leave. One guy came over to assist me. I pushed him away, saying: Don't grab me like this. It's not like I'm going to the execution ground. I can manage myself.

I wobbled across the street and headed home. Everything seemed so unreal, the people, the traffic . . . I didn't know how I got home. I stood by the wall, tears and sweat running down my face like rainwater. My wife kept shaking my arm and asking what had happened. I started to wail. She asked again: Old man, what happened? I clenched my teeth and yelled with all my strength: Guofeng is dead.

The next thing I knew, my wife fell to the floor and passed out. No matter how hard I tried shaking her, she didn't respond. She lay in bed unconscious for almost two days. When she came to, she just cried and cried, refusing to take water or food. She kept murmuring: Guofeng, how could you leave us like this?

On the morning of June 9, the local government delivered two train tickets to my house. The deputy Party secretary, who was supposed to accompany us, never showed up.

LIAO: Did he change his mind?

WU: Local officials here were nervous about my son's death. Nobody wanted to be involved for fear of losing their jobs. So the deputy Party secretary bowed out at the last minute.

LIAO: Let me interrupt one second. Didn't you say you received a telegram from Guofeng on May 31? When he didn't come home right away, did you have any premonition that something had gone wrong?

WU: Our only source of news was from TV. After June 4, all the TV channels began to broadcast the same tapes provided by the Central Television Station, saying that the army had imposed martial law to keep order and had successfully ended the counterrevolutionary riot. Who would have thought the People's Liberation Army could kill its own citizens? I naively thought that the government would arrest a number of student leaders as scapegoats. That was it. If Guofeng had the bad luck to get arrested, he would get some disciplinary action. After all, he was just a kid. Even if they threw him in jail or a labor camp for a couple of years, it wouldn't be a big deal. We had witnessed persecution before and there was nothing to be ashamed of.

LIAO: The whole world saw the tapes of the bloody crackdown. The Chinese were the last ones to learn the truth.

WU: Xinjing is a small town. The Communist Party did a good job of blocking news. We didn't know anything about the killings.

LIAO: Didn't any of his classmates from Beijing contact you about Guofeng's death?

WU: In the evening of June 8, right after I got home from the government office, we received a telegram from Xuzhou city, Jiangsu Province. It was sent by a relative's daughter. She was one year older than Guofeng and studied at the Beijing Second Foreign Languages Institute. She heard about Guofeng's death on June 4. But, at that time, the army had occupied the post office. It was also risky to send a telegram like that. So she and another student from Xinjing left Beijing on a train and arrived in Xuzhou. She sent the telegram from there.

To keep the story short, my wife and I left Chengdu for Beijing on the afternoon of June 9. We were overcome with grief and hadn't eaten for two days. We simply carried some water. After we arrived in Beijing, a woman, Comrade Zhang, met us at the station. She was the deputy Party secretary of Guofeng's department. After we exchanged greetings, silence fell. She put us up at the university guesthouse and said: Get some rest. We'll talk tomorrow.

The next morning, the department Party secretary briefed us on the situation surrounding Guofeng's death: on the night of June 3, university officials went from door to door, warning students not to leave campus because the army had already moved into the city. As an exception, students were allowed to play cards or mah-jongg if they wanted to. On that night, Guofeng had broken his ankle and was limping around in the dorm. He promised that he would stay in. However, after university officials left, Guofeng grabbed his camera and snuck out with one of his classmates. They rode their bikes and rushed out onto the street.

It was then that I found out about the camera. Starting from the death of Hu Yaobang, he had taken hundreds of pictures of the student protests. I found piles of pictures and undeveloped rolls of film under his pillow.

LIAO: Was he in Tiananmen Square that night?

WU: No. But as you probably remember, the protest movement lost momentum in late May. While most of the students in Beijing had returned to campus, thousands more from outside Beijing poured in and took up the spots in Tiananmen Square. On the night of June 3, when the government sent troops to Beijing, many residents and students came out again to rally support. My son and his buddy, a Mr. Li, left campus and soon they lost each other in the crowd. Li said he saw a large number of soldiers shooting at residents. He was so scared. He ducked into a small alley. Eventually, he found his way back to campus. But Guofeng never returned.

LIAO: Where exactly was he killed?

WU: Somewhere near Xidan, west of Tiananmen Square. The soldiers and tanks marched along Chang-an Boulevard, which leads to Tiananmen Square. They would shoot at residents who were taking pictures, shouting slogans, throwing rocks, or trying to set up roadblocks. Since Guofeng was carrying a camera, he was a prime target. They shot him on the spot. His bicycle was crushed by a tank. After those butchers marched away, some residents stepped out and carried him to a nearby hospital that was affiliated with the Department of Post and Telecommunications.

When I saw Guofeng's body, I begged the school authorities repeatedly to allow me to take him back to Xinjing. I had put the Party secretary in a difficult situation because the Party Central Committee strictly ordered that all victims be cremated right away. We told him that Guofeng's grandparents, his brother and sister needed to say goodbye to him. They still wouldn't budge. Eventually, I asked if I could take some pictures so I could show them to the rest of my family. The Party secretary had a meeting and then granted my wish, on condition that I keep those pictures confidential. He made me promise not to use the pictures to tarnish the image of our government.

Look at these pictures: He was covered with blood. The hole in his right chest was the fatal wound. Apparently he was struck by several bullets. Look at the holes in his shoulder, his arm and ribs. There is a cut here on his lower abdomen. The knife or bayonet was stabbed in and then slashed all the way down here. The cut is about seven or eight centimeters long. All his intestines were cut into pieces. A doctor who didn't want to disclose his name saw the picture. According to his analysis, the solider or soldiers had probably shot Guofeng several times. When they saw that the bullets hadn't killed Guofeng, one soldier pulled out his bayonet and stabbed him. I found two deep cuts on both of Guofeng's hands. He must have experienced excruciating pain and instinctively grabbed the bayonet . . .

LIAO: While you were in Beijing, did you talk with any of his classmates?

WU: Yes. They gave me some information but everyone was nervous. In that week, the top student leaders were put on the government's most-wanted list. Some had been arrested. The rest of the student partici-pants were forced to attend political study sessions. They had to pledge loyalty to the Party and denounce the movement as a counterrevolu-tionary riot. During my stay, the university authorities assigned four students to accompany us. They were nice and took turns consoling us with kind words. On June 12, my wife and I went to the morgue inside the hospital. A staff member washed the blood off his body and put some new clothes on it. Based on the tradition in my hometown, we wrapped his body around with a layer of white linen that we had brought with us.

LIAO: What was its significance?

WU: The white linen symbolized his purity. Even though Wu Guofeng was not married and didn't have children to carry on the family name, he was considered a dutiful son. On June 13, we held a wake at the hos-pital's memorial hall. His body was laid on a platform in the middle. Several of Guofeng's former classmates, friends, and even his teachers came. They walked around the body in tears. Nobody dared to say any-thing. After the wake, his friends helped us move the body to the Babaoshan Crematorium.

During that whole week, we were told the crematorium was abnor-mally busy. Bodies were being sent in nonstop. One guy working there said he had to work three shifts. When we got there, there was a long line. But the guy told us we didn't have to wait in line because there was a special order from the Party, saying that the bodies of college stu-dents were on the priority list. I guess the government didn't want the bodies of innocent students lying around. They could easily arouse sympathy from the public and contradict its statement that no students had been killed. So we were moved out of the line and through a back door. At the registration desk, an older man behind the window was busy writing. When I handed him Guofeng's papers, he didn't even raise his head and began to copy information. I was worried that he might make a mistake. So I said: Sir, Sir! Do you have any questions?

He waved his hands impatiently and said: Just stop pestering me, OK? I haven't slept for two days. I don't even have time to take a shit. Don't worry. I won't mess up. After the registration, we went to buy a wooden box to hold Guofeng's ashes. Guess what? The boxes were gone pretty fast. As my wife and I were discussing whether to pick a dragon design, a couple more were snatched by eager customers. Seeing that, we stopped our discussion and grabbed one right away and paid for it. Just to show you how weird it was.

LIAO: Despite the hectic situation at the crematorium, the government media still blasted out announcements denying that there had been any killings.

WU: Anyhow, we waited for several hours before we got the ashes. On June 16, we got on the train and returned to Xinjing on June 18. We set up a wake at our house, with Guofeng's picture and ash box on an altar. We also set up a memorial tent on the street. Relatives and friends came from all over to offer their condolences. On the fourth day, the township government sent an official over, asking me to stop the wake and disassemble everything. When I refused, he said to me: In the next two days, many village officials will be in town to hear important announcements by Deng Xiaoping and the Central Party Committee on the crackdown. Those hicks don't know shit about what's going on in Beijing. But when they are in town I don't want them to see the memorial tent. Your son's death contradicts what is contained in the official announcement. It could be a bad influence on those hicks. I know you are quite stubborn. It will get you into more trouble if you disobey the order. I thought about his words for a few minutes and then offered a compromise. I decided to dismantle the tent on the street, but insisted on keeping the memorial stuff intact at my own house. I knew many of Guofeng's high school friends were returning home for the summer holidays and would want to come visit. The township government agreed.

After the wake, I didn't bury his ashes. I kept the box at my own house. I believed that unless the verdict on June 4 was reversed, his spirit wouldn't rest in peace. But in 2002, Guofeng's little brother also died. Out of despair, I buried them together on the top of a mountain nearby.

LIAO: How did his younger brother die?

WU: His brother, the youngest in the family, was very considerate and thoughtful. After his elder brother, the future pillar of the family, died, he began to shoulder the responsibility of taking care of the whole family. He rose early and worked long hours to make money. He thought that if the family's financial situation was improved, the pain of losing his elder brother could be eased. Who could have known that the God in heaven was not on his side? Long hours of working damaged his health. Soon, he was diagnosed with uremia. I cobbled together all our savings and the money collected by Professor Ding from people in the U.S. to pay for his hospital bills. In the end, we still couldn't save him.

    Guofeng was the hope of several generations in the family. He was gone. So was his brother. It was just too devastating. Guofeng's grandma had high blood pressure. When she heard about Guofeng's death, she had a stroke and was paralyzed. She lay in bed for many years and died in 2002. His grandpa used to be very healthy. He was nine months shy of his ninetieth birthday when he heard about Guofeng's death. He couldn't pull himself out of the pain. He tried to commit suicide twice. The second time, he cut an artery on his neck and there was blood everywhere. Luckily, I discovered it and called the doctor. He was saved. While in the hospital, he deliberately fell to the floor and broke his collarbones. Two weeks later, he died.

    In 2002 alone, my family held three funerals. At the moment, my daughter has been laid off from a state-run factory. She has to raise two kids. Life is very hard. After my youngest son died, his wife, who is from a village nearby, went back to her parents and dumped her four-year-old daughter on us. Guofeng's mother hurt her head and suffered a serious concussion after she passed out at Guofeng's funeral in 1989. She can only do some simple house chores now.

LIAO: You are the only healthy person in the family.

WU: Not really. I'm suffering from kidney cancer. Not long after my youngest son became sick with uremia in 2002, I noticed a small growth on my waist. I didn't do anything about it because all of our attention was on my younger son. A year later, the growth was getting bigger. I began to see blood in my urine. The doctors recommended surgery. My right kidney was removed. I feel much better now. I just can't lift heavy stuff. I can't afford expensive Western medicine. So I simply take some cheap herbs. The surgery cost my family a fortune. Unless we are really desperate, I seldom call Professor Ding because she's very busy. Each time she gets a call from us, she knows that we need help. It's kind of embarrassing.

LIAO: How did you get in touch with Professor Ding and the Tiananmen Mothers?

WU: After Guofeng's death, I bought a shortwave radio so we could listen to overseas radio broadcasts. One day, I heard on the radio that Ding Zilin, a professor at Guofeng's university, had lost her son. She was try-ing to contact all the victims' families and seek justice for those who were killed on June 4. I tried but wasn't able to establish contact. Sev-eral years ago, Professor Ding's husband met a student at a party. The student grew up in Xinjing and told him about my son. So Professor Ding wrote us a letter, but misspelled my name. Luckily, with help from heaven, a friend working at the post office got hold of the letter. He delivered it to us. It was such a blessing for us to be finally in touch with Professor Ding. She said she had been trying to track us down for eight years.

LIAO: Does Professor Ding know what's going on with your family now?

WU: Our life is too hard right now. We live on two hundred yuan a month. We have to raise our granddaughter and support her education. She is our only hope. She is the only thing left after the loss of my two sons. Despite this, we don't want to bother Professor Ding. It doesn't matter if we live or die. Professor Ding has to live. She is the one who helps keep the issue alive. It's been sixteen years since the June 4 mas-sacre happened. Sooner or later, justice will be done. We probably won't live long enough to see the day. Whatever happens, we can't let the Communist Party get away with the bloody debt owed to families like mine.

THE FALUN GONG PRACTITIONER

One morning in December 2004, two neatly dressed women showed up at my door. Both of them seemed to be in their late fifties and looked like peasants from the nearby suburbs. One woman glanced around and whispered, We are not beggars. We are Falun Gong practitioners. The words "Falun Gong" stunned me. In the summer of 1999, after thousands of practitioners had staged a silent protest in Beijing against unfair treatment, the Party leadership saw the group as a threat to Communist rule, declared it an evil cult, and launched a massive campaign to eliminate Falun Gong in China.

Right at that moment, two "evil cult" members seemed to have arrived from another world. Each woman was carrying a bag that I found out later on contained stacks of Falun Gong literature. It took me a few seconds to compose myself. I had a daring idea. I invited them in, fumbled around for a notebook, and decided to interview Chen, one of the two women.

A week later, I heard another knock on the door. I looked through the peephole and saw two policemen outside. Worrying that the police were coming to get me for interviewing those Falun Gong members, I grabbed my stuff and jumped out my third-floor apartment window. Miraculously, I suffered only a few minor bruises. After that incident, I was on the run for four months and then moved to a small southwestern city.

—⚏—

LIAO YIWU: Before I let you in, could you check to see if anyone is tailing you?

CHEN: I think we are safe. I can normally sense it when I'm tailed.

LIAO: Good. Have a seat.

CHEN: Thanks for being open-minded enough to let us in. Nowadays, the government's brainwashing campaign and the threat tactics have made many people scared of being associated with Falun Gong. They become very nervous when they see a practitioner outside their door. Some even dial 110 to call the police. I don't blame them. Thousands of practitioners have been locked up and tortured to death. Who wouldn't be afraid? But people need to find out the truth about us. We are not a cult. The Communist Party is a true cult. No matter how the government tries to distort the truth by slandering and persecuting us, we believe truth will eventually prevail.

LIAO: How did you get started in Falun Gong?

CHEN: I'm a retired worker from a state enterprise in Hesheng Township, Wenjiang County. I was a Communist Party member for thirty years. After I retired, I lived on a meager pension, most of which was spent on medicine. I became ill very easily. I took so much medicine that my body became resistant to treatment. Each time I was hospitalized, the doctor would simply prescribe stronger and stronger medicine. I felt so helpless, thinking that I was going to die any minute.

On a sunny April day in 1999, I bumped into Liu, a former acquaintance of mine, on the street. I hadn't seen Liu for a long time and hardly recognized him. He used to be as sick and feeble as I was, with a hunchback. That day, he looked so different, healthy and younger. I was intrigued and stopped to chat with him. Liu told me he was practicing Falun Gong. I had read about it in a health magazine. He told me that Falun Gong combines Buddhist and Taoist meditation and exercises and was founded by Li Hongzhi. Practitioners referred to Li as Li *Laoshi* or Teacher Li. Liu also said that there were hundreds and thousands of followers inside China.

I was in a pretty desperate situation at that time. I would try anything that promised a cure for my illnesses. So when he told me about it, I said to myself: I will try it. What do I have to lose? So I borrowed a book of Teacher Li's teachings and joined a practicing group in a neighborhood not far from me. Every morning or evening, a large group of retired folks like me would gather in the courtyard, meditating and practicing Falun Gong. The movements are a little like those of tai chi. After the exercises, we sat together and read Teacher Li's book, which tells us how to cultivate our mind and be a good person.

Soon, I was so into it. I practiced many hours a day, and after three months, I began to feel the difference. So I went to the doctor and did some testing. The result showed dramatic improvement in my kidney and uremia. My arthritis was also getting better. As time went by, many of my illnesses disappeared.

LIAO: That was very dramatic and miraculous.

CHEN: Well, it's true. The only illness left was my asthma.

LIAO: Personally, I don't care whether it's scientifically proven or not. But when people practice together, it's like joining a therapy group. They can socialize, exercise, and talk about their problems. Depression and family spats will all be gone. The government can save lots of money on health-care costs. It's much better than sitting around a table playing mah-jongg and gambling, which seems to be the national pastime.

CHEN: You are absolutely right. After I benefited from Falun Gong, I also persuaded more of my neighbors to join our group. Everybody was happy—I mean the kind of happiness arising from our hearts, free of worries about trivial stuff.

On July 22, 1999, my neighbors and I were suddenly told to attend a meeting. At the meeting, a local official read an editorial from the Party newspaper, *People's Daily*. The editorial declared Falun Gong a cult and illegal organization, and urged all Party members to give it up. Believe it or not, I wasn't too shocked. My generation went through many big and small political campaigns. We all knew that the Party was capricious as a moody bitch. So we simply rolled our eyes and ignored the ban. Since we were not allowed to practice as a group in public, we simply did it at home.

Then the local government rounded up many people who refused to comply and put them in an auditorium. They were forced to read government propaganda materials and denounce Falun Gong publicly. The provincial government assigned a quota to each local public security bureau or government agency, ordering them to reform Falun Gong members. If a certain official exceeded the quota, he or she would be awarded a cash prize.

But later on, as more and more people refused to give it up, the actions of the government became frenetic. Local police began to search our homes for Falun Gong materials and treated each practitioner like a criminal. If one person was caught practicing, his or her whole family would be blamed and punished. After going through the Cultural Revolution, I couldn't believe a similar political campaign could be happening in China again. I decided to do something about it.

On January 15, 2000, a fellow practitioner and I traveled to Beijing to petition the government to stop the insanity. On the train, I was going through the petition in my mind again and again. I simply wanted to use my experience to tell the senior leaders in Beijing that banning Falun Gong was a mistake. That was it. I wasn't going to make trouble. After about twenty hours on the train, we finally arrived. Instead of getting food and finding a hotel, we simply walked directly to Tiananmen Square, which was about thirty minutes away from the train station. I was just eager to find the Citizens' Petition Office and tell my story. Before I reached the square, two policemen stopped us: Are you from out of town? When we said yes, they became suspicious and asked another question: Are you members of the Falun Gong group? We nodded our heads. Before we knew it, the two policemen swooped down on us, forced our hands behind our back, and dragged us into a police car. A couple of people had already been tied up there. We were taken to a branch of the Beijing Municipal Public Security Department near the Temple of Heaven. After two rounds of interrogation, police contacted authorities in Sichuan. Two days later, I was sent back home. Before my release, they confiscated six hundred yuan in cash from me. I overheard a certain Mr. Feng at the police station talking to an official who came to pick me up from Sichuan: Take this money as compensation for traveling all the way up here to get this idiot. When I reached home, the local police detained me in a small dark room for seventeen days.

LIAO: I heard people jokingly say that the Party had posted plainclothes policemen every five feet in Tiananmen Square because many Falun Gong petitioners like you displayed banners and practiced there in defiance of the government ban. Couldn't you have been a little more wary and told a little lie when police questioned you?

CHEN: Practitioners don't tell lies because it's a sin.

LIAO: I see.

CHEN: Not long after I was released from the detention center, three other practitioners in my neighborhood followed my example and traveled to Beijing to petition the government. Local public security officials suspected that I was the instigator. They came to my house, handcuffed me, and sent me to the detention center for the second time. I was locked up for another fifteen days. When I got home, I found a government seal on my apartment door. They forced me to move to a small, damp, and stinky shack. I was under their constant watch. Soon, the government stopped issuing my monthly retirement money. Instead, I was only given 120 yuan [US$15] a month to cover my basic necessities. They made my life very difficult, but I wasn't afraid. I still refused to denounce Falun Gong. Then, the government reduced my monthly pension from 120 yuan to 50 yuan, which was not even enough to buy a monthly supply of plain rice.

The more defiant I was, the more brutal and desperate the public security officials became. On July 1, 2000, I was ordered to show up at the township Party secretary's office for interrogation. The moment I walked in, Deputy Party Secretary Huang grabbed my coat and slapped me in the face again and again. That was still not enough to release his anger. He took a breath, balled his fist, and started to punch my face. In a few minutes, my face puffed up, covered with blood. My head was spinning and I fell to the floor. He then kicked my head with his pointed leather shoes. After that, I was dragged out of his office into the courtyard. Soon, a crowd gathered around me, with people kicking me like a soccer ball. I instinctively rolled around, covering my head, but had no place to escape.

LIAO: What prompted those officials to engage in such brutality?

CHEN: First, they were angry because I went to Beijing. It was a loss of face for local officials. Second, President Jiang and other senior officials had pressured local governments to brainwash and convert Falun Gong members. Failure to convert Falun Gong members could result in the loss of jobs for local officials.

LIAO: Did anyone step forward to stop the beating?

CHEN: No. Someone in the crowd even shouted: Come on and look! Another Falun Gong is getting beaten up. Hey, kick her some more.

LIAO: It's unimaginable. It was a lawless mob.

CHEN: I slipped in and out of consciousness, and could hardly see or feel anything. The buildings seemed to be swirling around me. I don't know how long the beating lasted. Then I heard an official say that it would give the township government a bad image if I was beaten to death in front of the government building. So a couple of guys pulled me by the legs and dragged me inside a meeting room. I gradually regained consciousness. I saw many people were peeping through the window. Someone shouted: Beat her, beat her. Emboldened by the shouts of the crowd, Deputy Party Secretary Huang, Deputy Mayors Zhang and Huang [no relation to the deputy Party secretary] began to take turns beating me. They forced me into a kneeling position, with my hands tied behind my back. They whipped me on the back and on my bare feet with copper wire.

LIAO: Were you still conscious during those beatings inside the meeting room?

CHEN: I was in and out. Deputy Party Secretary Huang threatened me by saying: You are the enemy of the people. I will not take responsibility if I beat you to death.

At seven o'clock that night, I awoke and found myself lying on the floor of my house. I had bruises all over my body. It was even painful to move my arms. Then I heard my seventy-year-old mother sobbing in another room.

A couple of days later, police ransacked my mother's house and took away all her valuable possessions, including a TV set, some antique coins, her clothes and bedding. Then they put us, Mother and me, on a truck, and drove us to a remote village to receive reeducation. In the words of government officials, sending me to a faraway place would prevent me from ruining the image of the township government.

LIAO: How could they be so ruthless?

CHEN: That was just the beginning. My mother and I lived in that village for about five months. I gradually recovered from the beatings. In the fall of 2001, before the moon festival, I teamed up with two Falun Gong practitioners in the village and painted a slogan, "Falun Gong Is Good," on the wall of a Buddhist temple. We were caught by a monk. Worrying that he could get blamed for the slogan, he called the police. Once again, we were detained inside a police station near the village. During the interrogation, I refused to tell the police my name and address because I was afraid of implicating my mother again. So the police locked me up in a jail with a bunch of criminals. To kill time there, I put two hands together, palm to palm, and began to do meditation. Two fellow prisoners, who had been instructed by the guards to keep an eye on me, immediately grabbed my hair. They yelled: Help, help, the crazy Falun Gong woman is conducting illegal activities again. Soon, one guard showed up and whipped me with a leather belt. He then ordered my hands and feet shackled. After that, he brought a two-piece wooden board with a hole in the middle, put my head through the hole, and locked the wooden board around my neck. Those shackles and the wooden board were specifically designed for prisoners who are suicidal or who were on death row.

For over ten days, I couldn't move. I couldn't even use the toilet on my own. After they finally removed the shackles, my neck, wrist, and ankles were abscessed. The lower part of my body was all swollen. It took another four months for the wounds to heal.

On April 25, 2002, while visiting a Falun Gong practitioner at a village near Chengdu, I was once again arrested by public security. After two months of detention, they put me on trial and sentenced me to two years in jail. On July 3 of that year, they transferred me from the detention center to an all-women prison outside Chengdu. Each prisoner was supposed to have a health checkup before being admitted. Because of the many beatings I had suffered at the hands of the police, I was in terrible shape. The prison refused to accept me. They worried that I could die during my incarceration. They didn't want to take any responsibility. So I was sent back to Hesheng Township, my hometown.

LIAO: All those beatings and tortures didn't do much to change your mind.

CHEN: When local police and township government officials heard about my return, they treated me as if I were a devil who was out to ruin their careers. They spent a whole night figuring out ways to control me. Finally, they reached a collective decision: Ms. Chen's obsession with Falun Gong has caused her to lose her mind. She is suffering from grave mental illnesses. On July 5, they tied me up with ropes, put me on a truck, and sent me to the Wanchun Mental Hospital.

LIAO: Did the doctor offer a diagnosis before your forced hospitalization?

CHEN: The township Party secretary said, The decision of the Communist Party serves as the most authentic diagnosis. Under pressure from local officials, the doctors put me inside a mental ward with thick iron doors. When the door clanked shut, I found myself in Ward A, which was specifically furnished for mental patients—iron bed, iron chairs, and an iron desk. The window was fitted with iron bars. I was surrounded by mentally ill patients, some staring blankly at the ceiling or shaking uncontrollably. Others were drooling or making weird noises, laughing or crying. I was so scared, and I begged the police chief who escorted me there to let me go home. He gave me the brush-off with a cold laugh: You are our VIP. We put you in this "resort" so you can relax and enjoy life. Do you know that it cost us 3,700 yuan [US$462] to put you up here? But it's worth it.

I knelt down, grabbed his leg, and begged: There is nothing wrong with my mind. He kicked me away and said: That's what they all say. All the people you see over here think they are normal. Oh well, go practice Falun Gong if you want. I heard there is another crazy Falun Gong member in this ward. She is a former government employee and her name is Yang. Maybe you and Yang can keep each other company.

After the police chief left, the nurses tied me up in bed for a whole night. The next morning, when the doctor saw that I was pretty obedient, they untied me and allowed me to walk around freely. I began to ask about Yang. On the second night, when the nurses were chatting after supper, I snuck out of my room and located Yang. She was thin as a stick, almost like a shadow. I struck up a conversation with her, and found out that she had been locked up in the hospital for over a year. She said she had long since given up Falun Gong. All day long, she simply imitated the behavior of those mentally ill patients. She had to act out crazily and aggressively, because if she didn't, some patients would come grab her hair, choke her, ride on top of her, and pee over her body. I reproached her: If you act like this all the time, it becomes part of you and you could become crazy like those people. She told me that she had tried to practice Falun Gong when she was thrown in there, but the nurses would stop her, and force her to watch the government propaganda video that condemned Falun Gong.

I felt so sorry for her, and told her about the stuff that friends had got from the Falun Gong Web sites overseas. I told her that thousands of people practice Falun Gong freely in Western countries and that the international community had condemned China for the crackdown. We chatted for a long time, and before I left we made a pact to resume our practice.

The next day, we got together inside my room and began to do the slow Falun Gong movements. One nurse found out and notified Dr. Deng, head of the psychiatric ward. He immediately ordered the guards to carry us to the treatment room for electric shock. They tied Yang onto the bed first, and then turned on the switch. Her body began to twitch violently, and she was screaming, "Save me, Teacher Li." Her loud screams were like something coming out of a tortured animal. I couldn't bear to watch her suffer. So I bent my head and closed my eyes. Dr. Deng grabbed my hair and poked his knee against my back, forcing me to watch and receive what he called "education." After more violent spasms, Yang's body weakened, her screaming became inaudible, and her skin turned from pale to blue. I lost control, and my body began to shake. I cried, How can you treat people like this? You should be condemned to hell. Dr. Deng dragged me out of the treatment room by the hair and said: If you continue to practice, you'll be next.

After that scary electric shock episode, the nurses put us in segregated areas, with twenty-four-hour supervision. We were locked up in a storage room next to the toilet. All night long, we were covered with mosquitoes. The next day, we were not given our food. Instead, the nurses put us on IV. Since our arms and legs were tied to the bed and couldn't move, the IV drops dripped very fast. One morning, the nurses injected several bottles of unknown liquid into our veins. I whispered to Yang: I don't know what kind of IV drips they are giving us! Yang replied: Don't you think they are injecting us with meds that will damage our brain? These people are animals and they can do anything to destroy us. Her words made me really nervous. It reminded me of a Japanese movie I had seen. The hero in the movie was fed drugs that damaged his brain. He became a zombie and jumped from a high building without knowing it. Then his enemies claimed that he had committed suicide.

The thought of that movie gave me the creeps. I began to scream, struggling to break free from the IV tubes. One nurse rushed in, pinned me down, and tightened the ropes around my legs and arms. The next day, they started to shove pills down our throats, saying that the medicine would cure us of our disobedience. I had no idea what those pills were. During the first several days, I refused to open my mouth. The doctor simply asked several guards and male patients to force my mouth open with a metal clamp, and wash down the pills with hot water. I choked and would begin to cough and vomit. After I stopped coughing, they would force my mouth open and do it again. My tongue and throat were seriously burned while my head and my face had scratches all over. A week after I took the pills, I became sleepy all day long. I couldn't stop drooling and had no appetite for food. Then I became too feeble to resist. When it was time for medicine, I would simply open my mouth voluntarily, swallow the pills like other patients did, and then doze off.

LIAO: So they finally subdued you and turned you into a mentally ill patient.

CHEN: All I could feel was exhaustion; my eyelids were so heavy that I couldn't keep them open. A month later, when the doctor reduced the dosage of my meds, I became easily irritable. Then the nurses transferred us to a new place to make room for the real mental patients. They put me and Yang in a room, where the windows had been nailed shut and covered with wooden boards. The nurses even unhooked the electric bulb. Later on, we found out that we were actually next door to the morgue.

I ended up staying in the mental hospital for 110 days. Yang actually stayed there for one year longer. One day, the director of the local Woman's Federation, a pseudo-government agency, came to visit me in the hospital. I was brought to a meeting room where visitors and patients were separated by an iron fence. She first inquired about my living conditions and then tried to persuade me to abandon my belief in the "cult." She said, Falun Gong has led to broken families, disgrace, and mental illness. I simply interrupted her by saying: I'm not mentally ill. I'm a normal person. I told her about how I was forced to take medicine. The director asked me to promise her that I would change. In return, she would tell the doctor to stop the medicine. But I refused to make any promises.

After the director of the Woman's Federation left, the doctor didn't stop the medicine, but he did reduce the dosage. At the same time, the director told the hospital to prohibit any visits from my relatives or friends.

LIAO: Why?

CHEN: Because they were worried that my relatives would find out about how I was being treated, and share it with the public. One day, my sister rode her bike for many miles to see me but she wasn't allowed to come in. So she started to shout my name as loudly as she could. A patient heard her and came to get me. By the time I rushed to the door, the guard had already chased her away.

LIAO: When did they discharge you from the hospital?

CHEN: At the end of 2002. A police car came to pick me up at the hospital and then sent me directly to a women's reeducation camp. I had to go through another health checkup and didn't pass. Again, the camp authority didn't want to accept me. The police told them: If she dies, nobody is responsible. Finally, the camp reluctantly admitted me.

LIAO: What happened later?

CHEN: One day, while we were out working in the wheat field, I escaped. After the camp authorities found out about it, they didn't even bother to send anyone to catch me. I figured they were just happy to get rid of me so they didn't have to bear any responsibility if I died.

Since I got out, I've been able to come to Chengdu and reconnect with more Falun Gong members here. Whenever I have the opportunity, I will secretly distribute Falun Gong pamphlets to as many households as I can. This morning, I walked for about twelve kilometers and dropped several hundred pamphlets inside residential buildings in the area. I still have some left and will finish these by the end of the day.

LIAO: How long did you stay inside the reeducation camp?

CHEN: I was sentenced to two years. I had two more months left before I escaped.

LIAO: Why did you bother to run away?

CHEN: I was worried they might change their mind and not let me go on my release date, on the grounds that I hadn't given up on my faith.

LIAO: I used to think that if every Chinese followed the principles of truth, benevolence, and tolerance, as preached by Teacher Li, we would totally resign ourselves to oppression. The Communist Party could rule this country unopposed forever. I guess I'm wrong.

THE ILLEGAL BORDER CROSSER

Unlike thousands of Chinese who hire smugglers to help them escape to the West, the forty-four-year-old Li Yifeng takes a different route. In the past several years, he has made several failed attempts to sneak across the border on his own, first to Myanmar and then to Hong Kong. He said he was a born border crosser.

Our interview took place recently at a teahouse near the Fu River in Mianyang city, Sichuan. Li had just been released from a detention center in the southern city of Shenzhen.

—◆—

LIAO YIWU: Where did you get this adventurous spirit?

LI YIFENG: I inherited the adventurous spirit from my father. My father was born in the late 1940s. He grew up in a small river town in the eastern part of Sichuan. As a kid, he used to sit alone by the side of the river and watch boats come and go. My mother told me that he would constantly ask himself questions such as: What's it like to be at the other end of the river? What's it like at the other end of the earth?

My father did very well in school and went to college. After graduation, he was assigned a job at the provincial cultural department. That was the place where educated folks worked. But when those educated folks got together, they began to talk about strange and subversive ideas, such as democracy or escaping to a foreign land. No wonder Chairman Mao never trusted intellectuals and initiated one campaign after another to purge them from the Communist ranks. Anyhow, the idea of traveling to foreign countries stayed with my father. Since Chinese were not allowed to move freely at that time, he began to explore the possibilities of illegal border crossing. His first experience was in 1962, when my mother was still pregnant with me. He left for the northwestern province of Xinjiang, home to the Uyghur and Kazakh ethnic groups. You probably would say that people were desperate to leave China in 1962 because of the famine. I don't think my father did it solely for that reason; he did it to satisfy his curiosity. After he arrived in Xinjiang, he picked up some odd jobs and waited for his opportunity. Eventually he moved to a small town which bordered the then Soviet Union, and started his cross-border adventure there. But luck wasn't on his side. He was caught. When the Chinese border police interrogated him, he pretended to be deaf and mute. The police mistakenly thought he was a member of the ethnic Kazakhs. They didn't shoot him for fear of exacerbating ethnic tensions. Instead, they detained him for several months. Upon his release, he moved back to Sichuan.

He then stayed with my mom for a few weeks until he became restless again. So one day he just disappeared. After he left, my mom moved in with her parents. Later on, my mom received a letter from him, saying that he was heading south to Shenzhen. In those days, Shenzhen was only a small fishing village bordering Hong Kong. Since the land border was heavily guarded, a local guide told him to sneak across via water. So my dad hid in the tall grass near the beach for a whole day. When night fell, he came out of the hiding place, jumped into the water and swam as fast as he could to the free world of Hong Kong. That crazy old man! After he had swum in the water for over a hundred meters, the guards detected him with the patrol lights. They began shooting at him. He got so scared he made his way back to the beach, where a group of border guards were waiting for him. They beat him and tied him up with a rope. Then he was arrested and sentenced to twenty years in jail.

In the Mao era, China was isolated from the rest of the world. Sneaking out to a foreign country was considered a cardinal sin, a crime so serious most ordinary people would not even dare think about it. My dad was quite unusual.

LIAO: What were the charges against him?

LI: They charged him with the crimes of betraying the motherland and engaging in counterrevolutionary activities. At the time of his arrest, I was still in my mother's womb. She carried me to visit my dad in prison and brought divorce papers for him to sign. Sadly, that was the kind of family I was born into. Do you remember an American movie called *Paris, Texas*? It tells the story of a guy who was unable to remember his past. He decided to find Paris, a city in the state of Texas, where his parents had supposedly met and made love. Since he was probably conceived during that encounter, the man was under the illusion that locating Paris, Texas, would bring back the memories of his past. To him, the city symbolized the perfect place where good things happened. So he abandoned his family and wandered around the country in search of that city. His journey was a precondition, a basic instinct and desire born from his blood. My father had such desires. So do I. The difference is that he paid a much heftier price. I'm lucky because things have changed. Nowadays, there are so many illegal border crossers. The government has problems stemming the trend. Penalties against us are not as harsh.

LIAO: The motives you just listed aren't too convincing. As far as I know, most Chinese attempt to leave China for economic reasons. They want to go to countries like America to make money. A few of them do it for political reasons. I don't know anyone who escapes China out of the basic instinct of a wanderer. Do you realize you are betraying your homeland?

LI: I always carry memories of my homeland in a bag: a couple of Chinese books, including a collection of Chinese poems, a Chinese dictionary, and pictures of some beautiful Chinese women. I understand the fact that if you have money, you can emigrate or travel to a foreign country via proper legal channels. But, sadly, I don't have money. Even if I did, I wouldn't want to go through various complicated channels or fill out all sorts of forms. I want to go wherever I want, and whenever I want. Writer Ai Wu's *Journey to the South* serves as my textbook. In the book, he describes how he impulsively left China in the 1940s and journeyed to Myanmar. He didn't tell anyone or go through any authorities. He just went like that. In my view, Ai Wu is the Jack Kerouac of China.

LIAO: Are you saying that you went to Myanmar to follow the steps of Ai Wu?

LI: Damn right. I picked Myanmar because of that book by Ai Wu. Since Myanmar is a Buddhist country, I figured that people would be nicer than the Chinese. Most important, going to Myanmar is not that difficult. If you follow the China–Myanmar highway, which starts in a small town called Ruli in the southwestern province of Yunnan, you can easily reach the border town of Mangshi. So, on that particular trip, there were three of us: me posing as a journalist, another guy claiming to be an official from Wulong County, and the third one, a former monk. So we put our money together and decided to go as a group. Through the former monk, we found a one-armed guide from Myanmar. His name was Yeshan. He was a monk. His job was to help those who wanted to enter Myanmar for a fee. At over 1.8 meters, he stood tall among us, and his yellow *kasaya* glimmered in the hot sun. We followed him for three days and covered over a hundred kilometers of mountain road. Since we could only walk at night, we were exhausted.

LIAO: When did this happen?

LI: That was in the summer of 1989.

LIAO: That was right after the government crackdown on the prodemocracy movement in Beijing. Many student leaders were on the run. You didn't do it for political reasons, did you?

LI: Not me. I'm not sure about the other two. But I doubt it. I was planning to find a job in Myanmar's capital city of Yangon and then look for some business opportunities there. If that didn't work out, my plan B was to join the triad in the Golden Triangle area. I wouldn't have minded smuggling opium. The profit was huge. So I was really motivated. The first part of the trip went smoothly. We didn't encounter any soldiers on the way. Then, on the morning of the fourth day, Yeshan patted me on my shoulder and said in his broken Chinese: You already inside Myanmar now. My job done. Goodbye. We were stunned. You can't leave us like this, screamed the "county official" who reacted faster than the others. He grabbed the monk's sleeve and said: All we see is this mountain. Heaven knows if this is Myanmar or not.

The "official" was right. It was so quiet. We were standing on the edge of a horseshoe-shaped ridge. We could vaguely see a river in the distance through the waist-deep bushes and grass. There was no way to tell whether we had entered Myanmar or not.

The three of us grabbed Yeshan and begged him not to leave us there. When the pleading didn't work, I took out a pocketknife to threaten him. Yeshan became very angry with us. He swung that arm of his at me and pushed me to the ground. The knife flew right out of my hand. That guy knew martial arts and none of us was his match. After he kicked our butts, Yeshan tossed the water bottles and the raw rice to us, pointed at a river down the mountain, and said in that broken Chinese again, Follow river and you no get lost. Make sure stay away from the Maoist guerrillas.

With those words, Yeshan walked away in big strides, his *kasaya* flying in the morning breeze like a sail. A couple of minutes later, he disappeared in the bushes. Things became so quiet. We got up and brushed the dirt from our pants. The "official" recommended that we go down the mountain at night, but both the former monk and I protested. Since we had already seen some rice paddies and houses in the distance, I figured that we were far away from the border and should be safe from the Chinese border police. There was really no need to do the night walk again.

After debating back and forth, I won. The three of us decided to walk on. We would go down the mountain at twenty meters apart. In this way, if one got into trouble, the others would have time to escape. I volunteered to go at the front. At the beginning, I could hear the footsteps of my friends behind me. Gradually, I could only hear the sound of my own footsteps. So I turned around and called out softly: Hey, hey, are you there? There was no answer. I then crouched down and walked back a little bit, hoping to find my fellow team members. I looked around and couldn't see anybody. Soon, exhaustion started to catch up with me. It was still early in the morning and not too hot. I lay down in the bushes. At first, I tried to stay awake. But soon I was sound asleep. At about noontime, I was awakened by the ants, which were huge in Myanmar. I jumped up and was sweating all over. The ants stuck to my neck like a bracelet. I smashed them with my palms, while continuing my way down. I was hoping to find a local who could help me out.

LIAO: Do you know the local language? How would you communicate with the locals if you ran into one?

LI: People living in the border areas can normally speak a little Chinese because there were lots of cross-border trading activities going on.

Also, in the late 1960s, during the Cultural Revolution, many Red Guards crossed the border to support the rebel forces in Myanmar, with the intent of exporting Mao's ideas and engaging in a worldwide Communist revolution. In other words, the locals were used to the presence of Chinese. I was told that locals wouldn't feel alarmed and call the border police if they saw a Chinese. Since the Chinese currency was accepted in the area, one could easily move around without problems.

LIAO: Sounds like you had done some thorough research before the trip. Didn't you tell me that you took these risky adventures simply because you preferred the lifestyle of a wanderer? But now you say you snuck across to be an opium smuggler.

LI: Well, I think it's a combination of both. On the other hand, what's wrong with leaving China for economic reasons? If a large number left China now, the Chinese population would be reduced and the government wouldn't have to shoulder a heavy burden of feeding that many people. If I were to make a policy recommendation to the central government, I would suggest we cut a swath of land through Mongolia and Russia, and build a highway directly to Europe. After the highway is completed, there is no need to advertise it. People would leave the country in droves.

LIAO: OK, OK, stop your grand ideas for a moment. Where were we just now?

LI: We were talking about walking in a jungle in Myanmar. Damn it, it was so scary because I couldn't find a regular mountain path. So I crawled and stumbled around in the bushes. I then checked my watch and realized that six hours had already passed. If things had gone right, I should have been close to the foot of the mountain. But I looked around and couldn't see anything, not even the Myanmar River, which I was supposed to follow. I fumbled forward and found a hidden path among the thick bushes. I was overjoyed. So I took the path and kept walking. A few minutes later, I noticed that the surroundings looked very familiar. I soon realized that I had somehow walked a circle and came to the spot where I had started six hours earlier.

As I was stuck there in the middle of the jungle, can you guess what I was thinking? The jungle reminded me of an old Chinese movie, *Bells Ringing Inside the Mountain*. The movie was about how the Chinese army fought gangsters and robbers in that region. I wish I could meet some gangsters on horses. I couldn't see shit. Looking back, it was kind of strange for me to be thinking of an old movie that I had seen twenty years before. Oh well. I sat down and pondered my next move. Then I heard a deep human voice: "Freeze." The sound sent cold shudders down my spine. My hair stood on end.

LIAO: Was it in Chinese?

LI: Yes, it was in standard Mandarin. I felt my head exploding. My poor legs suddenly lost control and flopped. I knelt on the ground. My body was trembling. About five minutes had passed, and I still hadn't seen anybody coming to get me. So I slowly raised my head and tried to see what was going on. Then, I heard the same voice again: Raise your hands above your shoulders. Bend your head. Toss out your weapons.

LIAO: You ran into the border police.

LI: In a way, they acted like the border police, except their uniforms looked kind of shabby. Four guys stepped out from behind the trees. But don't laugh when I tell you this—I was so scared that I had peed in my pants. For the next several hours, my pants reeked strongly of urine. My captors covered my eyes with a black scarf, tied both of my hands in the front, and then dragged me along with a rope. One guy pushed a gun against my waist. I don't know how far or how long I walked. When they finally removed the black scarf from my eyes, I found myself inside a mountain cave and surrounded by a group of men dressed in the Chinese military uniforms of the seventies. They stripped me and pushed me to the side of a table. A kerosene lamp was hanging from the ceiling, and you could hardly see anything beyond the interrogator who was sitting opposite me at the table. Everything was pitch-dark, very mysterious. Gradually, my eyes began to adjust to the darkness. The interrogator asked me: Your name? Age? Occupation? What are you doing here? Are you here to smuggle goods or for political reasons? How many partners do you have on this trip? I answered his questions one by one.

LIAO: Were you captured by the Chinese border police?

LI: No. They were called the People's Army, a guerrilla group affiliated with the Myanmar Communist Party. That group was very powerful in the 1960s and '70s. I heard they were divided into several military regions, with over ten thousand troops. The group occupied a large area in the China-Myanmar border region. The People's Army is in decline now because the world has changed. The fate of the Khmer Rouge in the neighboring area had had a devastating impact on the Communist forces in Myanmar.

LIAO: You got caught by the People's Army? You poor thing!

LI: I had strayed and ended up in the guerrilla territories without even knowing it. Damn, such bad luck. The strangest thing was that the bearded interrogator was from my hometown, the city of Chongqing. Remember what I told you about the Red Guards early in the conversation? That guy was a former Red Guard who had been sent down to work on a collective farm in Yunnan Province. In 1969, he escaped and crossed the border to Myanmar and joined the guerrilla forces. When he realized that he and I grew up in the same city, he began to loosen up and chat with me. He wanted to know about the changes happening in Chongqing. He told me that he had been away for over twenty years, but still missed his hometown. I secretly felt relieved at this unexpected turn of events and started to shoot the breeze with him. I told him about China's economic reforms, the students' democracy movement, and the popularity of cars. I said: Nobody believes in Communism anymore. Everyone talks about money, money, and money. We both talked in Sichuan dialect, swapping stories and jokes about Chongqing. Sometimes, we laughed so hard that tears came down. Other soldiers in the cave looked at us, puzzled and confused. Then my interrogator ordered his soldiers to prepare dinner for us—four dishes and a jug of liquor. I soon became tipsy. The interrogator reminisced about his younger days in China, about his passion for the Communistic ideals, and about his goal of spreading Communism around the world. He told me that the majority of his former comrades had been killed in guerrilla wars against the Myanmar government. I was truly touched by his stories and asked if he was planning to return home someday. He answered: Everyone, including you, is running away from home. What's the point of going back? To a certain degree, I said he and I shared something in common. We both were idealists, and were pursuing adventure in a foreign country. He strongly disagreed: Your ideals are different from mine. You are doing it for yourself, but I'm pursuing a goal to help mankind. My comrades and I are the only true Chinese Communists who are shedding blood in a foreign land, with the hope of establishing another Communist society. You probably call us rare specimens, but we are fighting for a noble cause.

As our conversation became more and more intimate, I began to broach the subject of having him release me. He sighed: We are fellow city men. Under normal circumstances, I would let you pass. Unfortunately, it's too late. My commander has been informed of your arrest. He has notified the Chinese border police. His words jolted me wide awake. Like a snake falling into an icy river, I was shaking all over, struggling for my life.

I slumped to the ground and knelt in front of him: I beg you to have mercy on me. If you can't set me free, why don't you shoot me now? The government will do the same if you send me home.

The interrogator pulled me up from the ground, and said: Cheer up, buddy! If they find out that you don't have other political motives for crossing the border, you probably will get two years in jail. To tell you the truth, I'm now the head of the regiment here. I have to set a good example in carrying out orders from above. Otherwise, I would lose my credibility among my soldiers.

LIAO: With words like that, I don't think you can argue much.

LI: Damn it. It was like a bad dream. After I woke up, I ended up in jail for two years. Look at my face now and you will notice that one side is more out of shape than the other. My chin is a little tilted. Those are souvenirs from my various border-crossing adventures. I got smacked and beaten up so many times. The pain and the excitement made me feel alive. Once, I was tied by a long rope to the back of a small tractor. My captors dragged me for many kilometers on a small mountain path. My clothes were shredded into strips, like a mop. While I was being pulled forward by the tractor, I thought of an American movie, in which the black slaves were tied to a wooden pole, waiting to be sold to another white owner.

The pursuit of freedom is the hardest thing in this world. In China, if you are dying of hunger, nobody gives a damn. But when you try to move to a new place to find food for yourself and look for a change of lifestyle, someone will immediately pounce and arrest you. In places such as Europe, the U.S., and Australia, people claim they have democracy and freedom. But the governments there will not grant entry to you if you don't have money or if you don't qualify as a political refugee. No matter how many times you tell them that you love democracy and freedom, they still don't give a damn. It's so damn hypocritical.

LIAO: Personally, I think Myanmar is a much worse country than China. Even if you had succeeded in crossing over there and had reached Yangon, you would have faced poverty just like you do here. It could be worse, don't you think?

LI: I have never been successful in getting over there. How would I know which is worse? A poet friend of mine once took the same path as I did. He got caught inside Myanmar because a local resident reported on him. He ended up in a Myanmar jail. Believe it or not, he was locked up in the same cell with a former leader of the Myanmar Communist Party. Within a year, he learned to speak English and Burmese, and obtained quite a lot of secrets of the Myanmar Communist Party. Those secrets were quite useless though.

Anyhow, he became friends with that Communist leader. Then he was forgotten. The government never put him on trial and they just left him in jail forever. One day, he began to scream nonstop. Thank heavens he did that. Otherwise, he could be rotting in there. He cursed and screamed in Chinese, English, and Burmese. That screaming really changed his fate. Later on, both he and the Communist leader were released. The Communist guy helped him get a visa. He was exported to Europe as a laborer. The last thing I heard was that he became a resident of Denmark. He is the luckiest border crosser I have ever heard of.

LIAO: His story is like a chapter in the *Arabian Nights*.

LI: My own story is like a chapter from the *Arabian Nightmares*. But let me tell you, during peacetime, sneaking across the border is the most adventurous and stimulating thing to do.

LIAO: Does it mean you are addicted to border crossing?

LI: I have done it four or five times. The most dramatic experience was the one I just told you. All the others were pretty ordinary and they all ended in failure. Penalty for border crossing has been reduced a lot in recent years. As long as you don't mess around with officials during interrogation, they will normally force you to pay a fine. That's it. Since I didn't have money to pay a fine, they would detain me for several months and then release me.

There is one more trip that's worth mentioning. It was in 1997. Since Hong Kong was about to be returned to China, I assumed that the Hong Kong–China border wouldn't be as tightly patrolled as before. I paid some money to buy a fake ID, and went to Shenzhen, like my dad did. Instead of swimming across, I decided to check out the land route. I took a stroll on the famous commercial boulevard that divides Hong Kong and mainland China. I looked at the Hong Kong side. The tall buildings and busy shopping areas were so mesmerizing, drawing me like a huge magnet. Like a complete idiot, I began to walk toward the barbed wire that was put up in the middle of the street to separate Hong Kong from the mainland. Two guards spotted me right away. They moved toward me with guns pointing. Without further thinking, I tossed my bag across to the other side of the street. The bag contained my fake ID and wallet. I thought the other side was Hong Kong territory and the mainland guard wouldn't dare to cross over to pick it up. They came over and one pointed his gun at me, ordering me to stand still. Then the other guard walked over to the Hong Kong side through a small entrance, and picked up my bag as evidence of my crime.

LIAO: At least your bag managed to cross the border.

LI: I told the guards: Hong Kong will be returned to China soon. It should be easier for Chinese to travel to Hong Kong. Why are you in such a rush to get me? They slapped me and told me to shut up. I was locked up in a detention center for two months. Luckily, they didn't find out about my real identity. Otherwise, they could have sentenced me for fabricating an ID card.

LIAO: You have just been released from a detention center in Shenzhen. Was it for another illegal border-crossing?

LI: Yes. I did odd jobs in Shenzhen for several years and then tried to enter Hong Kong on a train not long ago. I was caught because of my fake passport.

LIAO: You are hopeless. It must be in your genes.

THE GRAVE ROBBER

I met Tian Zhiguang on a cold November evening in 2002, near the front entrance to the Sichuan Provincial People's Supreme Court on Wenwu Road. He was in Chengdu to file a petition with the court against the local Public Security Bureau for "ruining his life through illegal detention." Tian had run out of money and was begging on the street. I took him to a restaurant nearby and bought him a bowl of noodles.

Over the meal, Tian told me he had just turned thirty-three. He was known among his fellow villagers as the "grave robber," even though he had never put his foot inside a grave.

—※—

TIAN ZHIGUANG: I remember a fortune-teller once telling me: "You come from a family that includes generations of peasants. You are predestined to be tied to the soil and to earn your money through hard labor. But should your calloused hand touch anything valuable, you are bound to get in trouble." As you can see, fortune is not in my destiny. It's not like I don't want to make lots of money. I'm just not smart enough to handle wealth.

LIAO YIWU: Tell me about your life.

TIAN: My family lives in the Xijiashan No. 2 Village, which is under the jurisdiction of Jiangan County, near the city of Yibin. My village is pretty famous. During the Qing dynasty [1644–1911], a local scholar, named Xi, successfully passed the imperial examination and was promoted to be a mandarin. He bought a plot of land in an auspicious location and built a large mansion. A century later, the mansion remains well preserved. Because of the Xi mansion, the village has acquired a new name, the Xijiashan Rural Residence, and has attracted tourists from all over the country. Our village is also well-known for the cranes. Each year, thousands of white cranes migrate to the area and roam around.

My family has a house in the northwestern corner of the village, near the foot of a mountain. Both my parents are still alive and I have three siblings. My elder brother is already married with kids. My younger brother and I now live at home.

My bad luck started in 1993 after I had turned twenty-four. According to the local tradition, it should have been the time for me to get married. My girlfriend and I had been dating for over a year. She wanted to marry me because my family was quite well off. We earned pretty good money by collecting and selling crane eggs. So, at the urging of my girlfriend, I started preparing for our wedding. In the fall of that year, my family managed to raise five thousand yuan [US$625], and invited a local contractor and some craftsmen to add a new wing to our house. On the first day, my younger brother and I were assigned to work on the foundation by digging a hole in the ground and pouring concrete into it. Not long after we started, my brother accidentally hit something hard. We dug around carefully and discovered two big pottery containers. They were so heavy and hard to lift. My brother and I carried them into our house. We unsealed the covers and found shiny gold coins, in both of them!

I couldn't believe my eyes. I called all my family together. We emptied the pots, dumped all of the gold coins onto the floor, washed off the dirt, and then piled them up on the table. We counted and counted—there were one hundred of them. My goodness, my whole family was in a total blissful daze. Everything just felt so unreal. We truly believed that we wouldn't have to worry about money for the rest of our lives.

Oh well, as the saying goes: walls have ears. Apparently, our screaming caught the attention of the contractors. They had seen everything through the window. Those three bastards were consumed with jealousy. They immediately contacted the police. Half an hour later, several police cars arrived and surrounded our house from every direction. Of course, we didn't know that. At that moment, my whole family was still caught up in the excitement of our newly gained wealth. We were literally shaking with ecstasy. Suddenly, the door burst open. We saw fully armed police everywhere, as if they had just descended from heaven. Without any explanation, they shoved us aside and snatched the two pots of gold. Then, they tied up my whole family with one long rope, me, my parents, my younger brother, and my nephew, and herded us into a police truck.

At the Public Security Bureau, police interrogated us for a whole night. The next morning, they decided that my parents and my nephew were not directly linked to the case, so the police released them. My younger brother and I were transferred to a detention center in Yibing. Special detectives were called in to interrogate us in three shifts for several days. Police charged that we had stolen the gold coins from the grave of the Qing official. A Mr. Bai, who was the chief interrogator, put a gold coin on my palm and asked me to examine the head of the coin carefully. I looked at it closely and noticed several characters: "Minted in the sixth year of Qing Emperor Tongzhi's reign by the Xi family." I didn't realize those gold pieces were minted in 1867. My family members were so carried away with the discovery that none of us saw those characters on the coins.

I told the police repeatedly that my brother and I had found those gold pieces under our own house. On hearing that, Mr. Bai gave out a cold laugh: These gold pieces are clearly part of the treasures inside Mr. Xi's tomb. How could those gold pieces end up buried under your house? They didn't have legs, did they? He also said that there were many Ming [1368–1644] and Qing tombs in the vicinity of the village. About 70 to 80 percent had been looted by an organized group of robbers. He said my case was only the beginning of a large-scale investigation. The government was determined to protect cultural relics as well as to wipe out the crime syndicate. Police hoped to piece together all the clues from my case and capture the ringleader. They suspected that my brother and I were both grave robbers.

I was dumbfounded. I had no clue as to what Mr. Bai was talking about. He said sternly: Don't attempt to put on a show. 'Fess up. Cooperation will lead to leniency. We know that you and your brother are not the ringleaders. Who is behind all these lootings? Are you hoarding any other precious cultural relics, such as porcelain, jade, or pottery? How many have you sold on the market? My mind was completely fogged up; I couldn't have cooked up stories even if I had wanted to. I just kept saying: I don't belong to any group and I haven't stolen anything. Then, Mr. Bai became really nasty: I initially thought you guys were just a bunch of hicks. Didn't realize you are pretty experienced in coping with interrogations. If you refuse to cooperate, we can keep you here forever. Don't blame me if you get the tougher punishment.

LIAO: How did the gold pieces end up under your house?

TIAN: From the unexpected discovery of fortune to our sudden arrest, everything happened so fast. We didn't even have time to think about things such as who had buried those gold pieces under our house. We still don't know.

Anyway, since the interrogation didn't yield much of a result, the local police refused to release us and detained my brother and me for three and a half months.

The days were long and miserable. Initially, the guards thought I was some kind of a big shot—the head of a triad specializing in robbing graves. They were a little fearful of me and treated me nicely. One guy even offered me a quilt when it became chilly in the evenings. Several weeks later, they found out that I was only a country bumpkin. Then things started to get nasty. The guards secretly instructed my fellow inmates to straighten me out. Under the guards' prodding, the "big boss"—a tall burly guy in my cell—began to orchestrate the initiation ritual that I hadn't gone through in my first week of detention. They stripped me, forcing me to lie down on my stomach. Then about twenty inmates walked over, spat on my ass, and then stomped on it. They called this "granting the knighthood." I was later told that prisoners had gotten the idea from a Hong Kong kung fu movie about a fictional kingdom of beggars. After I was "knighted," two prisoners placed a big plastic chamber pot on top of me. They called that "tortoise carrying the shitload." Both of my hands were pressed under the container. Each time I tried to move my hands or my body, the toilet container would tilt and urine would spill over onto my body. One guy, who had been assigned to be my torturer, would kick my head if the container tilted. He kicked it so hard that my hair was soaked in blood.

LIAO: How could they be so brutal?

TIAN: That was just the beginning. Each time the inmates walked over to relieve themselves, they would sit on the container and step on my body. The nicer ones would only put their feet on my shoulder or back. Those evil ones deliberately put their feet on my head. I began to scream with pain, begging for mercy. But the big boss wouldn't let me go. With the help of two guys, he managed to sit on the container with both of his feet up in the air. By then, he had moved all his body weight onto me. I yelled loudly: You are killing me. You are killing me.

My loud screaming startled the big boss. He jumped off and asked his lackeys to cover my mouth. But it was too late. One guard on duty heard me. He opened the cell door and pulled me out of there. My whole body was soaked with urine. Luckily, the guard was a new graduate from the local police academy. He was young and still had a strong sense of justice and sympathy. He ordered other inmates to fetch me some hot water so I could wash and change. The guard then called the big boss to his office for interrogation. The big boss was all smiles and said I was having stomach pains and accidentally knocked over the urine container. The guard turned to me, and asked if it was true. I immediately nodded my head. The guard was skeptical but had to believe his story. He called the clinic and asked the nurse to give me some pain medicine and then issued a warning to the big boss: Next time, if there are horrible screams from your cell, I won't hear a word of explanation. I will just tie you up and put you in solitary confinement.

LIAO: You were lucky to have met a sympathetic guard.

TIAN: When the big boss and I were sent back to the cell, he tossed me a cigarette butt and said: You were quite a guy. You didn't betray me. Go rest up for a couple of days. I will give you a new assignment. Why don't you clean the floor?

LIAO: How did it work?

TIAN: The big boss assigned the chores to all inmates in my cell. If he didn't like someone, he would assign the person to dump and clean the chamber pot. Two people were needed for the job. Those two had to stand at attention by the container all day, one on each side. When the big boss or his friends needed to take a dump, the two guys had to help him take off his pants, and then stand in front of him to shield the big boss from public view. If the big boss wanted to spit while sitting on the pot, he would grab one of the guys by the collar and spit into his shirt. Compared with those two toilet helpers, I was really lucky. At least I was promoted to be the floor cleaner and didn't have to serve as a human spittoon.

LIAO: I've been in jail once and know something about initiation rituals. But I've never heard about the ceremony you told me. I guess prisoners are getting more creative when it comes to torturing people.

TIAN: For a while I thought I was doing OK. Two weeks later, the detention center launched a large-scale "Confession Leads to Leniency" campaign, which encouraged us to confess our own crimes and report on others. One day, about three hundred detainees from nine cells were called to the courtyard for a meeting. Leaders from the local Communist Party, the Public Security Bureau, and the People's Court showed up. We lined up in neat horizontal and vertical rows and sat on the floor, both legs crossed and back straight, just like soldiers in training. One by one, the leaders gave their speeches. All of them were saying the same thing: You should seize opportunities to confess. Confessions will lead to reduced sentences. If alleged murderers voluntarily confess their crimes and if the details they provide can be confirmed by authorities, they will get life imprisonment instead of the death penalty. At the end, the prison chief reminded everyone that the new policy would last for only two weeks. Once the campaign was over, no matter what kind of confession a detainee made, no leniency would be granted.

I sat there quietly, listening very attentively. I didn't even dare cough or fart. The courtyard was surrounded by fully armed guards, and two machine guns were aiming at us from the window of a building nearby. At the end of the meeting, I suddenly heard my name called by the head of the Public Security Bureau. "Yes, sir!" I immediately got up and stood at attention. He looked at me with a fake smile, and said: Tian Zhiguang, I want you to think hard and take advantage of this opportunity, understand?

Overnight, the chief's remarks turned me into a top celebrity thief. Once again, everyone began to think I was a big criminal. After we were back in the cell, a guard whispered something to the big boss, and then delivered some pens and notepads. Every inmate was supposed to put his confession in writing. The big boss pulled me aside and whispered: You are a lucky guy. Even the head of the Public Security Bureau knows you. If you confess, he will probably let you go home tomorrow. I shook my head and answered: I don't have anything to confess. The big boss slapped my head: You dumb ass. This type of campaign only happens once a year. If you don't take advantage of it, you will end up in jail forever.

Then, he continued to lecture me: Those officials out there are all liars. Under normal circumstances, they trick you into confessing, promising you the reward of a reduced sentence. Once you tell everything, they never keep their promise. You probably end up with a bullet in the head. However, this campaign is different. The media has written about it. If those officials renege on their promises, they will lose face and credibility. After hearing his lecture, I told him the same thing: I don't really have anything to confess. The big boss finally lost patience with me. He tossed me a pen and a notepad, and said: Don't try to fool me. You'd better tell everything to the authorities. Just blame everything on your accomplices who are on the lam. Your confession will benefit me. I can take credit for extracting the truth out of you. If I'm lucky, I can get my sentence reduced.

I was left with no choice. I took the pen and began to agonize over my confession. The cell was like a classroom and every "student" was asked to write a paper. The big boss walked around the room, making sure that every inmate was following instructions. I wrote in detail about what I had already told the police. After a whole day of nonstop writing and rewriting, we finally turned in our "papers." The next morning, we were told that half of the inmates had failed to produce any new stuff. The big boss became mad, really mad. He told his lackeys to slap and kick us. Then he ordered us to kneel down, put our notepads on the floor, and then bend over to revise our confessions. It was very painful to kneel and bend like that for hours. Two older inmates couldn't take it after ten or fifteen minutes. They began to moan with pain. The big boss dragged the two guys to the chamber pot and dipped their heads in urine. He then forced them to resume. Every now and then, he would yell at us: Your confession needs to be sensational. Don't try to simplify and whitewash. The more serious your crimes are, the better it makes me look.

Under the intense pressure, my fellow inmates began to fabricate stories of rape. Having grown up in the countryside, I was an honest bumpkin. I wasn't good at making up stories. I kept writing the same thing. The big boss became really irritated. He lit up a cigarette and poked the burning end of the cigarette at my eyelids. I began to scream. He ordered another inmate to seal my mouth with Scotch tape. He then grabbed my hair and said: Are you fucking with me? I have the backing of the prison authority, do you know that? He threw me onto the floor and asked other inmates to kick me. After about ten minutes, he told them to stop and unsealed my mouth. He asked again: Are you going to do it or not? I got up, knelt in front of him, and said: Sir, I don't really have anything to write.

Again, he grabbed my hair, and asked one inmate to pry my mouth open: You have a very stubborn tongue. He stuffed four or five burning cigarette butts right into my mouth. They hurt but I couldn't spit them out because two guys were holding my head and chin. I coughed violently and tears ran down my face. The big boss asked again: Are you ready to confess or not? If you don't, I'm going to light up this whole packet of cigarettes and stuff them down your throat.

I caved in and became creative. I admitted that I had robbed graves before. He asked: How many times? I raised both hands and showed him eight of my fingers. He smiled: Very good!

Believe it or not, my imagination began to run wild. Even though there were many grammatical errors in my report, I did it very vividly. I said that I started robbing graves at the age of fifteen and had been in the business for nine years. I used chisels, hammers, and flashlights as tools. Each time I robbed a grave, I would hide the excavated treasures, such as gold, jewelry, and other valuables, under some shrubs. I would then dig them out five or six months later, after the coast was clear.

I also said that I used a special compass to locate tombs. The compass helped me to detect how much treasure was buried inside.

Before dinnertime, I showed my newly fabricated confession to the big boss. He was very satisfied with the information. He then handed them over to the guard on duty. As a reward, I was given a bowl of spicy pork. I was so hungry and wanted to swallow it all. But my mouth and my tongue still hurt from the cigarette burns. Every bite brought excruciating pain. It took me two hours to finish that meal.

The next day, one guard put the handcuffs on me and shoved me into a police car. I was supposed to take four police detectives to my hometown and uncover those hidden treasures. The car jolted along the bumpy road for about four or five hours. We passed Xijia Mountain and then came to a crossroad. The police asked me which way to go. I pointed randomly to a small side road. The police car drove right on. Then the car came to a sudden stop. I realized that we had come to a dead end, in front of a run-down farmhouse

The police became impatient. They waved their guns at me: Where the hell is it? I stammered: It—it's somewhere around here. They kicked me out of the car. I had no idea where we were. I simply pointed in the direction of a hill nearby. The police parked their car on the side of the road and all four of them followed me. My mind was running blank. All I did was to amble forward into the bushes, jump over small streams, and climb steep slopes. About twenty minutes later, we saw over ten tombs scattered around a cleared area. I sat down, exhausted. I pointed at the tombs and said, There they are. The policemen were panting, gasping for air. They asked me: Which one? I simply drew a circle on the ground, and said: From here to there. One guy took out a small military shovel from his backpack, and a piece of elaborate-looking equipment. Seeing that the police took my words really seriously, I began to tremble with fear. I walked around those tombs, pretending I was trying to remember where I had buried my treasures. The guy with the detecting equipment followed me. Others were digging frantically. An hour later, nothing had turned up. As darkness fell, the head of the group lost his patience. He seized the collar of my shirt and yelled: Where in the hell did you bury your treasures? I put both of my hands up: Sir, I really don't know . . . Before I even finished my sentence, he punched me in the face. I fell into the bushes. I struggled to get up, and knelt in front of him: Sir, please forgive me. I lied and I deserve to die. One guy tried to hit me with his shovel, but was stopped by the group leader.

By the time we walked back to the parked car, it was already after midnight. On our way back, I told them about the tortures I had gone through and explained to them why I had to lie. Nobody listened to my story. One guy even pointed his gun at my face and said: If you don't shut up, I'm going to blow your head off.

LIAO: You certainly played a big practical joke on the police.

TIAN: I had no choice. Otherwise I would have to swallow a whole pack of burning cigarettes. My body could have been turned into a furnace.

LIAO: What happened later on?

TIAN: The big boss in my cell blamed me for trashing his opportunity of getting a reward. He and other inmates stripped me naked and ordered me to stand by the chamber pot for twenty-four hours. Each time I tried to doze off, they would use cigarette butts to burn the hair under my armpit, on my legs, and around my genitals. It was so painful but I didn't dare to make a noise for fear that the guards would hear it. If they had, it could have gotten me into more trouble with the big boss. I passed out a couple of times from the pain, but the big boss wouldn't give up. He ordered one inmate to inject some peppery water up into my ass. I begged him: Please have mercy. I promise I will confess this time. Nobody believed me. I said: No. I swear to Chairman Mao that what I'm saying is true. If I lie, my mother will turn into a whore for the Americans. My desperate begging made everyone laugh. He softened his tone by saying: If I can't get you to confess, the guards will give me a hard time. I'm glad you understand.

I then fabricated more stories in my second round of confession. Before I gave it to the guard, the big boss reviewed it and forced me to put a statement at the end of my confession. It read: If I tell lies this time, I'm willing to subject myself to any type of punishment from the people's government, including the death penalty.

LIAO: You were really bold.

TIAN: What would you expect me to do? I knew very well that the authorities would take a couple of days or so to read my confession. Then it would take another day before they decided to drive me out to find the hidden treasures. That would buy me several days of peace. I could also get some food. As for what consequences those lies would bring me, I didn't even care to think. After two days of peace and quiet, I was on the road again, in a police car. Once again, we ended up with nothing. The police kicked me and slapped me and tied both of my hands tightly behind my back. I was locked up in solitary confinement for several days. When I was back in my cell, the big boss ordered more beatings. I passed out many times. Each time after I regained consciousness, I would beg and scream: I'm going to tell the truth this time, I swear to Chairman Mao. They never trusted me again. Several times, when I saw the guards passing by in the hallway, I would reach my hands out through the iron bars, trying to get their help. They simply ignored my plea.

But one day, things suddenly began to change. Two guards came and took the big boss away. At the end of the day, he came back, subdued and silent. When the other inmates saw that, they all got scared and sat around him quietly. I picked my usual spot by the chamber pot, anticipating another round of beatings. But nothing happened. At bedtime, several of his lackeys tried to massage his back and made his bed for him, but he simply pushed them away.

LIAO: Could it be that some high-level officials were coming in for an inspection?

TIAN: Not exactly. The next day, all inmates were called to the courtyard for a meeting, just like the one we had had before. After the meeting started, five inmates were paraded onto the podium. Two guards pushed them down onto the ground, with their faces down and their hands tied behind their backs. It turned out that during the "Confession Leads to Leniency" campaign, a guy in Cell Six had died from severe beatings from his fellow detainees. He was a midlevel executive at a state-run enterprise, and was a chief suspect in an embezzling case. Police interrogated him for a week, but he wouldn't admit any guilt. The guards secretly asked inmates to roughen him up a bit. That poor guy wasn't up to it. After getting hit and kicked on the chest by a couple of bullies, his face turned blue. But those guys still wouldn't stop. One tall guy grabbed the former executive by the feet and held him upside down while another one punched him in the stomach. Soon, his body became limp and he began to spit blood. By the time the guards found out, the executive had already died. His death leaked out to the media. To prevent future embarrassment, the local government ordered prison authorities to crack down on big bullies inside the detention center. But who were the real murderers? Not those bullies. They were coerced by the guards, none of whom was taking responsibility.

LIAO: This practice of ordering prisoners to extract confessions from fellow inmates has been around for a long time, from the Qing dynasty to the present.

TIAN: Yeah, that's what everyone says. But that doesn't mean it's legal. After the meeting, the big boss in my cell was scared shitless. He knelt down, kowtowed to a little portrait of the Buddha that had been smuggled in by an inmate: He then told his lackeys to be careful during future tortures: We should focus on those areas where we can cause pain and discomfort without killing the person. He then patted me on my shoulder: Thank God you didn't die in my hands.

The next day, right after breakfast, the loudspeaker inside each cell was suddenly turned on—we were told that the bullies were going to be paraded around inside the detention center. We all gathered around the iron bars and looked toward the hallway. Soon, the bullies in Cell Six came, and stopped right in front of us. They recited a couple of lines, like robots: My name is so and so and I'm a bully. I illegally tortured my fellow detainees. I deserve severe punishment. Please do not follow my example. After that, they were dragged away to another cell. It was quite a festive occasion. Several guys in my cell started to applaud. The big boss gave them a nasty look, and they immediately stopped.

The campaign worked in my favor. During the next week, it was very peaceful and the big boss was nice.

Before I even had the chance to witness the execution of those bullies, my brother and I were released. My poor brother was locked up in a separate cell and suffered internal injuries from the bullies. When we got home, we found out that our mother had gone insane. She would sit by the door all day, without moving. She peed and shat in her pants. My dad moved in with my elder sister's family. He would come in to cook for my mother every couple of days and clean. My brother and I used to be very energetic. But after we got out of jail, our health got really bad. We looked like ghosts and didn't have the strength to do any physical labor. On top of that, we were shunned by everyone in the village because people thought we were thieves. My brother had blood in his stool for a long time, but he doesn't have money to see a doctor. I've been having bladder problems for nine years and I'm impotent. I think about women all the time, but just can't get it up. I don't think I'm capable of having kids to carry on the family name. Someone needs to pay for our sufferings.

LIAO: How?

TIAN: I became a beggar and wandered in the county for quite a while. One day, I overheard someone talking about a newspaper report that said that a peasant had won a lawsuit against the local Public Security

Bureau. I was inspired by the story. I changed into some clean clothes, and went to seek advice at a law office. I told the lawyer in tears about my detention and the tragic impact on my family.

LIAO: What did the lawyer say?

TIAN: He was very sympathetic to my situation, but declined to take my case. He said it would be very hard to sue the local Public Security Bureau because no one would be willing to testify on my behalf. He said my own account was insufficient. That made me really mad. I had to seek justice somewhere. I took the case to the local court myself and they wouldn't take it. I then went to file petitions to higher levels of government, seeking 200,000 yuan [US$25,000] in compensation. Nobody listened. So I came to Chengdu to file a petition with the provincial supreme court. I want to sue the police for illegally detaining me. I also want to sue the detention center for secretly encouraging detainees to extract confessions from their fellow detainees. Those bullies in the detention center had turned the Communist jail into a living hell. Last, I want to sue the local Public Security Bureau for embezzling the gold coins. Nobody knows where the confiscated gold coins have gone. Those involved in the case should be liable for the loss of the coins.

LIAO: Sounds reasonable to me.

TIAN: So far, nobody has yet handled my case. The Communist Party and this government are very cold-blooded.

THE SAFECRACKER

A week after the lunar new year in 1991, I accompanied a lawyer friend to a jail in Chongqing and visited the famous robber Cui Zhixiong. The date set for his execution had been postponed for forty-five days. According to him, "I got lucky and picked up another Chinese New Year for free."

Cui was thirty-nine years old, with heavy brows and big round eyes. He was quite strong. Using a Chinese cliché, I will describe him as having a tiger's back and a bear's waist. Even in the cold winter he was wearing only a shirt and summer pants. He was heavily shackled, but didn't look at all frazzled and weary like other death row inmates I had met.

After my interview, I set aside the tapes and notes. I revisited our conversation in 1998, when he had long been turned into ashes.

—⚉—

LIAO YIWU: How did you end up here?

CUI ZHIXIONG: I have committed the worst crime under heaven. I have cracked many safes and stolen millions of yuan. I'm waiting to be executed. This is the second time I've been locked up in a prison. Three years ago, I got busted for the first time and was locked up at a detention center on Gele Mountain. That was an old-style prison built by the Nationalists in the 1940s. Even after fifty-some years, the structure was still solid. The walls were built with steel-reinforced concrete, and there were four watchtowers, one at each corner. The daily activities of prisoners were confined to a rectangular courtyard, which was surrounded by a two-story building. The back of the prison bordered on a deep cliff.

To get to the prison, a car had to climb a long circuitous mountain road. After you passed the entrance, you found yourself in a small courtyard. Outsiders were allowed to come in only after going through a thorough body search. On the ground floor, there was an interrogation room, a kitchen, a public bathhouse, a storage room, and a latrine. The second floor housed all the prison cells—sixteen altogether, including one for women. A circular corridor, which cut through the prison wards, was so dark that lightbulbs had to be turned on during the daytime. My prison cell had a window in the ceiling. If I jumped high enough, I could touch the window bars. When I did a chin-up and hung on to the window bars, I could see in the distance a hill covered with pine trees.

LIAO: How did you get so familiar with the local geography?

CUI: I am a born thief. I can remember the details of any locale after one visit. Besides, I was locked up inside that detention center for over two months. I knew every piece of brick and stone. The first day I entered the detention center, I began to work on a plan to escape. I was told that nobody had ever managed to escape from that prison. Only a fool would believe that. Even stones have cracks. I had broken into so many safes and frequented so many forbidden areas. Nobody had stopped me. I was quite confident that I could find a way out.

During the first month, I had to go through interrogation every day. I didn't have time to focus on any escape plan. Later on, I began to cooperate with my interrogators. I would confess a little here and a little there. The interrogators became very happy. Sometimes, when I offered them some secrets of safecracking, they couldn't digest them all. They would spend a couple of days researching. As a result, I was able to take a break.

LIAO: Under normal circumstances, a detainee has to go through all sorts of "procedures" to have his attitude changed. Did they ever beat you up?

CUI: You are right. A new prisoner would have to go through various tortures designed by the guards and his fellow inmates to break him. I lucked out. Since the prosecutor needed me to help out with some of his other cases, he personally brought me to see the head of the detention center and told him to take good care of me. So I was spared the "procedures." Anyway, after the pace of my interrogation slowed down,

I had time to think about how to escape. First, I had to find opportunities when I could be left alone. When many people huddle together, even a magician can't make himself disappear in front of them. Prisoners did everything together. Apart from three meals, every inmate was allowed to go out for one fifteen-minute break in the morning and one in the afternoon. When the inmates stepped out into the courtyard, the guards would watch everyone from inside the towers perched on top of the four corners of the wall. One way to avoid attention from the guards was to hide inside the latrine. The latrine, which was opposite the public bathhouse, was dimly lit. Its stinky smell was overwhelming. Inside, there was a row of holes on the ground so people could squat on them to take care of their business. Those holes were connected to a huge human-waste pond at the back of the latrine. The stinky latrine was the perfect place for a loner like me.

LIAO: No other prisoner used the latrine at break time?

CUI: There was a big wooden shit bucket inside each cell. People normally did their business in there. During our breaks, two inmates were responsible for carrying the buckets out, dumping the contents, and washing them. Therefore, when everyone rushed into the courtyard, people in charge of the buckets would try to finish their tasks as soon as possible so they could go breathe some fresh air or stealthily swap some petty goods with others. So I could squat inside the latrine alone for over ten minutes without arousing any suspicion.

It took me two trips to the latrine to finally figure out an action plan. The first time I was in there, I noticed a tiny ventilation window. From there, I could see a wall right in front of me. There was no way I could get out that way. Then, I found out about the human-waste pond behind the latrine. I began to wonder whether the pond was built inside the jail or outside. It couldn't have been inside because I had never seen prison staff clean out the pond. But, if the pond was outside, was it an open one or was it covered like a manhole with a lid on it? How big and heavy could the lid be?

One day, as I was squatting inside the latrine, I vaguely heard noises coming from outside the prison. I held my breath and pushed my ear against the wall. It sounded like someone was scooping out the human waste. The person might have been a local peasant because I could hear a horse-drawn cart. It was obvious that it was an open shit pond outside the prison wall. At that moment, all my blood rushed to my head. My brain was buzzing. I had a plan in place.

The next step was to calculate the route and the speed of my escape. My daily breaks were about fifteen minutes each. It usually took five minutes for inmates from six cells to empty the wooden shit buckets in the latrine. That would give me ten minutes to go inside the latrine and complete phase one of the plan. At the end of the break, there would be a roll call. If they found someone missing, guards would check the courtyard and cells and then form a search team. That would probably give me nine to ten minutes to carry out phase two of the plan—running away. Then the guards would usually spend time dividing the team into several smaller groups so they could search separately. That would probably add two additional minutes. In other words, during the escape and chasing process, I would have twelve minutes to run away from the guards.

LIAO: Wow, it was like in a thriller movie.

CUI: The stuff in a movie is nothing compared to my adventure. When they sent me to the detention center a couple of months before, it took the police car twenty minutes to get from the bottom of the mountain to the top. If my escape was successful, I could run down the mountain in a straight line in roughly the same amount of time. I had rehearsed this escape episode in my mind over ten times.

Things worked out really smoothly. I remember clearly that it was on May 6, 1988, three days before my thirty-sixth birthday. That afternoon, I wrapped in a small plastic bag a vest, a pair of shorts and shoes, as well as a small towel. I tied the bag around my waist and put on a large uniform. After a guard blew the whistle for afternoon break, I joined the crowd in the hallway. Two minutes later, I was inside the courtyard. I held myself against a wall and glanced up at the guards inside the watchtowers. They were chatting. I then quickly crept into the latrine and almost bumped into two inmates walking out with a bucket. I deliberately made a lot of noise unbuckling my pants and they didn't even look back. I squatted over the last hole from the door. I could hear a guy come in and take a piss at the urinals near the latrine entrance. There was no time to waste. I took off my uniform and carefully slid my body down into the hole. I couldn't look down because the stinky smell went directly into my nose, bringing tears to my face. The squatting hole was pretty small. I had to let my legs down first, and then squeeze my body down slowly, with two hands firmly clinging to the edge. Then I slowly lowered my upper body and then my head down. I found myself dangling in the air. I didn't realize the hole was so deep. I clenched my teeth and counted one, two, and three. Then I let go with both hands. The next thing I knew, I had plunged into the shit hole like a heavy bomb.

My heart beat so fast. It was going to explode. My basic instinct to survive overcame everything. I ducked my head down inside the shit and swam forward. I could feel a rat jumping over my back. Time seemed to have frozen. Goddammit, it seemed forever. I began to tremble involuntarily. I didn't dare to open my eyes. I could hardly move because the human waste was too thick. I just splashed forward little by little. I felt I was drowning. Soon, I touched some barbed wire. I raised my head and opened my eyes. I was outside! I was about five meters away from the edge of the pond. A barbwire, connecting with the prison walls on both ends, ran through the middle of the pond. I reached my hands down and tried to see how I could get through. It turned out that the wire didn't reach all way down to the bottom. I dove headfirst into the shit and swam under the wire. By the time I got out, I had two big deep scratches on my back and legs. Since I had pretty strong wrists and arms, I grabbed the edge and managed to drag my body out. I thought I had stayed in the shit pond forever. Actually, the whole operation took less than six or seven minutes because I could hear the prisoners inside were still on break.

I quickly stripped, opened up the plastic bag, wiped myself with that towel, and then changed to my vest, shorts, and shoes. Apart from the stinky smell on my body, I looked like a jogger. I dashed down the mountain on a small wooded path. My legs moved like they were equipped with wings. I jumped over dead trees and big rocks. I think I must have broken the world distance running record. I fell and rolled down a sloping mountain path several times. I got up and moved on. I ran into five or six tourists coming down from the mountain. I smelled so bad. They all covered their noses and ran away from me. All that time, I thought I heard the sirens of police cars. It turned out I was just hallucinating.

Next to the Martyrs' Cemetery at the foot of the mountain was a foreign languages college. I ran right onto the campus and passed through the students' playground. Since I was only wearing a vest and shorts and had muscled arms and legs, people thought I was a professional athlete. Nobody detected anything suspicious. I snuck into a dorm building. It was empty because students were either in class or outside. I cleaned myself in the public shower room, and snatched some clothes that were hung out to dry outside a dorm window. After I left the university, I realized that I was in a place called Shapingba. I knew that there was a large hospital nearby. I stopped a taxi and jumped in. After he drove for about a hundred meters, I could hear the sound of sirens. The search team had already arrived. About two hundred meters away, I noticed traffic police stopping cars to check passengers inside. I immediately beckoned the driver to stop. I said apologetically, Sorry, sir. I forgot to bring my wallet. He turned his head back and said: Do you want me to take you back? Before he even finished his sentence, I had already jumped out of the car. I ran in the direction of the hospital. After I walked in, I roamed around the patient ward and saw a morgue behind the labs. I lifted a latch on one of the back windows and climbed in. I looked around and found that the room was about twenty meters long and thirty meters wide. There were six stone platforms for corpses, and three were occupied. A couple of bodies were stacked inside a fridge with glass doors. Since I had no safe place to go, I simply lay down on a stone platform and covered myself up with a blue plastic sheet.

It was pretty hot in May, but after lying down on a slab of stone for a couple of hours, the dampness began to seep through my bones. The morgue was dimly lit. The stinky smell of the bodies floated in the air. All my dead neighbors in that room seemed to have been killed in traffic accidents. I could see pools of blood on the slabs. I waited for the sky to turn dark. Anxious as I was, time seemed to move very slowly. A breeze came and the door kept swinging back and forth. I was shivering with fear. If anyone came in, I would have been finished. If that person dared to remove the sheet on top of me, I would thrust out my claws and choke him to death.

LIAO: How long did you stay inside the morgue?

CUI: It felt like eternity. I started by counting my heartbeat. When my heart beat fast, I considered three as one second. When it slowed down, I counted one beat as a second. Later on, I counted myself into a sleep. I was awakened by some noises in the adjacent room. It was the sound of chopsticks banging on tin bowls. Apparently, it was dinnertime for the guard. The thought of dinner stimulated my stomach, which began to have terrible spasms. It hurt so much that I wanted to get up and move a little bit to distract myself from the pain. But I controlled my urges and held myself still a little longer. The guard spent the next two hours eating and drinking tea. Before he went to bed, I could hear him humming a tune from a traditional Sichuan opera. Strangely enough, I can now remember the tune and the words very clearly.

Things began to quiet down after the guard went to sleep. So I got up. My body was almost frozen stiff. I left the morgue. As I was passing by the hospital cafeteria, I noticed it was open for night-shift workers. Then, two nurses walked out, chatting and laughing. I hid behind a small grove of shrubs. As they passed by, I picked up a small piece of stone on the ground and threw it at one of them. It hit her right on the wrist. "Who is it?" She was startled, and dropped her food to the ground.

The two women screamed and ran back into the cafeteria for help. I ran away as fast as I could, and went back to the morgue. I stayed there for a little longer until it was quiet on all fronts. When I came out again, I accidentally came across half a bottle of water on the side of the road. I picked it up and dumped the water into my mouth. It felt really good. I then came to the place where the two nurses dropped their food. I cupped the food up and swallowed it. My stomach suddenly felt a surge of stabbing pain. I squatted down and rested for a few minutes. I then walked stealthily into the patient wards. I checked each floor for food. When I came to the fifth floor, I saw the doctor's office was open. Nobody was inside. I walked in, quickly changed into a white gown I found in the closet, put on a surgical mask, and picked up a stethoscope from the desk. Then I visited a maternity ward, pretending I was a doctor on call. I ended up with quite a few treats: I had stolen over a thousand yuan from various patients and managed to get some cakes and fruit.

After I came out of the hospital, I walked into a military medical academy next door. I stole a set of military uniforms that were hanging outside a dorm building. By that time, it was almost dawn. A big shuttle bus was parked right in front of the building. I found a piece of metal string, bent it, slid it in to open the lock, and got inside. I made myself comfortable on the last row of seats. Exhausted as I was, I soon dozed off. Then I felt someone tugging at my clothes and pushing me to a corner seat. I woke up and realized that the sun was already up, and the bus was filled with students in military uniforms. A guy sitting next to me asked: Which class are you in? I couldn't answer him, but randomly pointed to a building outside. He said: You work at the computer lab? I nodded.

From the conversations I overheard on the bus, I realized that it was Sunday. The bus carried the students, including me, all the way downtown. The trip went well, without any glitches. For the first time in a long while, I saw groups of pretty girls on the street. I tasted freedom.

LIAO: You were even bold enough to sleep on a military bus. Weren't you afraid of getting caught?

CUI: I couldn't go back to the hospital, and it was not safe to loiter on the street. Walking around inside the military medical academy at night was even riskier. The shuttle bus was the only place to go.

LIAO: What happened afterward?

CUI: They never caught me. I was a free man again, wandering all over the country, stealing and breaking into safes. I had stolen so much money that I didn't know what to do with it. I decided to settle down and live as a recluse. I purchased a couple of houses in Beihai. But I never felt safe. I wasn't at all excited about starting another business because I hated to associate myself with businessmen. They are boring people. Moreover, I had just reached the peak in my profession. If you wanted me to change jobs, I just couldn't get myself to become enthused about the idea. So, I just idled around. When I had nothing to do, my mind began to go crazy. I dreamed about prisons and policemen every night.

LIAO: Were you ever married before?

CUI: I had a girlfriend. She was a big fan of the Taiwanese pop singer Tong Ange. I loved his songs too. I wanted to marry her but couldn't. You don't have to tell your girlfriend about your profession, but you need to share everything with your wife. That's the Chinese tradition, isn't it?

LIAO: How did you get caught this time?

CUI: Two years had passed since I escaped. I thought the coast was clear. I returned to Chongqing. One day, I made a bet with a couple of old buddies, saying that I could easily break into a new type of high-tech safe at a large company. There I went. I walked right through the main entrance. I broke into the treasurer's office. Within ten minutes, I located the safe and cut off the office alarm system. I stuck a razor-thin knife into a small crack, and with the sound of a click, I cut off the alarm on the safe. No shit, was that what they called the new advanced laser protection technology? Breaking that damn thing was the easiest job I had ever done. I was a little carried away by this initial success and began to let down my guard. I leaned against the safe, chewing bubble gum. I even blew a big bubble. After I opened the safe door, I found there were about 500,000 yuan [US$60,300] in there, plus some bundles of newly minted hundred-yuan bills. On the spur of the moment, I used my cigarette lighter and began to burn those hundred-yuan bills one by one. Then, the police arrived before I even finished with one bundle.

When I was arrested, I felt as if my heart had finally dropped to the ground after hanging on a high cliff for a long, long time. I felt my mind could finally rest. I stood up, stretched my hands out, and asked the police to handcuff me. Then, after they shackled me, I said calmly: Let's go.

LIAO: Now that you are on death row, how do you feel?

CUI: I think a lot about my escape three years before. It was too miraculous. However, nobody can escape his fate. While I was on the run, my body was set free, but my mind wasn't. I owe society too much. I never used the stolen cash to help those who really needed it. So many poor children can't afford to go to school, so many unemployed workers have nothing to support the family . . . What's the difference between those corrupt officials and me? There's none. OK, so much for the story. You are an intellectual and you understand that: whatever you do, you need passion and motivation. I have lost my passion and motivation to live. I'm ready to exit this world.

THE BLIND ERHU PLAYER

On a chilly night in October 1996, I walked into a hot pot (Chinese fondue) restaurant on Wangjianmu Street in Chengdu. After I sat down, I saw a waiter leading a blind street musician inside. The musician was holding an erhu, a two-stringed Chinese violin, and feeling his way around the tables. He kept bowing to customers. I felt so sorry for him and ordered a tune. To my surprise, he played it beautifully.

The erhu player said he was sixty-three and refused to disclose his real name. He called himself "Nameless Zhang."

LIAO YIWU: Master, you played so beautifully. Could you play me another tune, "Water from the River"?

NAMELESS ZHANG: You need to pay first. According to the rules here, you pay ten yuan per tune.

LIAO: Here is fifty yuan [US$6.40]. Please feel it and make sure it's authentic. Normally speaking, one cannot put a price on music. That's all I can afford. I need to leave some to pay for my meal.

ZHANG: Sir, you are a pro. If you want to hear more, I can play for you all night long. Playing the erhu is like a writer burning the midnight oil. The longer you play, the more you are into it. "Water from the River" is such a sad piece. Why don't I play you "Chirpy Birds on the Empty Mountain"?

LIAO: That's fine. Here is a toast to you. Throughout my life, I have loved two kinds of musical instruments: one is the erhu and the other, the flute. Look at the erhu; it only has two strings, but can express all the stories and emotions of human life. I grew up in Lijaping village, which was hemmed in on three sides by mountains. We used to live in a little run-down courtyard house at the foot of the mountain. When I see you play, all my childhood memories come crowding back. I remember a village teacher who liked to sit on the threshold of his house on rainy days and play the erhu. He also played it when the moon was out. His music always evoked in me a melancholy mood. Nowadays, I can only hear his music in my head.

ZHANG: Your remarks make me cry. I have been selling music on the street for many years now. I can play all kinds of tunes with various techniques. But the majority of listeners have no ear for good music. They are just pretentious eaters who are simply looking for fun and something to enliven the atmosphere. I could handle their requests very easily. But playing music for a pro like you makes me nervous. The music has to come from my heart.

LIAO: Tell me about yourself. How did you lose your eyesight?

ZHANG: As soon as I was pulled out of my mother's womb, I began to struggle in the dark. I don't know what sins they had committed, but all my three siblings were born blind. My family had a reputation in the region as "a cursed dark hole." When I was three years old, my father thrust an erhu into my hand, and forced me with a whip to practice. Playing the erhu was a blind person's rice bowl. It was not as romantic as you have just described. When I turned seven, my parents couldn't stand the fact that all their children had been born blind. They both swallowed poison and committed suicide. At their funeral, I was draped in a white mourning outfit; I sat beside their bodies and played the erhu nonstop. I was hoping to get enough donations and buy coffins for them. I sat there and played for three days. Their bodies were decaying and I was also on the verge of exhaustion. But I didn't dare to stop, feeling as if a whip were hanging over my head. Even now, I still associate my memories of my father with that thin whip that inflicted so much pain on me. Eventually, friends helped bury my parents. My siblings and I were adopted by another blind family. At the age of thirteen, I began to wander around the street to make a living as a musician. I started out in my hometown, Qiaolai, and then traveled all over the province.

LIAO: Is it easy to move around for a person like you?

ZHANG: Blind people have their own community. Each time I arrive at a new place, I have to pay my respects to the chief of the local community. I butter him up with flattering words, and then hand over some money as a gift. With this bribe, he will designate a blind kid to be my guide. The kid will lead me down boulevards and small lanes with instructions about where to make a turn and who lives where. He will also tell me which household is rich and more likely to hire musicians, what the temperaments of people in the household are, and when is a good time to visit. There are rules for everything. By the time you memorize them you can start your own business.

LIAO: Those must have been the rules and customs before the Communist revolution. We are now at the end of the twentieth century. There are street artists everywhere, some singing and playing musical instruments, others performing acrobatics. They don't seem to follow any rules. Most of them change venues constantly. If they see a busy area, they start their gigs right there. Sometimes, the police will kick them out. During the holiday season last year, five blind musicians showed up in front of my house with their erhus, and together they played "The Sun Comes Out and People Are Happy." I ended up giving each one a red envelope with crisp new bills in it.

ZHANG: They were not real musicians. Ours is a big city. Fake musicians wander from district to district, swindling money out of residents. We do have rules within our community. Street musicians are gradually forming a guild with professional rules. Everyone is hoping to make money with real skills. The market for quacks and fake products is getting smaller.

LIAO: What do you mean by "professional rules"?

ZHANG: First, street musicians need to have their own fixed venues or territories. Second, street musicians need to elect their own guild chiefs. In China, everyone used to belong to a government work unit, which offered them jobs and housing. Street musicians also need to be organized and regulated. For example: I've been playing music near the Wangjianmu area for almost seven years. Everyone recognizes me and knows that I treat my music seriously. People are willing to order tunes from me and pay for them. I'm sure you'll see blind musicians in other areas such as Chunxi Road or Wuhou Temple Road. I don't care and have no intention of finding out who is performing down there. All I care is to do a good job here. I assume street guitarists, violinists, beggars, bicycle repairers, or shoeshine boys in this territory will share my view. If someday we want to move to another territory at random, we have to negotiate. Otherwise, we could be kicked out.

LIAO: Aren't you worried about the hard economic times when restaurants around here close down one after another?

ZHANG: I have known many restaurants to close, but that hasn't affected me that much. I have never been short of clients. There are many entrepreneurs who dream of making it big in the restaurant business. The closing of one store means the opening of another one. This area never remains idle. When a Chinese restaurant closes down, a Western restaurant opens up in its place. A seafood restaurant closes down, a hot pot joint opens. The Wangjianmu area used to be the burial site for a young emperor during ancient times. It has good feng shui and is full of prosperous human spirits. In the summertime, the hot pot vendors line up the street, and it's hard to squeeze by. While I perform there, the smell of spices is very distracting to my sense of surroundings. There is the danger of me walking right onto someone's hot pot stove. When all the hot pots are boiling and set in motion, so is my music, which is sometimes lost in the din of the street. I asked a friend to get a speaker for me. I hook up the erhu to the speaker. I carry the speaker on my back while I play. I'll do anything to make restaurant goers happy so I can make some money.

LIAO: Don't you feel you are wasting your life playing here?

ZHANG: My life? I have never pondered these profound issues. For a blind person like me, every day is the same, unless I get sick or injure myself by bumping into a wall. When I was fifteen, I was playing at a teahouse one day. Suddenly, firecrackers filled the air like ear-shattering bombs, and completely drowned out the sound of my music. I didn't stop and kept playing until the owner grabbed my hand. He said the teahouse was empty and everyone was gone. I felt my way outside. People were beating gongs and drums. I was told that the Communist troops had entered the city. That was it. Didn't realize the Nationalist government had been toppled. Later on, after the Communist government was established, I was given some money and sent back, along with many migrant workers, to the countryside in Sichuan. I was assigned to work as a musician for a local cultural bureau. I spent a year learning Braille and I even had a girlfriend.

LIAO: How did you get yourself a girlfriend?

ZHANG: That was 1957. Folk music was in. The tunes by the well-known blind erhu performer and composer Aibing were very popular in China. I rode on the popularity of Aibing, and was invited to perform on the stage for a large crowd. I also played for some music professors. One company made records of my music. Then local officials wanted me to recruit a student. I told them that I didn't want anyone who had normal eyesight. Those who could see would never have the opportunity to enter the world of the blind.

So they sent me a female blind student, who was three years younger. We practiced day and night to prepare for performances at folk music concerts. One day around noontime, I was taking a nap. I felt something moving on my face. At first, I thought it was a fly, and tried to chase it away with my hands. Then, I touched a soft hand, the fingers caressing my nose and my eyes, sending burning sensations all the way to my heart. I reached out my hands and touched her as if I were in a dream. Her braids were so thick, her eyes were so big, her eyelashes were so long, and her skin was so smooth. We finally embraced and held each other close. Around that time, my music reached a peak. I didn't feel that I was playing. I felt as if someone inside my heart were playing for me. I could see my lover in my music. She was beautiful. Wouldn't it be nice if I could take her with me to wander around the world?

LIAO: Did you get married? Did you have children?

ZHANG: We had sex and she became pregnant. During those years, premarital sex was considered immoral and illegal. You could end up in jail for that. Since we were disabled people, the director at my work unit didn't prosecute us. But he forced my girlfriend to have an abortion so we could avoid bad repercussions among the masses. But we wanted the baby and my girlfriend refused to undertake the procedure. We applied for a marriage license. The director said that it was a special case and he needed to have meetings to discuss it. After several meetings, he still couldn't make a decision. Meanwhile, my girlfriend's pregnancy was getting more and more prominent.

Not long after, Chairman Mao's anti-Rightist movement started. My director was labeled a Rightist, and he lost his job. Some of his former subordinates charged that my girlfriend had been impregnated by the director. They didn't think a blind person like me could have sex with a woman. We never got the marriage license, but instead ended up being the target of public humiliation. I was labeled a corrupt element of society because I tried to defend my director. Thank God I was blind; otherwise I would have been tortured to death by those fanatics. My student had a harder life. Several guys pinned her down and coerced her into having an abortion. She was also labeled as a degenerate element of society for having sex with the director.

LIAO: What happened later?

ZHANG: We broke up. It was fate and I couldn't escape. It would have been different if it had happened today. People's attitude toward sex is different. Also, if a blind person can marry another blind person, wouldn't it be a perfect match? It could help solve many social problems. At that time, the whole country was like a big prison. The Party controlled every aspect of our life—eating, drinking, pissing, shitting, birth, marriage, and death. By the way, my student died in the famine of 1960.

LIAO: People are more open-minded than before. Dating and premarital sex are no longer political issues. You are also free to sell your music on the street. I assume nobody asks you to pay license fees.

ZHANG: Pay a license fee? To whom? I think the government should impose a social welfare tax to support people like us. I've been laid off from the Cultural Bureau since the 1960s. If it hadn't been for those political campaigns, I would have been a celebrity and probably a professor at the Chinese Academy of Music. They have an erhu department, you know.

LIAO: What's so special about being a professor? No profession grants you more freedom than that of a street musician.

ZHANG: Being a street musician without any professional affiliations is nice, but not stable. You never know what will happen the next day. By the way, why don't you start to "enjoy" this freedom?

LIAO: With you being my guide, I will start enjoying this freedom tomorrow. I will bring my flute and let's do a duet together. You can collect all the money. I hope you can introduce me to more blind musicians.

ZHANG: Why?

LIAO: I want to find an agent who can help us find sponsors and organize a blind musicians' concert. If you can get twenty blind musicans, we can make it happen.

ZHANG: Good idea. I will go back and discuss it with the head of the guild.

LIAO: Are you telling me that there is another blind musican older than you are?

ZHANG: No, he is younger and he is not blind. He is the head of the local triad, who controls this territory. We call him "Mr. Big Guy for the Blind." He is the only one who can go and negotiate with musicans at the Wuhou Temple Road, Chunxi Road, and the Western Gate Bus Terminal areas. By the way, do you have money? He charges a lot of money for the service.

LIAO: Don't be too obsessed with money. It ruins my initial impression of your erhu music.

ZHANG: It's getting late. Let me start playing.

THE STREET SINGER

I first met Que Yao at a nightclub in 1995. We were both guest performers that night. I was a flute player and he was a pop singer. A friend told me that he was blind in one eye. That was why he wore a pair of designer sunglasses all year round, day and night. He looked kind of cool with his sunglasses, reminding me of Wang Kai-wai, the Hong Kong movie director, whose credits include In the Mood for Love. *Que Yao sang like a woman in a pretentiously soft falsetto. I found his style repulsive, but the crowd at the bar swooned all over him.*

In the ensuing years, I saw him perform at various venues and got to know him a little better. On a recent Saturday afternoon, I interviewed Que Yao at a teahouse near Chengdu's Huangzhong Residential District.

—✳—

LIAO YIWU: Is Que Yao your real name?

QUE YAO: Of course. That's my first name. My family name is Qi. I was born on April 11, 1969, right after the Communist Party concluded its Ninth Congress. Chairman Mao designated Marshal Lin Biao as his successor in the new Chinese constitution. The whole country showed up on the streets to celebrate. To mark the occasion, my parents named me Queyao, or Leap for Joy, for Chairman Mao's choice of a successor. You know, it was at the height of the Cultural Revolution. Each time Chairman Mao issued a new edict or a quotation, whether it was during the day or in the evening, people had to go out into the street to celebrate with singing and dancing.

LIAO: I remember those days. Were they Communist Party officials?

QUE: No, far from that. They were ordinary folks—both of them were blind. For many years, I felt so embarrassed about my parents that I never talked to anyone about them. It wasn't until I turned thirty that I realized how stupid that was. I had a very interesting childhood. I grew up in a small town in Sichuan. My early memories were of sausages shuffling back and forth on a machine. I was three and my mother had me tied on her back. She worked at a sausage factory run by the local welfare agency. All the workers there were disabled—the blind, the deaf, and the crippled. Both my mom and dad were employed there. Between the two of them, they earned twenty-seven yuan [US$3.50] a month, barely enough to support a family of five, including me and my two sisters.

My parents used to be street musicians. My mom played the erhu, a two-string Chinese violin. My father was quite a well-known storyteller. His storytelling, interspersed with singing, was accompanied by the daoqin—a traditional instrument which has become almost extinct nowadays. It was like a drum, made from a meter-long thick bamboo cylinder, with the open end covered in pigskin. He would tap the drum, singing and talking to its lively rhythms. Most of his stories were taken from Chinese classical literature, such as "The Warrior Conquered the Tiger." People loved the suspense and colorful descriptions. My father had had a large following. When the Cultural Revolution started, the government banned him from performing because his stories were considered feudalistic and antirevolutionary. As a result, he and my mom were assigned to work at the sausage factory.

My hometown was situated along the Yangtze River in poverty-stricken Yunyang County, near Chongqing. Before the Cultural Revolution, people living in the remote, isolated countryside and small towns didn't have access to various forms of entertainment. Street performers and local operatic troupes filled the void. But, after 1966, street performances were declared illegal and local opera troupes were only allowed to stage the "Eight Revolutionary Model Operas" mandated by Mao's wife, Jiangqing. Apart from that, people spent their evenings attending Communist meetings. Sometimes, they might witness public executions of counterrevolutionaries or murderers and rapists. That was it. People were bored to tears.

Beginning in the early 1970s, there was a period of political relaxation. That was the time when Lin Biao, jealous of Chairman Mao's supremacy within the Party, attempted to assassinate our Great Leader.

After the assassination plot failed, he escaped in a hurry to seek asylum in what was then the Soviet Union. But his plane crashed in Mongolia after running out of fuel. Do you remember that? Who knows how he died. Anyhow, the extreme days of the Cultural Revolution were pretty much gone. That led to a revival of traditional operas, music, and plays at private venues such as weddings, funerals, or birthday parties. The revival offered opportunities for former street performers like my parents. So, they organized a small troupe consisting of seven or eight blind musicians. The troupe would carry simple props and perform at private functions. They even traveled across the border to Sichuan Province and performed on market days in rural areas outside the city of Yichang. They could earn twenty to thirty yuan [US$2.50 to $3.00] a day. Sometimes, they might run into the local militia or members of the Market Regulatory Committee. When that happened, all their "illegal" income would be confiscated. They could be detained for a couple of days and had to attend public denunciation meetings. Somehow, they became used to the risks.

I went on tours with my parents at the age of four. Troupe members would carry their musical instruments on their backs while walking in a single line—one hand holding a stick and the other holding on to the shoulder of the person ahead of them. I served as their guide and led them from village to village. Can you imagine a four-year-old, with a shaved head, walking at the front of a group of blind musicians? I was often bored and tired, reduced to picking my nose and yawning. We would leave very early in the morning and walk ten to fifteen kilometers a day for a gig. On the way, our group constantly attracted the attention of adults and kids. They would follow us and poke fun at us. I felt so embarrassed and wished I could disappear. Well, most of the gigs were associated with funerals. It was a local tradition for rich people to have a lavish and festive funeral with bands and chanting monks. The event normally lasted from three days to a week, attracting hundreds of people from around the region. In a way, funerals provided a rare occasion for entertainment. At a funeral, the family of the dead would set up a stage in the middle of the courtyard, right next to the coffin. Various groups would take turns performing traditional operas or story singing. At a gig like this, my dad would do a dozen shows, each one lasting two to three hours. It was pretty challenging and could easily strain the performer's voice. But my dad had a voice of steel. He practiced long hours every day for many years. He could handle the long hours without any problems.

LIAO: Did they do it all night long, without stopping?

QUE: My dad would do three shows a night. There would be a two-hour break between shows. He would normally find a quiet spot and doze off a bit. All his shows were classic Chinese tales about the imperial court or touching love stories, which Chairman Mao called "historical trash." But ordinary folks loved the "historical trash." One of the most popular pieces that my dad performed was called "Courtesan Li Yaxian." The story goes like this: In the Tang dynasty [618–917], a young scholar named Zheng Yuanhe traveled to the capital city of Chang-an to take his imperial examination. If he could pass, he would be eligible for a high-level government post. As he passed the prosperous city of Yangzhou, he visited a brothel and encountered the famous courtesan Li Yaxian. He became so infatuated with her that he decided to stay. As one might predict, Zheng missed his exams and squandered all his allowance. Seeing that he was penniless, the madam threw him out on a cold snowy night. Zheng had almost frozen to death when two beggars saved him. They took pity and taught him to survive on the street by singing the famous "Beggar's Song." Meanwhile, courtesan Li was saddened and dismayed to see that her lover had lost his motivation to succeed in life. Li stabbed her eyes out and scarred her face so he would leave her to pursue his future at the imperial court.

LIAO: What a story, with all its ups and downs.

QUE: Many local opera troupes picked segments of the story and converted them into different operatic versions. For example, in Beijing opera, it was called "Beauty Stabbing Her Eyes to Motivate Her Wayward Lover." In Sichuan opera, it had a different version, "Beggars Wandering the Street," which focused on Zheng's life as a beggar. All these versions drew from the same story. For his own performance, my dad took the plot of the story and borrowed the librettos from various operatic versions. The result was a poetic masterpiece, with singing and storytelling. He dramatized every twist and turn and could hold people's attention for hours. Believe it or not, my dad was illiterate. He learned all the librettos by listening. "Temptation abounds in the vast expanse of the red dust / The lover's heart is entangled by all consuming lust / What is the meaning of life for butterflies and bees? / To be drawn to pretty flowers to fulfill their destiny and needs."

LIAO: I'm amazed you can still remember those librettos.

QUE: As a kid, I didn't have any friends and spent lots of time hanging out with blind musicians. During those gigs, I would watch them until I dozed off. As time went by, I began to pick up a lot of the librettos. I once fantasized acting in one of the operas someday.

LIAO: Did you intend to inherit your father's trade?

QUE: When I was young, I was so ashamed of associating with blind musicians. My dad had forced me to learn the erhu. Under his instruction, I practiced for hours. My little soft hand hurt so much. But if I stopped, he would beat me. Since my heart wasn't in it, I only learned to play a couple of popular revolutionary songs, such as "Chairman Is the Red Sun." Looking back, I wish I had persisted. My parents were born blind, but they were smart and highly motivated people. My mother could play five different types of musical instrument. During the Cultural Revolution, she was forced to read four thick volumes of *Chairman Mao's Selected Works* in Braille. Soon, she memorized most of Mao's articles and won a prize. As for my father, he became very popular in the late 1970s, after Mao died. Many traditional performances came back with a vengeance. My father was invited to work with several opera companies in adapting old operatic pieces and writing new ones. He even performed several gigs on the radio.

LIAO: So you didn't do too badly growing up among the blind musicians, did you?

QUE: Not exactly. I picked up a lot of bad things too. One time, I fell asleep at my parents' gig at a funeral. The host family put me on a bed next to the coffin. Then the bed began rocking and I woke up. The son of the deceased was having sex with a girl from the opera troupe. At the height of their passion, unaware that I was awake, the girl accidentally sat on my leg. I was so scared that I didn't dare to cry or breathe. My legs were totally numb. Also, I was only five years old when I learned that taking white arsenic could help a woman abort an unwanted fetus.

LIAO: That was quite an education you got. What has happened to your parents?

QUE: My dad died in 1980, when I was eleven years old. Like many people who grew up along the Yangtze River, he enjoyed swimming. Since he was blind, I had to accompany him all the time. I would either swim by his side or stand on the pebbled beach to help him with directions. For example, if I saw a big swirl coming, I would scream "Danger." If he swam too far out, I would call "Turn around." One day, while watching him from the shore, I became tired and fell asleep. I didn't hear his loud call for help. It turned out that he had had a cramp in the leg and drowned. When his body was pulled out, it was all black and blue, very ugly. I was very sad. All the onlookers pointed their fingers at me: This kid is so dumb. His dad called for help for a long time and he didn't even wake up. I remember that my mother and my twin sisters hunched over my dad's body and wailed for hours. I simply stood there, without shedding any tears. I felt so guilty.

After my dad passed away, my whole family collapsed. No matter how hard my mother worked, she still couldn't support three of us kids. So when I was fifteen, I dropped out of school and got a job at another local welfare factory for the disabled. Once again, I was thrown into the circle of the disabled. My job was to vulcanize a type of cheap but highly toxic rubber and then pour it into molding machines to make soles for shoes. The workplace was like a poisonous hell, but workers on the production line never had any protection. Each month, we were given protective gloves, masks, and jackets, but most of us sold them for cash. I was paid 120 yuan [US$15] a month, quite a handsome salary. But soon, I began to suffer severe upper respiratory problems because of that poisonous smoke we inhaled every day. I coughed a lot and my voice turned raspy and hoarse. Eventually I quit, joined a band, and sang at dance clubs. That's how I began my singing career. I guess I must have got the genes from my dad. I didn't have any training but I was quite good. Initially, I did a lot of popular love songs because my raspy voice was perfect for it. Later on, I began to sing rock. Around that time, I met a rock musician by the name of Chen. He had a big influence on me. He was in his thirties and performed electric guitar. I went to visit him in his apartment one day. There was no furniture, nothing, except a bed and a globe. He also had some copies of the travel magazine *Windows to the World.* When I commented on the absence of furniture in his apartment, he pointed to his head: All my wealth is inside here. He wanted to travel around the world. Chen always ganged up with other guys in stealing and fighting. His defense was that many Western artists lived similar lifestyles. He admired Bob Dylan and John Lennon. I totally fell for his crap. At the age of eighteen, I teamed up with some musicians and formed a touring band. We traveled all over China, from the cities of Guangzhou, Xian, and Wuhan, to Nanchang, Luoyang, and Urumichi in the far northwest. Wherever we went, we just performed on the street. I played guitar and was the lead singer. Initially, I was pretty shy at this new "venue," but soon I started to like it. We did a lot of hard rock. The music was so loud that we were always surrounded by a large young crowd. We put a collection box on the ground. At the end of the day, we would split the profits. We didn't make too much money, but all of us had a great time.

One day, I met a college student who watched me perform and really liked our band. When he learned that I composed my own songs, he was impressed and strongly recommended that I attend a music academy to have some formal training. I was seduced by the idea. So our band stayed in the same city for a long time. The college guy and I started hanging out together. Since it cost a lot of money to attend the music academy, he figured out a way to help me save money. He asked his parents to set aside a room for me and I moved in. Each time I earned some money on the street, I would hand it over to him and he would put it away in a bank. Since I didn't smoke or drink, I did save quite a bit. But then I realized that having money was not enough. To enroll in the music school, students had to take the National College Entrance Exam. I was a high school dropout and there was no way I could get in. But I didn't regret my efforts. At least I got to fantasize.

Later on, I continued to travel. In each city I passed through, I would always see a church. Out of curiosity, I walked into one and stayed through a service. I was touched by the sound of hymns. Before I left, I stole a copy of the Bible. I read it and was really into it. So I began to dream of going to a divinity school and becoming a composer serving God. I could write all sorts of hymns, you know.

LIAO: I assume that the door to God's service should be open and free to all. At least you don't have to pay tuition.

QUE: Well, I began to read the Bible and write hymns in my spare time. One day, I summoned enough courage to set up an appointment with a young minister. When I showed him my work, he glanced through it and handed it back to me with a look of contempt. He said: We have many beautiful hymns already written by grand masters. Your job is not to compose, but to learn. I wouldn't give up. I cleared my throat and sang a hymn that I had just written. But he wasn't impressed.

LIAO: Didn't realize you turned yourself into a gospel singer and writer.

QUE: I was pretty persistent. I met another minister in Yichang, Hubei Province. He was touched by my sincerity and piety. He recommended that I apply to the Jinling Divinity School in the southeastern city of Nanjing. I got the address from the minister and went on the road again. I felt very motivated. Four months later, I finally arrived in Nanjing and met with the school president. I told him about my family, my childhood, and my experience with God. I also asked for advice on my plan to receive education in Christianity. The president kept a stern face and seldom looked at me throughout the conversation. Occasionally, he would force a smile out of politeness. After my presentation, he said coldly: This school is the most prestigious Christian higher educational institute in China. To get in, you need to go through political background checks. Also, you have to pass the National College Entrance Exam. Then, if you meet these two requirements, you will need to work here as a volunteer for two years before you can officially start.

LIAO: Political background checks? I guess the government wants to make sure you are patriotic and support the Communist government.

QUE: I begged him, saying: Can I work here as a volunteer and take classes while you go conduct my political background check? The president said that he couldn't allow such a precedent. He also shared with me his concern that many people had attempted to attend the divinity school and used the experience as a springboard to go abroad or to marry a foreigner. Their motive had nothing to do with serving God. While he was lecturing me, I felt so uncomfortable. It was true that I had other motives. I wanted to change my life as a street musician. Was there anything wrong with that?

LIAO: Did he point out a new path for a strayed sheep like you?

QUE: Well, he told me to go back to Yichang and discuss my passion with the local church belonging to the Three-Selves Patriotic Movement. In China, the Party has created its own "Catholic" and "Protestant" churches in every city. They are called the Chinese Patriotic Catholic Association and the Three-Selves Patriotic Movement, which is Protestant.

LIAO: Yes, I'm aware of it. It's strange that the Chinese Catholic church does not listen to the Vatican, but to the atheist Communist Party.

QUE: It was understandable. Since nobody in China believes in Communism anymore, our leaders fear foreign religions could threaten the Party's rule. Let's not get into a political debate about it. Anyway, I followed his instructions and went back to Yichang. I sought help from an official of the Three-Selves Patriotic Movement. He said he could offer me the opportunity to volunteer in his church, but I had to get official approval from the Yunyang county government. I asked if the church could issue an invitation letter, but he said he couldn't. So the road to God was blocked. My passion for religion was officially over.

LIAO: If you really had a passion for God, why didn't you join the hundreds of underground churches? You could compose hymns for them.

QUE: The government has banned the underground churches. Many people have been arrested. It's too risky.

LIAO: What happened after your spiritual pursuit ran into obstacles?

QUE: Life went on, without God. After a while, I felt tired and decided to settle down. First, I stayed in Chongqing. On October 8, 1992, I played a gig under a viaduct in the Shapingba district. My singing attracted quite a large crowd. But then, little did I know that the performance on that day would "throw me in a sewage ditch."

LIAO: Isn't that the code phrase for "got busted by the Municipal Regulatory Agency?"

QUE: Yes. Every street performer can tell you about their experiences with MRA. I had been busted before and always managed to get away with minimal loss. But on that day, things were quite out of control.

LIAO: I've heard many stories of corrupt MRA officials.

QUE: They are like state-supported robbers. Vendors need to bribe them big-time to get a permit. If you don't have a permit, they smash all your equipment during their regular checkups. Since we used expensive sound equipment, the damage could run up to several thousand yuan.

LIAO: You were certainly much better equipped than your parents' band.

QUE: Our income was proportional to our investment. We wanted to make it big and make more money. But when the uniformed MRA robbers showed up that day, they shattered all my dreams. This is how it all happened. As I told you before, my hoarse and raspy voice was perfect for the new Chinese rock songs. My favorite was "Descendants of the Dragon" by the Taiwanese composer-singer Hou Dejian. In the 1990s, that song was very popular. The majority of the young folks wouldn't know the first two lines of the Chinese national anthem, but they could sing every word of "Descendants of the Dragon." So, when I performed the song that day, several hundred people immediately gathered and began to sing along. It was quite a spectacle. Soon, the crowd was getting bigger and our collection box was filled with one-yuan and five-yuan bills. After I finished, people applauded and requested three encores. As I was enjoying the moment of success, loud sirens could be heard all over the area. Then, several police cars and jeeps pulled in under the viaduct. Over twenty MRA officials and police jumped out of their vehicles. Since we had a huge crowd, which was wildly excited, the police and the MRA guys had a hard time dispersing them. The audience became really unruly. I could see the police were mad as hell. They accused me of instigating trouble and began kicking at the speakers and microphones. They smashed the drums and came to get my guitar. Since I had a brand-new guitar, I was stupid enough to clutch it to my chest and not let go. Two policemen tried to punch me and seize it. Several onlookers saw this and began to throw beer bottles at the police. That really incensed them. Soon, four or five police joined forces and began to hit me and other people with batons. I fell to the ground, with blood all over my face. My guitar was broken into pieces.

After the crowd was finally dispersed, the police handcuffed and threw me into the back of a car, and then locked me up at a detention center.

LIAO: What about the other people in the band?

QUE: They were detained for a day or so and then released. Since I was the head of the band, they charged me with "resisting arrest and instigating trouble." One officer said I deserved severe punishment.

LIAO: How did they treat you at the detention center?

QUE: At first, I was locked up with thirteen other guys in one room. I was still recovering from the bad beatings. I had a fever and lay on the floor, totally delirious. On the second day, two bastards saw that I was getting better. One guy pissed in a big bowl and then came over to me. He and his friend pried my mouth open and fed me the urine with a spoon. I spat it out but they kept slapping me. A guard heard my scream and stopped by. He yelled: You bastards, what are you doing to that guy over there? The guys immediately got up and stood at attention: Sir, we are feeding him Chinese herbal soup. The guard got curious: What kind of herbal soup? They answered: It's urine from a virgin boy. You know that a virgin boy's urine can help heal the body's injuries. The guard burst out laughing: You guys are virgins? Hope you don't pass on your STD to him. Then he walked away without stopping the torture.

LIAO: That was so disgusting.

QUE: At the end of the first week, the guys in my room found out that I was a singer. They were thrilled. One guy, who was the head of the gang in my cell, immediately put me to work. He ordered me to sing any songs that he requested. For a whole afternoon, I performed over forty songs. I almost lost my voice, and those bastards still wouldn't stop. Eventually, they all began to sing along. The whole detention center became a festive concert hall. I became a pop star among detainees. The "celebrity" status enabled me to dodge many of the physical attacks inflicted upon new arrivals.

The head of the gang was a well-known underworld assassin. Before his arrest, he had been hired by many businesspeople to go collect debts. For those who refused to cough up the money, he would cut off their ears or chop off their hands. People were really scared of him. He made me his perfect bitch. After he got tired of my singing, he came up with new ideas. In the evenings, when the guards were away, he would force me to dress in drag. A guy made a wig out of straw. Another one tucked two bowls into my shirt as fake breasts. Within a few minutes, they turned me into a bar girl. I used a tube of toothpaste as a fake microphone and was ordered to do strip dances. I was also forced to perform oral sex on him several times. Luckily, I was only detained there for two weeks. Then, I received an official notice from the court—I was sentenced to two years at a youth reeducation camp on the outskirts of Chongqing.

At the camp, we planted rice, tended orchids, and picked tea leaves. The hardest part was carrying buckets of human manure on shoulder poles from the delivery trucks to the field. My daily quota was fifty trips. Since I was short and thin, the job was killing me. So one day I talked with the camp director and asked if I could use my singing skills to educate and motivate other detainees. In return for my services, I could be spared some of the shit-carrying jobs. He thought it was a good idea and agreed to let me carry the manure three days a week rather than six days. He gave me a whole list of songs to perform. Among them were "Turning a New Chapter in Your Life," "Physical Labor Is Glorious," and "Socialism Is Good."

LIAO: You told me that you lost one of your eyes at the camp. How did it happen?

QUE: One day, I didn't fulfill my manure-transporting quota and had to work extra hours. At about 8 p.m., I was getting really tired and dizzy, but I continued without taking a rest. Then I collapsed and fell on my face. I felt a sharp pain in my left eye. I realized that a piece of rock had pierced it. I screamed and passed out. When I woke up the next morning, I was in a hospital. They operated on my eye and took the eyeball out. At that time, I was three months and four days away from my release from the camp. Because of my injury, they let me go earlier. So I was back on the street, half blind and penniless. I thought about my blind parents. Could it be some sort of inescapable fate?

LIAO: Do you believe in fate?

QUE: I was only in my twenties when that happened. If I had resigned myself to fate, I wouldn't have had the guts to change and survive.

LIAO: Well, you've changed. You are quite an established avant-garde street musician.

QUE: My music has a lot to do with my life. The most important accomplishment for me is that I have rediscovered myself. In the past, I was embarrassed by my parents and never bothered to delve into their music and their art. Life behind bars and performing on the street have given me a new appreciation for street music. I have found street life a rich source of my musical inspiration. I constantly bring a tape recorder with me and record the clash of street sounds and noises. I then add this lively mix into my own singing.

LIAO: I listened to the CD you sent me. I have to say it's a very interesting concept.

QUE: I'm back with the people whom I knew the best. In the summer of 2000, at the Sichuan Folk Art and Music Festival near the Big Buddha Temple [Dafosi] in Chengdu, I had the opportunity to perform on the same stage with Zou Zhongxi, a master in folk music. He was already in his eighties and completely blind. Like my father, Master Zou was also a storyteller-singer, but he played a three-piece wooden clicker called a jinxianban. The clicker snapped and flew between his fingers, and the variations on the rhythms enhanced his storytelling. My father used to be a big fan of Zou. He would carry a radio and listen to Master Zou's performance for hours. On that day, I played my father's daoqin and then Master Zou performed "The Warrior Conquered the Tiger" with his jinxianban. When he was recounting the part where the warrior finally tamed the fierce tiger, he was so emotionally charged that I could almost see light shooting out of his blind eyes. That was really amazing. After the performance, I went to my father's tomb. I felt that I had finally done something that would make him proud.

*I've always doubted the existence of sleepwalkers until recently,
when I came across an essay by the poet Niu Han. In the essay,
he wrote: "As a member of the so-called intellectual elite, I was
beaten severely on the head by Red Guards during the Cultural
Revolution. There was severe bleeding in my brain, and eventually, the blood pinched a nerve and I began to sleepwalk. The
habit of sleepwalking has tortured me for almost half a century
and has become part of me. I sleepwalk during the day or night.
I have become a person who can never wake up from his sleep."*

*Several years ago, I was introduced to Li Ying, a veteran
Communist official. During our conversation, I learned that
her novelist husband, Guan Dong, also suffers from sleepwalking. Thus, we began a long chat.*

—⚋⚋—

LIAO YIWU: I heard that your husband, Guan Dong, has written a short
story that has a character who sleepwalks. Is the story autobiographical?

LI YING: You are not the first person to ask that question. I wouldn't say
the whole story is autobiographical, but the part about sleepwalking is.
Unlike the poet Niu Han, who suffered during the Cultural Revolution, my husband began sleepwalking under different traumatic
circumstances.

In 1948, China was still ruled by the Nationalists under Chiang
Kai-shek. Guan Dong was a college student who was very actively
involved in the student movement against government corruption.
Once, he took part in a street demonstration and scuffled with police.
He was arrested and put in jail for over forty days. Finally, under public
pressure, the government ordered his release. On the day when prison
authorities told him that he could go home, he was asked to sign some
papers, and was led down a dark hallway where he saw several dark
shadows move toward him. Guan Dong immediately turned around

and wanted to run. But he was blocked from all directions. His attackers held thick wooden sticks. One guy hit him right on top of his head. He let out a loud scream and passed out. After he regained consciousness, he found himself inside a spacious room of a hospital. The thugs had dumped him outside on the street and strangers brought him in. I was working as a nurse at that hospital.

That incident made him a celebrity and a hero overnight. The public began to pressure the government to investigate the case. Many believed that the government sent those thugs to beat up Guan Dong in order to intimidate other student activists. While at the hospital, several pro-Communist organizations sent representatives to visit him. Newspapers carried his story with big pictures of him. His room was always filled with flowers, most of which were sent by women. With such care and encouragement from the public, he recovered very fast. At the beginning of 1949, the Communist takeover was imminent. The Nationalist government was collapsing fast. It was chaos everywhere. Guan Dong wanted to go back home but the doctor advised him to stay on for a couple more months.

They put Guan Dong under my care. As time went by, I began to fall in love with him. One day, I was carrying a medicine tray and was about to leave the nurses station when I heard a loud scream coming from Guan Dong's room. It was as loud as the siren from a train. I was so startled that I dropped my tray, spilling meds all over the floor. I dashed toward his room and kicked the door open. Many of the medical staff also rushed over. Guess what? He was standing by the window, calmly smoking a cigarette. He acted as if nothing had happened. He didn't know why so many people had shown up at his room. He patted me on the shoulder, all smiles: What's the matter? Why is everyone here? Has anything happened?

I thought he was play-acting and became too angry to say anything. Later on, the doctor called me into his office and said: Are you sure you want to marry this guy? Guan Dong will probably never recover from his injury. Right now, there are still some blood clots inside his brain. Our hospital will not be able to remove the clots because we don't have the skills and technology. Therefore, whenever the blood pinches the nerves, he could experience memory blackouts. The episode you just saw, I mean the scream, may be the first of many such future outbursts. I was stunned, and asked if this would happen frequently. The doctor said: The same symptoms will appear when he is nervous, under stress, or overexcited. But luckily, Guan Dong is a strong person. He is an optimist. I think he will handle it OK. Nowadays, technology is developing fast. Once the conditions in our hospital have improved, we'll be able to operate and treat his illness.

That was what the doctor told me in 1949. Little did I know that his illness would drag on for over forty years without a cure. I've gotten used to his sporadic loud screams. There was one more torturous symptom that the doctor didn't mention: sleepwalking. Under normal conditions, Guan Dong has a very calm demeanor. He is a very considerate person. However, during sleepwalking, he displays another side of him—he is full of passion and excitement. He does it in a very quiet and almost soundless manner. Just like what Freud described in his book, all human dreams are abrupt and incomplete, and have a lot to do with life in our early years. Guan Dong cannot remember his dreams. I will normally tell him what I have witnessed. That's how he got to incorporate the details into his short story.

LIAO: When did he begin to sleepwalk?

LI: It was in the third month after we got married. I remember the date very well because it was right before the Communist troops moved into Beijing. Like many residents, Guan Dong was very excited because he was an idealist, believing that the Communists could change the old corrupt regime. On the night before the troops officially marched into the city, we had made arrangements with other friends to meet the next day for a celebration ceremony on the campus of Beijing University.

An hour or so after we went to bed, I woke up. I found Guan Dong had left the room. Then, I heard some faint noises coming from the public bathroom down the hallway. I slowly opened the door, and walked barefoot to the bathroom. I saw him standing in front of a mirror, shaving. I called out to him in a low hushed voice, "Guan Dong, Guan Dong." He didn't answer me and continued with his shaving. In a few minutes, he began to wash his face very quietly. After the washing and shaving, he slowly turned around. I could see his chin was bleeding; his eyes stared straight ahead. Since he is much taller than I am, his rigid stare passed over my head. I began to realize what was going on. Since his doctor had warned me not to wake him up during his sleepwalking, saying it could cause sudden death, I rushed back to the bedroom and pretended to sleep. I was praying that he would come back to bed. But he didn't. He walked into the room, made a 180-degree turn as if in a military exercise, and walked stiffly out of the door. He was in his underwear and barefoot.

I put on clothes and followed him closely. He took a familiar path in front of the dorm building. I was afraid that he could follow this tree-lined path that led to the patient ward. That would be horrible. He passed through the garden and walked in the direction of the morgue next to the Infectious Disease Ward. I didn't know what to do except to follow him. We didn't have cell phones then, and there was no way I could call a doctor on duty to help me out. He stopped in front of the morgue, pushed the door open, and walked inside. Guan Dong made a mess inside the morgue. He pulled two corpses out from the refrigerators and then held them standing against the wall. I knocked on the door of the guard and begged him, with tears in my eyes, to help me out. Luckily, the guard didn't freak out. He picked up a thin wooden stick from the floor and walked inside. He edged closer to Guan Dong, standing side by side with him. Then, as Guan Dong was raising his arm, the guard slipped the thin wooden stick into Guan Dong's hands. The guard held one end of the stick and Guan Dong held the other. The guard began to lead Guan Dong by the stick and, strangely, he followed. After the guard led him into our dorm, Guan Dong jumped onto the bed and soon began his thunderous snore.

LIAO: That sounded pretty dangerous. Did your husband ever hurt you during his sleepwalking?

LI: He never hurt anybody during sleepwalking. When it first happened, I informed the doctor at my hospital. With their approval, I managed to put a couple of sleeping pills in his water cup and asked him to drink the water before he went to sleep each night. I also asked my neighbor to lock our door from the outside. In this way, even if he sleepwalked, he would end up walking around the house. He is not a detail-oriented person at all. He didn't know about the sleeping pills, but just said his water tasted a little strange. He never bothered to probe further. As time went by, I began to notice a pattern. As long as his mood and emotions were under control, he was OK. Guan Dong loved writing. After the new Communist government was established, they needed young people with a pro-Communist background to work in the publishing industry. Guan Dong was soon hired by a newly formed publishing house. Unfortunately, not long after he started his job, the Korean War broke out, and China joined North Korea to fight against the U.S. Guan Dong signed up with the troops without telling me. After he told me about his decision, I was shocked and tried to stop him. I couldn't tell him the truth about his illness. I was afraid he would be too traumatized.

I concocted a lie, saying that he couldn't go because I was pregnant. After he heard the news, he only laughed. In those days, young people were asked to put the interests of the country above everything else. The fact that his wife was pregnant was not a legitimate cause for deterring a husband from joining the army. So I went to ask for help from the president of the hospital, hoping he could write to the army about Guan Dong's illness. But the president was under investigation by the new government. They suspected that he was a spy for the old Nationalist regime. I wouldn't give up. I eventually located the doctor who had treated Guan Dong and dug out his old files. I excitedly clutched his files and ran over to the recruitment center. After I handed over his medical records to officers there, they told me he had already left with the troops. I was so worried. I went over to the train station and got myself a ticket to the North Korean border. Before the train reached its destination, it stopped at a small station. Some soldiers got on and asked all passengers to get off. Only those with special passes could stay on the train. I was told that the war had already started.

During the first three months, Guan Dong did a terrific job as an embedded journalist. He wrote some wonderful articles for the newspapers at home. More important, if needed, he could pick up a gun and fight like a soldier. He was a sharpshooter and was even awarded a medal. But soon he was charged with being a "U.S. spy" and was sent back to China.

Do you know why? One night, his unit was carrying out an assignment to ambush the enemy troops. As he and his comrades were hiding in the bushes, he suddenly jumped up, dropped his gun, and let out a loud scream for no reason at all. As you may have guessed, the enemy was alerted. They fired a firebomb, and within seconds the bushes where the Chinese troops were hiding were lit up. The whole plan was sabotaged and there were heavy casualties on the Chinese side. The commander had to request reinforcements so his unit could retreat. During the retreat, a bullet hit Guan Dong's leg. His comrades, who were so mad at his irrational behavior, tied him up and dragged him out of there. Later on, the hospital record that I submitted to the military saved him from being tried in a military court. He returned to Beijing, full of guilt and regrets. That guilt has haunted him all his life. However, if it hadn't been for the bullet wound in his leg, he wouldn't even remember that he screamed before the enemy fire.

LIAO: By then, Guan Dong was well aware of his illness. What did he do?

LI: He was a little depressed for a couple of weeks. He would drink alone at home. He kept saying to me: I didn't hurt you, did I? If I'm too much of a burden to you, we can file for divorce. I comforted him with the patience of a nurse: Since you love me so much, you won't hurt me. Dreams are mostly the reflections from your conscious behavior. You are a kind person, and the kindness will reflect in your subconscious behavior. That's why I'm not afraid. Guan Dong stared at me for a long time before he finally said: I hope you are not lying just to make me feel better. My outburst in North Korea led to the deaths and injuries of many of my fellow soldiers. I'm the one who should have been killed. I hugged him and said: Guan Dong, you need to snap out of your depression and cheer up. We are still young and I'm sure we'll find a cure for your illness. He was touched, and finally he said: With you by my side, I'm sure I can recover. Many years have passed and I can still remember these words vividly.

LIAO: What happened later?

LI: Guan Dong went back to the publishing house. He got along with everyone, and his boss liked him a lot. Each time he asked to take a leave of absence for treatment, his boss would give permission and provide financial help without giving him any hassles. We traveled to Shanghai and Guangzhou, and even sought help from experts in the Soviet Union, which was China's close ally in the 1950s. Nobody dared to operate on him. We had no choice but to wait for a miracle. To avoid doing any damage during his sleepwalking, Guan Dong would tire himself out by staying up very late editing manuscripts. Before he went to sleep, he would lock the bedroom door from the outside, hide all the sharp metal instruments, and then drink several shots of liquor to ensure sound sleep. He would always sleep on the living room couch.

In 1957, Chairman Mao launched his anti-Rightist campaign. Since all the writers and administrators at the publishing house enjoyed pretty close relations, the leadership only singled out a few "Rightists." Apparently, that didn't satisfy the municipal authorities, which set quotas for every government-run organization. Since the campaign's primary target was intellectuals, the municipal government had specifically allocated a large quota to Guan Dong's company, which had a large number of editors and writers. According to Mao, writers and editors were the most dangerous ones who harbored ill feelings toward the Party. To fulfill the quota, the publishing house reluctantly named two more people who confessed that they had expressed dissatisfaction with the Party in their diaries. Then Guan Dong's boss, Mr. Wang, received a notice from the municipal government that they needed to come up with one more Rightist. If the publishing house didn't name another one, the municipal Party leadership would send a task force to investigate the company. In the end, under pressure from above, Mr. Wang made a plea at a staff meeting: If we still cannot find a Rightist, I will turn myself in since I'm responsible for every decision here. Upon hearing that, Guan Dong became impatient and stood up: You can't do that. You have a large family to support, your parents, your children and grandchildren. If you are labeled a Rightist, all your children will be implicated and their future will be ruined. Why don't you pick me to fill the quota? I don't have children. Mr. Wang asked: What does your wife think? Have you talked with her? Guan Dong answered: I don't need to. In the past, you've been so generous to me when it came to treating my illness. It's a good time for us to pay you back. I'm sure my wife would agree. We are honored that we could do this for you. Mr. Wang said, But you have not done or said anything against the Communist Party. I can't make any accusations against you. Guan Dong hesitated and said: Why don't I say something against the Communist Party now? Since everyone is here, they can testify against me. If this still doesn't work, I can say that as an editor, I used to edit all the articles written by the Rightists and counterrevolutionaries.

LIAO: That was very altruistic.

LI: He was a hero for a couple of minutes and ended up paying a hefty price in the next twenty years. Not long after he was labeled a Rightist, he was kicked out of the publishing house and we were sent down to the countryside outside Beijing for reeducation through hard labor. Before our departure, Guan Dong went back to his work unit to say goodbye to his former colleagues. It was barely two months since he had made himself a Rightist, but people seemed to have forgotten all about how it had happened. They all shunned him like he was carrying some infectious disease. A female co-worker used to be Guan Dong's good friend. When they bumped into each other in the courtyard, the woman thought he was going to attack her. She became so frightened, and while running away, she fell into a sewage ditch. The reaction from his former co-workers shocked Guan Dong. His everyday smiles disappeared. After he got home, he downed half a bottle of liquor and passed out. A few hours later, his sleepwalking resumed. This time, he broke the window and jumped out. Fortunately, we lived on the first floor of an apartment building and he didn't kill himself. This latest recurrence made him really depressed for a while. While we were in the countryside, he worked hard in the field all day. Before he went to bed at night, he would tie himself up in bed. He did that brutal thing to himself for many years until we were allowed to move back to Beijing in the late 1970s, after the central government reversed its verdict against him.

LIAO: Do you have children?

LI: No, we don't. At the beginning, we were too busy seeking treatment for his illness. After the Great Leap Forward in the late 1950s, famine hit China. With people dying in the millions, it was senseless for us to even consider having children. After the famine passed and food became relatively abundant in 1964, I told Guan Dong that I wanted to have a baby. But he was worried that his Rightist label could taint the future of his kids.

LIAO: How did the famine affect you and Guan Dong?

LI: Many Rightists suffered or died in the famine. Since I worked at a rural hospital, doctors and nurses were allocated more food than ordinary peasants. On top of that, Guan Dong constantly went to harass the county officials for extra food. Since we didn't get to eat meat, our only source of protein was placenta, which I picked up from my hospital. Locals didn't want to touch the stuff for superstitious reasons. We were quite lucky that we survived.

LIAO: Now that medical conditions have greatly improved, has Guan Dong been able to find a cure for his illness?

LI: I assume that he could go have the surgery now but he doesn't want to spend the money. He said jokingly that the devil had already inhabited his brain for many years. If the doctor took it out, there would be an empty hole in his brain and he wouldn't like it. What nonsense! He is already in his seventies and he still acts like a kid. We have taken quite a lot of preventive measures. We have a small courtyard house. We always lock the door in the evenings so he can't walk too far in his sleep. Sometimes, he would get up in the middle of the night, shave, and read in his study. One time, I got up quietly and took a peek through the door of the study. Unexpectedly, he began to talk: My dear, what are you doing there? I was so startled. Guess what? He was not sleepwalking, he was awake. He just doesn't sleep that much these days.

Guan Dong remains young at heart. In the late 1980s, the government was planning to shut down a well-known youth magazine because the editor published an article that allegedly contravened Party policy. The decision aroused anger from many intellectuals. When Guan Dong heard about it, he put on a T-shirt and ran barefoot to the office of the Party official who had played a key role in the shutdown. Guan Dong sat in the conference room and began to scream and cry. He made quite a commotion in there and drew a large sympathetic crowd. When everyone gathered, he gave a speech on why the Party shouldn't suppress freedom of speech. He was so crazy. Since he was retired and had experienced so much in life, they didn't know what to do about him.

Recently, while he was reading late at night, he came across a magazine article about sleepwalking. He was so excited that he woke me up, and said: Look, it says here that in South America, there is a village for sleepwalkers. People work at night and sleepwalk during the daytime. If tourists visit the village at noon, they will see many people sleeping under the trees or sleepwalking on the street. The village is so quiet. The village will come to life after dusk. The shops are open. People get up and then resume their nightly business. By midnight, the whole village is lit up like daytime. The circus will come in and the whole place is packed with locals and tourists.

LIAO: I've also heard about that story.

LI: Guan Dong doesn't believe it's a story. He truly thinks this place exists. He is now collecting materials, hoping he could visit the village before he dies. He says: That is the home for sleepwalkers. If you don't sleepwalk, you are considered a freak. Isn't that great? I assume that Gabriel Garcia Márquez must have visited the place. His book *One Hundred Years of Solitude* is written in such a dreamlike style. Sometimes, in my dreams, I thought I have written lots of great stuff on paper. When I wake up the next day, it is still a piece of blank paper. Nothing has been written down.

LIAO: It seems that sleepwalking is both a misfortune and a blessing for Guan Dong. In a way, sleepwalking offers him some sort of dreamlike world that he can escape to, I mean, temporarily away from this murky world we live in. A pure and innocent person like Guan Dong deserves to live in heaven.

LI: Despite all the hardships we have encountered in life, I think Guan Dong has always been living in heaven.

THE MIGRANT WORKER

In recent years, millions of peasants have migrated from the poverty-stricken rural areas to big cities in search of better job opportunities. Many of them end up working on construction sites or at clothing and toy factories. According to a Chinese government statistic, about 114 million rural laborers, known as min gong, or "peasant workers," swarmed into China's major cities in 2003.

In Chengdu, the Nine-Eye Bridge area has the most crowded labor market. The line of job seekers stretches as far as several blocks. On a recent winter morning, I disguised myself as a recruiter and visited the area, hoping to talk and get some stories out of the migrants. However, the trick did not work because nobody had the time to chat. Later that evening, I bumped into Zhao Er on a side street near the New South Gate. Zhao, in his forties, was one of the migrants who took shelter on the street. He came from the northern part of Sichuan. He wouldn't tell me his real name. I heard his shelter mates call him Zhao Er, or Zhao the Second.

—m—

LIAO YIWU: How long have been away from home?

ZHAO ER: Seven years.

LIAO: Are you homesick?

ZHAO: Of course. I have a wife and a bunch of kids.

LIAO: What do you mean when you say "a bunch of kids"? Don't you guys in the rural areas have to follow the one-child policy?

ZHAO: Of course we have to abide by the policy. In my village, you have to pay a fine of 3,000 yuan [US$380] if you have an additional child. I don't have no money to pay. What can they do? Not much. It's not like in the old days when officials would penalize the violators by razing their houses or forcing women at childbearing age to have loops inserted into their wombs. Once they put the loop in, it was very hard to get it out. Some desperate peasants used chopsticks but still couldn't pull it out. Since Western countries criticize China for treating women like animals, the local government has stopped the practice, or at least they don't do it openly.

There used to be a well-known comedy skit that made fun of country folks who ran away with their pregnant wives to faraway places so they could breed more kids. That was such an exaggeration. Come to think of it, it takes money to run away. Who is paying for the transportation? Nowadays, it's hard to sneak on and off trains without a ticket. I have three daughters. They were all born in the village. Since I had violated the policy, a family planning official visited my house, which was a dump. It was so dark inside my house, she couldn't see nothing. She tripped over a makeshift stove and became panicked. At that time, my wife was breastfeeding our third daughter. The other two kids seized the official's coattails and begged her for candy. She ran out as fast as she could. After that visit, she never bothered us again.

LIAO: If you were so poor, why did you keep having children?

ZHAO: I am penniless. I have no luck with money at all. That's my fate. But my dick is not willing to accept fate. That stuff down there is the only hard spot in my body. The more seeds I plant, the more likely it is that I can change my fate and fortune. Also, unlike you city folks, we peasants don't have money to go visit the nightclubs. In the evenings, when it's dark and boring, we have nothing else to do except to pin our wives down and go "nightclubbing." If you are not extra careful, accidents will happen. Your wife's stomach will get big again. Who do I blame? My wife badly wanted a son. The more she wanted a son, the more damn daughters she bred.

LIAO: Do you save money to send home?

ZHAO: Yes, I used to send money regularly. But I haven't done that for over half a year now.

LIAO: Without the money, what are your wife and kids supposed to do at home?

ZHAO: They have to figure out their own ways to survive. My wife knows the township pretty well. When times are hard, she drags the kids along, begging from door to door. She probably gets more income than I do. Children in the countryside are not born with silver spoons in their mouths. When they get to the ages of two to three and start to walk steadily on their own, they begin helping out with household chores or go out begging for food. I find that kids growing up in rich families are more difficult to raise. They look damn healthy and fat, but end up in hospitals every other day. My kids, on the contrary, never get sick. They are tempered by wind and rain. They are just like young trees. When you just leave them alone, every time you turn around, they get a bit taller.

LIAO: As a father, how can you be so guilt-free about this?

ZHAO: I can't even take care of myself. Life at home might be hard but at least they have a home. I have to sleep on the street. Look at these folks around me here. They're all much younger. I'm an old fart and have to put up with a lot of crap here. This location is close to the Nine-Eye Bridge Labor Market. I need to be there early tomorrow. If I'm lucky, I can probably get a job with a restaurant nearby. Early in the day, I was planning to look for a construction job. Construction is hard work, but the pay is slightly better. When my stomach gets empty and the cold air moves in, all I crave is a restaurant job where I can get a bowl of hot noodles for free. Over there, near the funeral home, there is a noodle place run by a plump lady. She charges three yuan per bowl of noodles, with free refills on the noodles, not the sauce. Once, I was so starved that I ended up eating seven bowls of noodles!

LIAO: Sounds like you are more attached to your noodles than to your own daughters.

ZHAO: Hey buddy, can you spare a couple of yuan so I can get a bowl of noodles?

LIAO: Here is ten yuan. Be quiet and don't make any fuss. Otherwise, the other guys will come asking for money from me. By the way, do you always sleep on the street like this?

ZHAO: You can't call this "sleeping on the street." This is a rainproof plastic tent. Down here, I'm sleeping on a waterproof sheet. When I put a quilt on top of the sheet, it's like sleeping on a comfortable bed. Being frugal can save me from future starvation.

I lived on the street when I first arrived in the city. Later on, I started a tricycle business and had money to share an apartment with a couple of other guys. Then, after several of my tricycles were confiscated, I went broke. I couldn't afford the rent. I thought of getting a cheap five-yuan hostel room early this evening, but by the time I got there, the place was full.

LIAO: Where is this place? Why is it so cheap?

ZHAO: Near the Nine-Eyed Bridge. There are a bunch of plastic tents and some shabby houses. During daytime, it is a market. Vendors use the tents as stalls for their merchandise. In the evening, the tents are converted into bedrooms, with all sides sealed. For a bigger tent, you can squeeze seven or eight people in there. In the wintertime, when bodies are crammed in together, you get pretty warm. Sometimes, it's so warm that you sweat simply by blowing a fart. Each day, before dusk, the owner will stand outside the tent to collect money and get as many people in one tent as possible. Her favorite saying is a spoof on an old quote from Chairman Mao: "We come together from all corners of the earth, united by a common goal of starting a Communist revolution." She changed it to: "We are all travelers, coming from all corners of the earth. For one common goal of making money; we are now squeezed together." Even that damn place was fully occupied tonight. Last week, I got a nice paid spot deep inside a shabby building. But around midnight, I got up to take a dump. When I returned, I found the spot had been taken. I tried hard to squeeze in but got kicked out by seven or eight pairs of feet. I was so mad. So I wrapped myself in a quilt and sat by the door until morning. Sleeping over here is not bad at all. At least it's spacious. If this were summer, it would be even better.

LIAO: How did you end up in the city? Do you own any land at home?

ZHAO: No, I don't. About ten years ago, my parents' family was allotted a
small piece of farmland. When I got married, the village didn't have any
land left. Even if we had, we wouldn't be able to make money on the
crops. The local government levied all sort of taxes. Many young people
left the village to search for jobs in cities. I did the same thing. I got my
first job at a coal mine, not far away from my village.

LIAO: Were you employed by a township-run coal company?

ZHAO: No. I worked for a small privately owned coal company, which
piggybacked on the state mines. If the state company dug coal from
one side of the mountain, my boss would secretly dig from the other
side. The whole mountain looked like a beehive, with all sorts of holes.
The local government was aware of our illegal mining activities but
turned a blind eye. Most county officials took bribes from the private
company owners.
    We would normally dig a tunnel with a tiny entrance. We had to
crawl inside with a basket on our back. The coal mine was shaped like
a wine bottle. As you went down the tunnel, the place got bigger. It was
always pitch-dark down there.

LIAO: Didn't you guys have cap lamps and a pneumatic coal pick?

ZHAO: We were illegal miners and didn't have fancy equipment like that.
We simply tied a flashlight to our heads. As for the pneumatic coal
pick, we couldn't use it at all. Once you plugged it in, the vibrating
noise was too loud. It was dangerous because the vibrations could
cause the mine to collapse. The structure of the coal mine was made of
cheap wood sticks—any type of shaking could topple it. Nowadays,
you hear a lot about people dying inside mines. I know exactly what has
caused the accidents. There is no safety protection. Those private mine
owners are brutal bastards. They never care for workers' safety. I
worked for the coal company, on and off, for three years. My daily
salary was about two or three yuan. My face was smeared with so much
coal dust. As time went by, the dust seeped into the skin around my
neck and the back of my ears. I couldn't get it off. It wouldn't help even

if I tried to rub the skin off. I was tired all the time. Sometimes, when I got home, I fell asleep while eating.

LIAO: Why did you leave?

ZHAO: In the 1980s, I could pretty much make ends meet by working in the mine. However, in the mid-1990s, everything became so expensive, but our salary remained the same. Sometimes, I worked seven days a week and the money I got couldn't even buy enough food for my family. On top of that, county officials also charged us all sorts of fees. We worked our asses off only to fatten the pockets of those bastards. Then several state coal companies in the region went bankrupt because they had bad management. The laid-off state workers clenched their teeth with hatred each time they saw us. They felt that we had stolen their jobs. We were worried that those angry state workers could become desperate and block the entrance of our coal mine. We could all be dead inside. Aiya, as a result, many of us fled. In my village, many young guys moved to the cities to work on construction jobs; many women worked as nannies. Some women became whores. I don't blame those poor women. Luckily, my wife had three kids, otherwise, she would also be turned into a whore. Two months ago, I ran into a shoeshine woman near the Nine-Eye Bridge. It was getting dark but she was still busy peddling her service: "shoeshine, shoeshine." She somehow looked familiar. I went up closer and found out that she was the wife of my fellow villager, Dog Mouth Zhang. It turned out that she was polishing "yellow shoes."

LIAO: What's that?

ZHAO: It's the code name for prostitution. Those women will come out in the evenings and look for clients in the name of polishing their shoes. Once a guy stops and shows some interest, she will start polishing his shoes first, and then reaches up to fondle his ankle, while haggling over the price. For fifty yuan [US$6.40], she is willing to offer a full service. Of course, if a chick is young with full breasts, the transaction is easier. An older woman will have a hard time. My friend, Dog Mouth Zhang's wife, is almost thirty and has several kids. Her boobs sag to her waist! She will be lucky if she can sell herself for twenty yuan.

In this area, the young, pretty, and slick-tongued chicks go pick up clients at nightclubs. The older and ugly ones conduct their businesses at hair salons, or on the street. Let me tell you, those hookers from the countryside are picking up new things very fast. Shortly after they arrive in the city, they begin to drop their accents and speak standard Mandarin, powder their faces, and flirt by swinging their little butts. Some hookers even pay money to buy a fake college degree. Having a college degree can get them a rich guy. Then they will make up lies by saying that they hope to earn more money so they can change to a new career that matches their degree. So much bullshit!

Every now and then, I will indulge myself and get a hooker. I normally pay ten or sometimes twenty yuan. One day, I was really short of money. I tried to bargain down to five yuan but ended up getting a smack on the head with a shoe brush. That bitch stood up, with her hand on her hip, and said: You are much older than I am. Why don't I pay you five yuan to get a piece of your ass?

LIAO: You are such a jerk.

ZHAO: Don't you think I earned my money easily? When I first arrived in Chengdu, I worked at a construction site, pouring concrete and digging dirt. After more than a year, I had saved two hundred yuan [US $24]. With the help of a friend, I bought a tricycle and used it as a cab to drive people or deliver merchandise. It was kind of exciting. One bad thing was that we couldn't get city registration because I wasn't a city resident. I had to dodge the police constantly, like a chicken dodging a wolf.

LIAO: How long did you drive a tricycle?

ZHAO: For over two years. The city confiscated three of my tricycles.

LIAO: There are over ten thousand unregistered tricycle cabs in the city. Those registered tricycle cabs are complaining that you guys are stealing their business.

ZHAO: We made our living through hard labor. It's better than stealing or robbing people. I'm kind of mad that migrants like me are being treated like thieves. In those days, when someone yelled, "Police are coming," everyone would pedal away as far as our legs carried us, like geese hit by a bamboo stick. We would all dive into the side streets. I seldom got caught.

But greed is my weakness. Each time, someone offered me a high price, I forgot about the risks. On one occasion, a woman customer wanted a ride from the Intercity Bus Terminal near to the Baiguolin area. I didn't want to go. So I called out a random price—ten yuan. I didn't think she would agree to it. But she did. I was still reluctant to go, but she begged me and called me, "Sir, sir." She was kind of cute and her pleading softened my heart. I figured it was Sunday and the route around the second ring road would be okay. So I decided to take her.

It was in the summer. Out-of-towners love to take tricycle rides: cheap and cool. The second ring road was pretty dusty, but the scenery wasn't bad. I offered the woman my umbrella so she could shield her face from the sun. Soon, I was sweating. I took off my shirt and bared my back. She told me to be careful, not to catch a cold. When a customer started to be real sweet, I couldn't help chatting away. I just couldn't shut up. I told her about the best park in town, the shop where she could get good bargain prices, et cetera. I acted as if I were a Chengdu native. In reality, I was just bragging for the heck of it.

As I was making a turn near Zhongxin Road and sliding down a slope, a couple of police motorbikes blocked my way. I was scared shitless. I turned around and tried to go back up the slope. I pedaled very hard and several times the tricycle slid back down. That woman was also scared and tried to jump from the tricycle. She poked my bare back with the umbrella. My back was bleeding but I didn't dare to stop. She then raised the umbrella and beat me with it. She was also kicking me. That umbrella cost me eight yuan, but soon it was in shreds. Later on the police motorbikes caught up and cornered me. Damn it. I had just paid off my tricycle loan. I clung to my vehicle and wouldn't let go. Tears and sweat ran down my cheeks. The police didn't give a damn about how I felt. They threw the vehicle onto a truck waiting nearby. I ran after the police for a couple of blocks, begging and crying. It was useless. I had lost my vehicle and my umbrella. I didn't even get to collect the fare from that woman. She even had the nerve to ask me to compensate her for the emotional trauma I had caused her. That bitch! During the next several hours, I walked around the city aimlessly. I felt so empty inside.

their dirty business after midnight. They attack residential buildings one by one. All they need is a rope with a hook at the end. Most Yi guys are skillful mountain climbers. With the rope, they can climb walls easily. When they steal, they take anything they see: sausages, preserved meat, clothes, even diapers that people hang on their balconies. They just dump everything into their shawl. Once they break into a house, they take all the things that move. For big items, such as refrigerators, washing machines, they generally smash them. People hate them. Every year, the police will raid those places where Yi people gather and send them back to their hometowns in the mountains. After a couple of those raids, the neighborhood will be quiet for a month or so. Then the pickpockets will return. The residents in the area are facing a new set of problems.

LIAO: Have you ever seen any thieves in action? They are pretty rampant in big cities now.

ZHAO: Yes. Those thieves rob people in broad daylight. They snatch earrings and necklaces. Sometimes, they will grab a woman's hand and try to pull the ring from her fingers. The easiest victims are those well-dressed girls, carrying purses as big as your palm, and swinging their asses to the point of blinding you. Hey, within seconds, their purse is cut open. If they scream "Thieves," they may end up getting beaten up. Once, I drove a businessman and we were passing Moping Road. My client looked strong and big. He was chatting on his cell phone. Pulling him on a tricycle needed lots of strength. I was soon out of breath. At that point, six or seven people jumped onto my tricycle cab, one grabbed the big guy's neck and another wrestled his arm. The tricycle was almost turned upside down. Damn. Within minutes, all the pockets of that businessman's suits and pants were searched. His belt was pulled out. They even patted his underwear to make sure he didn't hide money there. In the end, he begged them not to take his shoes because he wouldn't be able to walk home. The thieves completely ignored his plea, saying that they wanted to see if there was any money hidden inside. That businessman was left with nothing. He ended up covering his face and crying like a woman. Many people saw those thieves, nobody stepped up to help.

LIAO: What were you doing? Why didn't you call the cops?

ZHAO: How could I get away? I was so shaken that I began to have cramps in my legs. Also, there are so many thieves nowadays. What could I do? I wasn't looking for trouble. All I cared about was my tricycle. If those guys broke it, it would cost me a bundle to have it fixed. On the other hand, that business guy was as stupid as a bear. From his looks, you would assume he would know some Chinese martial arts. Nope. Later on I tried to push him out of the cab, but he wouldn't move. So I drove him home. But when I asked him to pay the fare, he started to swear at me.

LIAO: You certainly know how to protect yourself.

ZHAO: Sir, are you being sarcastic? I'm already a homeless person, and I don't possess any superhero qualities. Sir, are you a reporter? Superman was a reporter. China needs selfless supermen at the moment. Crime has gone up and people are desperate. China's economy seems to be developing very fast, but there are still too many poor people. Too many people want to strike it rich. I'm lucky that I didn't turn into a thief.

Oh well, it's been raining for quite some time now. I wonder what the weather will be like tomorrow. Maybe I should go pick up an odd job at a construction site if it's sunny. Who knows!

Translator's Acknowledgments

Following his release from a Chinese prison, Liao Yiwu asked a blind fortune-teller to forecast his future. The fortune-teller felt around Liao's face, inquired the date and time of his birth, and told Liao that his future would start to look promising because he would be assisted and blessed by several *guiren*, or noblemen.

Translating and bringing Liao's works to English readers has certainly proved the wisdom of that fortune-teller. *The Corpse Walker: Real-Life Stories, China from the Bottom Up* wouldn't have been possible without noblemen and noblewomen.

My gratitude goes to Philip Gourevitch and his editorial staff at *The Paris Review* who first introduced Liao's works to the West by publishing three excerpts in their magazine. Philip's unwavering confidence in Liao's works and his enthusiastic support motivated and helped me get to where we are today.

I owe a special gratitude to Esther Allen at the PEN Translation Fund for discovering Liao's works and jump-starting my career as a translator. I want to thank Sarah Chalfant for her generous support.

Liao's friend Kang Zhengguo deserves a special note. As a volunteer "agent," Kang has diligently looked after Liao's interests overseas and served as a conduit between Liao and the outside world. I also want to express my admiration for Chen Maiping and Cai Chu at the Independent Chinese PEN Center for tirelessly championing Liao's works abroad and for courageously promoting freedom of speech in China.

My friends Doug Merwin, Professor Robert Crowley, Monica Eng, Carolyn Alessio, Bill Brown, Liang Xiaoyan, Chen Xiaoping, and Zhou Zhonglin have helped me a great deal in getting the book off the ground. Professor Crowley meticulously read the first draft of every translated story and offered valuable editorial suggestions.

Both Liao and I are very lucky to have Peter Bernstein as our agent. I found Peter at a very challenging time in my career. With a reassuring and easily accessible style, Peter patiently helped me navigate the publishing process.

Last and most important, I want to express my gratitude, on behalf of Liao, to our editor, Erroll McDonald, for granting us the flexibility and creative freedom we needed in the translation process, and to Lily Evans and Robin Reardon for moving the process along smoothly.

ABOUT THE AUTHOR

Liao Yiwu is a poet, novelist, and screenwriter. In 1989, he published an epic poem, "Massacre," that condemned the killings in Tiananmen Square and for which he spent four years in prison. His works include *Testimonials* and *Report on China's Victims of Injustice*. In 2003, Liao received the Hellman-Hammett Grant from Human Rights Watch, and he received the Freedom to Write Award from the Independent Chinese PEN Center in 2007. He currently lives in China.

ABOUT THE TRANSLATOR

Wen Huang is a writer and freelance journalist whose articles and translations have appeared in *The Wall Street Journal Asia*, the *Chicago Tribune*, the *South China Morning Post*, *The Christian Science Monitor*, and *The Paris Review*.

LIAO: Why didn't you do your business outside the second ring road, as was required by city ordinance?

ZHAO: There were too many migrants outside the second ring road. The neighborhood was not safe and many people took rides without paying, especially members of the local triad gangs. They would constantly collect protection fees from us. For us illegal tricycle cabdrivers, we couldn't go report to the police if we were blackmailed. Near the Wukuaishi region, all pickpockets have formed their own gangs. Sometimes, they use knives in gang fights. A guy got stabbed and his intestines were pulled out. Since it was too expensive to send him to a big hospital, his fellow gang members used my tricycle and took him to a small clinic to have his stomach sewed up. Hey, let me tell you that shitty doctor wore a pair of old reading spectacles and worked on the wounds like he was sewing shoes, pulling the strings in and out. The guy was dripping blood. So the doctor put a basin under the operating table. It was scary, but miraculously, the guy survived.

    The most brutal bunch are those ethnic Yi people. During daytime, they all squat by the side of the road, a whole bunch of them in their black shawls, like a flock of bald eagles. No local gangs dare to touch them. They call those Yi guys "dark clouds."

LIAO: That's very vivid.

ZHAO: The ethnic Yi people are very unique. Unless they are desperately hungry, they won't rob a pedestrian. But if they see a pickpocket stealing, they will immediately follow him like a dark cloud. Then they spread their black shawls and surround the pickpocket guy and scream, "Wow, Wow, Wow." If the guy is smart, he will turn over his money. If he tries to fight back, the knives of the Yi guys are faster than you can imagine. Those knives have been soaked in poisonous liquid. Once you get a cut, it becomes infected and takes months to heal.

LIAO: In other words, those pickpockets have become the slave workers for the Yi guys.

ZHAO: Almost. That's why you never see any pickpockets in places where the Yi guys stay. Well, those Yi guys are not angels. They normally do

A NOTE ON THE TYPE

This book was set in Fairfield, the first typeface from the hand of the distinguished American artist and engraver Rudolph Ruzicka (1883–1978). In its structure Fairfield displays the sober and sane qualities of the master craftsman whose talent has long been dedicated to clarity. It is this trait that accounts for the trim grace and vigor, the spirited design and sensitive balance, of this original typeface.

Rudolph Ruzicka was born in Bohemia and came to America in 1894. He set up his own shop, devoted to wood engraving and printing, in New York in 1913 after a varied career working as a wood engraver, in photo-engraving and banknote printing plants, and as an art director and free-lance artist. He designed and illustrated many books, and was the creator of a considerable list of individual prints—wood engravings, line engravings on copper, and aquatints.

Composed by Creative Graphics,
Allentown, Pennsylvania

Printed and bound by Berryville Graphics,
Berryville, Virginia

Designed by Soonyoung Kwon